The Control Data Corporation's Early Systems

The Control Data Corporation's Early Systems

By

Stephen H. Kaisler

Cambridge Scholars Publishing

The Control Data Corporation's Early Systems

Series: Historical Computing Machine Series

By Stephen H. Kaisler

This book first published 2023

Cambridge Scholars Publishing

Lady Stephenson Library, Newcastle upon Tyne, NE6 2PA, UK

British Library Cataloguing in Publication Data
A catalogue record for this book is available from the British Library

ISBN (10): 1-5275-1966-X
ISBN (13): 978-1-5275-1966-4

TABLE OF CONTENTS

LIST OF FIGURES

LIST OF TABLES

CHAPTER ONE

CONTROL DATA CORPORATION

Source: Worthy 1987

Control Data Corporation (CDC) was founded in the summer of 1957 to develop high performance computing machines for the scientific and engineering environments. Several engineers, including William C. Norris and Howard Engstrom, left Sperry Rand Corporation to found CDC in Minneapolis, Minnesota. The new company was financed by the sale of 600,000 shares of stock at $1 per share. Control Data was the first computer company to be publicly financed in the United States (Worthy 1987).

The new company occupied an old warehouse. Over the next several months, other engineers from Sperry Rand joined CDC. Norris and his team worked in an area where "floor space was divided by temporary chipboard partitions". Years later, these partitions still stood and remained unpainted as the company continued to grow (Worthy 1987).

By the late 1950s, IBM had gained control of the computing marketplace. Other competitors, such as General Electric, RCA, and Bendix, tried and failed to compete with IBM, and eventually withdrew from the market. Norris, realizing the futility of competing with IBM, recognized a niche existed in which IBM was not providing systems – the high-performance scientific computing arena. Norris and his team determined "to design and build the most power computers the world had ever seen" to fill that niche.

Through the early 1960s, CDC made several acquisitions that brought in needed technologies and skilled personnel. In the 1960s, many computer systems were leased rather than purchased outright – following a model pioneered by IBM, which guaranteed a continuous inflow of capital. To support such a model, debt was incurred to finance the leasing operation, but this had an effect on the balance sheet and investor perception of the company's financial stability.

One of these acquisitions was Commercial Credit Corporation (CCC) of Baltimore, Maryland in 1968. CCC retained its corporate autonomy (due to financial regulations), but provided CDC with a source of capital for financing computer leasing.

CDC made a decision to manufacture its own peripherals as it realized that a large portion of the cost of data processing systems was allocated to peripheral equipment. CDC's computer systems required high-performance mass storage systems with significant capacity to match the speed of its computers. Such devices were not available from other companies, so CDC had to design and build its own. Its success allowed it to become a source in the Original Equipment Manufacturer (OEM) market for companies that did not have to capability to build their own peripherals.

CDC also realized that software was becoming a major expense to many organizations. Norris realized that many small to medium companies would buy a computer system if it came with software that could do what they already did and what they needed in the way of applications. CDC began developing software applications that ran on its computers that addressed the needs of many corporations. It also modified software applications from companies that it had acquired.

CDC also realized that many corporations needed high-performance computing, but only in less amounts than an entire machine would provide. Such computer systems were too expensive to purchase for many firms that could use only some of that computing power. Norris decided that "he wanted to sell a little piece of a big computer at a time". As a result of an anti-competition suit against IBM, CDC gained control of the Service Bureau Corporation (SBC) in a settlement (Worthy 1987).

SBC enhanced CDC's ability to offer a suite of services and systems to its customer base. SBC more than doubled CDC's service business both in quantity and breadth of offerings by adding business data processing services to complement its engineering and scientific applications services. Most importantly, it brough a highly qualified and talented management and staff to augment CDC's management.

By 1969, CDC's timesharing service, which was offered to small and medium companies, was large enough to spin off into its own division, called CYBERNET. With SBC's personnel and expertise, CDC became a prime competitor in the time-sharing arena.

Norris had always been interested in seeing how computers could aid in education. Norris, learning of interesting work at the University of Illinois, offered to install a high-speed CDC computer for the group working on PLATO. PLATO evolved from the late 1960s into a powerful system to support instruction by computer until it became a commercial offering.

As Norris planned to retire in the mid-1980s, he appointed Robert Price as President and Norbert Berg as Deputy Chairman of the Board. The three of them formed a Corporate Executive Office with Price and Berg running the company and Norris offering advice and assistance as needed.

By the mid-1980s, pressure from competitors and the minicomputer vendors prices significantly undercut the large, powerful CDC machines. CDC exited the OEM disk drive market, and lowered its prices in other areas. The reduction in profit margins meant less support for research and engineering for new systems.

Competition from Cray Research at the high end of supercomputing, and IBM and DEC in the middle ground, along with financial and management constraints imposed by the SEC and its lending banks, presented CDC management with significant problems. CDC had to slow or severely reduce some of its products and manufacturing facilities, which further eroded its financial viability. Among the divestitures were Commercial Credit, remote data processing, the ETA division, and its training and education programs.

The result was a slimmed down company that focused on computing and systems integration services. In 1992, it changed its name to Ceridian Corporation and spun off computer operations into Control Data Systems, Inc. CDSI focused on systems integration services. By the mid-90s, the mainframe supercomputer manufacturer had ceased to exist although the name Control Data was used by CDSI.

William C. Norris (1911 – 2006)

William C. Norris, the founder of Control Data Corporation, was born in Nebraska in 1911. By high school, he had become interested in physics and electrical engineering. He graduated from the University of Nebraska in 1932 with a degree in electrical engineering. Upon the death of his father, he returned home to run the family farm.

At age 30, he joined the U.S. Naval Reserve where he was assigned to a unit whose responsibility was to intercept, analyze, and decode German and Japanese radio transmissions to try to locate enemy submarines. In 1946, he received funding from a group of investors to found Engineering Research Associates in St. Paul, MN. ERA was purchased by Remington Rand in 1951.

In 1955, after Sperry Corporation bought Remington Rand, Norris became General Manager and Vice President of Sperry Rand, a consolidation of four computer divisions. Lacking support from Sperry executive management, he formed Control Data Corporation in 1957 where he became President. CDC developed a niche in high performance computer systems for scientific and engineering applications. Between

1960 and 1979, CDC acquired over 80 small companies that greatly expanded its technical expertise and market. In 1986, Norris retired from CDC after anointing his successors. In 1986 he received the National Medal of Technology for advances in microelectronics and computer technology.

See Also:
William Norris: Computer Pioneer, Maverick Social Activist; *Jones Telecommunications and Multimedia Encyclopedia*, 1999
Worthy, James C. "William C. Norris: Portrait of a Maverick", *Ballinger Publishing Company*, Cambridge, Massachusetts, 1987

This volume discusses the early CDC systems through the CDC 3000 series, while fast, were not in the supercomputer category. We pick up the CDC story in Volume II as CDC focuses all its efforts on the supercomputer marketplace.

Caveat: This volume is neither exhaustive or comprehensive, but represents my best judgement as to describing the functions and capabilities of the CDC early systems.

1.1 CDC Systems Overview

Norris, Engstrom and others had become disillusioned with the company support they were getting for the development of computer equipment at Sperry Rand Corporation and decided to start their own business. Norris and colleagues set up shop in the old Minneapolis Star and Tribune Company warehouse. Initially, Control Data started out as a subcontractor for components used by the big computer companies. Norris's goal was to build the most powerful computers the world had ever seen.

The true history of CDC perhaps begins with the hiring of Seymour Cray in 1958. He developed a modular circuit configuration that could be used in high-speed digital computers. Using Cray's work, in the late 1950s Control Data Corporation produced the world's most powerful computer, the CDC 1604, at that time. At the same time, Cray sketched out the design for a small computer (e.g., a minicomputer) – the CDC 160 - with a 12-bit word size that could serve as a personal computer or a front-end to the CDC 1604. The CDC 160 influenced the design of the PPs for the CDC 6600, which is discussed in Volume II.

In June 1958, Control Data got its first order for the new computer from the U.S. Navy Bureau of Ships. The computer was delivered in January of

1960. When CDC announced the CDC 6600, IBM immediately countered, announcing the development of its own supercomputer, the IBM System 360/80. The CDC 6600 was billed as a 'supercomputer', defined as a machine that with its relative power, in any given time period, possessed certain performance and architectural capabilities that made their creation unique within the general framework of computer systems (Lincoln 1982)

Orders for the CDC 6600 stalled, waiting to see what IBM was going to come out with. But IBM's machine only existed on paper, and when this became apparent after a year, CDC filed an antitrust suit against IBM. The same month the suit was filed, CDC released its next supercomputer, the 7600, which dared IBM to try anything. IBM did nothing this time and the 7600 was one of the most successful computers ever built. Five years later, Control Data won the lawsuit against IBM.

When Cray left CDC in 1972, CDC invested over $300,000 in his new company, Cray Research, Inc. CDC further developed the STAR computer system, somewhat oriented towards business data processing, and delivered it commercially as the Cyber 203. A follow-on model, the Cyber 205, was successful. Another group of engineers left CDC with management approval to set up ETA to develop a new generation of supercomputers. Eventually, CDC reeled ETA back in when it felt its prodigy was encroaching too much on the parent's market.

The development of microprocessors, the emergence of superminicomputers and minisupercomputers, threatened CDC's long held niche. Competitors included Digital Equipment Corporation (DEC), IBM, and Cray Research. CDC started losing money; William Norris stepped down in 1986 as Chairman. But, in an attempt to recover, CDC sold Commercial Credit, its remote data processing bureau, its training and educational services division, and closed its ETA division.

By 1992, it spun off its computer division to a company called Computer Data Systems, Inc. and changed its name to Ceridian, which emerged as a provider of computing and systems integration services. Both still exist, but the mainframe computer manufacturer, a world leader in supercomputing for almost 40 years, no longer exists. Ceridian was eventually bought out and its new owners appear to be committed to eCommerce and human resource management solutions.

In 2007, CDC published an overview of its first (and last) 50 years (CDC 2007k).

We will not discuss the Omega 480, which was similar to the IBM 370 Series in instruction set and architecture. This machine was not very successful for CDC before it collapsed. We also will not discuss the CDC 924, an early CDC computer system of which only a few were manufactured and, apparently did not much influence the rest of the CDC computing systems.

Note: Cray Research computer systems are discussed in a forthcoming volume entitle *The Cray Dynasty*.

1.2 Two Volumes

CDC was an early and important innovator in high-speed computing in the United States. The amount of information available to describe CDC computers, and their operating systems, and application necessitated the two volumes of which the first describes the early CDC systems and suite of peripherals which were shared across the computer families. Volume Two: *Control Data: The Need for Speed* describes the supercomputer era of CDC and its operating systems.

CHAPTER TWO

CDC 160

The CDC 160 was one of the first transistorized computers to become commercially available (the other being the Digital Equipment Corporation PDP-1). The CDC 160 was packaged as a standard, double pedestal office desk. According to Dolan Toth (Lincoln 1975), the CDC 160 was designed at the same time as the 1604. Apparently, Seymour Cray wanted to build a big computer while CDC management wanted to do something smaller. Toth thought that Seymour was out sick one day and when he returned, he brought with him the design for the CDC 160, which, in effect, was a scaled down version of the CDC 1604. So, both machines were built concurrently. The CDC 160 design was based on the "Big Character" machine which was a test setup for checking out memory circuits and component design for the CDC 1604. Figure 2-1 depicts a CDC 160 console and tape units.

The CDC 160, along with the IBM 1620, established the solid-state minicomputer era by using discrete transistors and magnetic core memories. They were both announced in 1960. Although solid-state meant smaller machines, it also meant higher prices - $60,000 for the CDC 160 versus $74,500 for the IBM 1620. Both machines were intended for process-only applications, but the CDC 160 evolved into data acquisition and general-purpose data processing applications. Both machines used parallel logic which reduced the time to execute instructions – for the CDC 160 to 12.88 microseconds. The CDC 160 was also the first to implement relative and indirect addressing in order to overcome its short word length of 12 bits (Koudela 1973).

Although the CDC 160 was not designed as a satellite computer, its small size made it useful as a machine for handling unit record equipment. Thus, when the 1604 became operational, one of the first uses for the CDC 160 was to hook it up to the CDC 1604 to handle low-speed I/O requirements. This was accomplished by dual-porting a magnetic tape unit that could be controlled by both machines (Lincoln 1975). Later, CDC developed a high-speed data transfer channel that allowed the CDC-160 to be used as a front-end machine for other CDC computers (CDC 1965ad).

CDC also packaged the CDC 160 in a brown cabinet. It was then sold by National Cash Register (NCR) as the NCR 310. About 50 machines were sold in this packaging, according to Toth (Lincoln 1975). Over 150 machines were sold in either the CDC 160 or 160A configuration.

The base cost for a CDC 160A, an improved version of the original model, was about $110,000. This included the CPU, minimal memory, a high-speed paper-tape reader, a medium speed punch, and a Flexowriter. An assembler and a 4K FORTRAN compiler were available.

A CDC 160 could have attached up to 40 magnetic tape units. It supported high-speed printers, punched card readers and punchers, paper tape readers and punchers, and plotting and digital display equipment. Two CDC 160A computers could share the same magnetic core memory but operate independently. Table 2-1 presents the basic characteristics of the CDC-160.

Note: The IBM 1620 will be described in more detail in a forthcoming volume entitled *Early IBM Minicomputers: The 1130, 14xx, and 1620 Machines*.

Note: NCR computer systems will be discussed in a forthcoming volume entitled *The Other Dwarves*.

Note: This CDC 160A computer system has been variously referred to as the CDC 160A and the 160A. For simplicity, I have chosen to refer to it as the CDC 160A.

Figure 2-1. CDC 160A Console and Tape Units
Source: CDC 1961v

Figure 2-2 depicts a CDC 160A being used at Goddard Space Flight Center circa 1963.

Figure 2-2. CDC 160A at Goddard Space Flight Center
Source: NASA GSFC, No Date
Courtesy of the U.S. Government

Table 2-1. CDC 160A – Basic Characteristics

Characteristic	Value/Explanation
Internal Representation	Fixed Point Binary
# Bits/Word	12
# Instructions/Word	1
# Instructions	
# Bits/Instruction	12
Instruction Type	One-Address
CPU Technology	Transistor
CPU Registers	Six including Accumulator (A), Program Counter (P), Transient (Z)
Main Memory	Magnetic Core: 8K to 32K words; access time 6.4 microseconds
Add Time	Fixed Point Binary: 12.8 microseconds
Multiply Time	External Arithmetic Unit
Divide Time	External Arithmetic Unit

2.1 CDC 160 Architecture

The CDC 160 was a 12-bit computing machine. Four octal digits could be represented in each word. Indeed, it can be rightfully called the first minicomputer as it preceded the PDP-1 and strongly influenced the design of the PDP series. It was used in either stand-alone mode, as depicted above, or as a front-end to a CDC 1604 computing machine. Figure 2-3 depicts the CDC 160A processor architecture.

2.1.1 System Registers

The CDC 160A had several addressable registers, e.g., accessible by the programmer. The addressable registers are described in Table 2-2 (CDC 1965ad).

Table 2-2. CDC 160A Addressable Registers

Register	Description
A	The A register was used in all arithmetic, logical, and shifting operations.
P	The P register contains the storage address of the current instruction. P's contents are advanced by 1 or 2 unless a jump has occurred. If P contained either 7776 or 7777, adding 1 advanced to address 0000.
Buffer Entrance Register (BER)	During buffered I/O operations, BER holds the address to or from which address was being transferred. The contents of this register may be transferred to storage and to the A register.
Buffer Exit Register (BXR)	During buffered I/O operations, BXR holds the last address + 1 to or from which information was transferred.

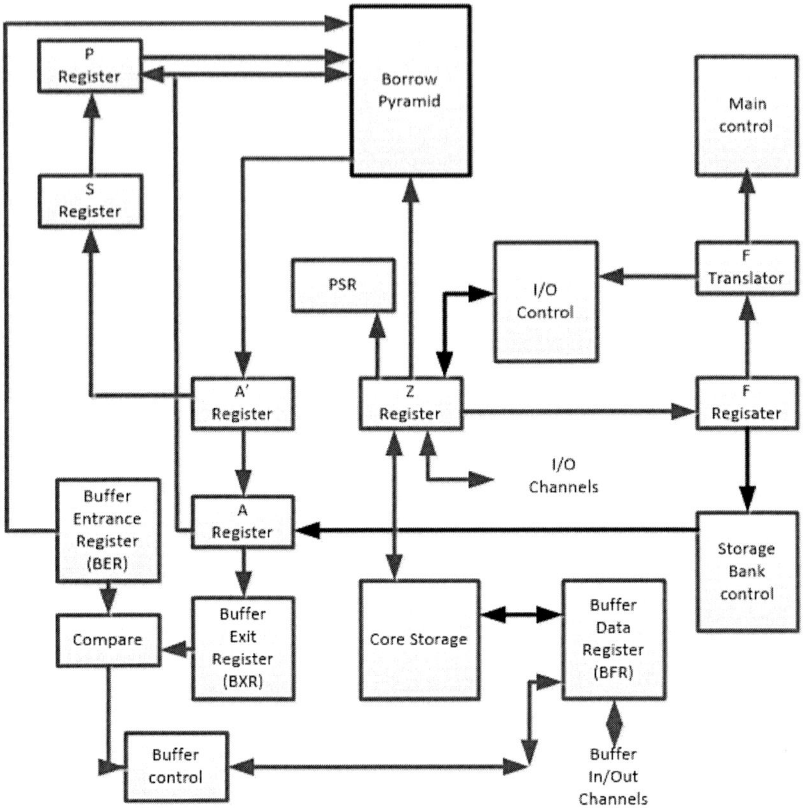

Figure 2-3. CDC 160A Processor Architecture
Source: Adapted from Control Data 1963b

Table 2-3 presents the non-addressable registers.

Table 2-3. CDC 160A Non-addressable Registers

Register	Description
Z	A buffer register holding data during transfer between storage and peripheral equipment. Also used in arithmetic operations.
S	This register contained the storage address currently being accessed for instructions or operands. Prior to any memory access, the storage address to be accessed had to be loaded into S. It supported direct addressing of 4K words.
F	This register contained the function code (upper 6 bits) of the instruction being executed
Buffer Data Register (BFR)	During a buffer operation, the BFR contained the word being transferred
A'	This registered acted as an auxiliary transmission register for information moving data between other registers. The output of the borrow pyramid was stored here.
Punch Storage Register (PSR)	The 8-bit PSR contained the character being punched on the paper tape punch.

2.1.2 Arithmetic Unit

Source: CDC 1961v

The CDC 168-2 Arithmetic Unit, depicted in Figure 2-4, which was accessed as an I/O device, performed add, subtract, and shift operations as well as multiply and divide operations with 27-bit precision. Multiply and divide were performed in fixed point. This unit enhanced the performance of the CDC 160A by performing arithmetic operations faster. Typical speeds for the arithmetic unit were 205 microseconds for addition and subtraction, 280 microseconds for multiplication, and 350 to 420 microseconds for division.

Figure 2-4. CDC 160 Arithmetic Unit
Source: CDC 1961v

2.1.3 Main Memory

The CDC 160 memory consisted of two, four, six, or eight banks of magnetic core storage each with 4096 words. The minimum memory was two banks yielding 8192 words. Each bank was assigned a number, 0 through 7, when it was installed. Associated with these banks were four registers of three bits each, called the *storage bank controls*. Each control register could be set to reference any one of the banks. Each bank had its own set of addresses numbered 0000 to 7777 octal. The four registers are described in Table 2-4 (CDC 1965ad).

When the computer attempted to reference a storage bank control that had a nonexistent bank, the CDC 160A would halt with a fault interrupt.

Two CDC 160A computers could be coupled through a dual-ported memory bank. Synchronization between the two machines was the responsibility of the programmer.

Table 2-4. CDC 160A Storage Bank Control Registers

Bank Control Register	Usage
Relative Bank Control (r) (RBC)	The RBC was used to specify the bank from which all instructions were to be fetched.
Direct Bank Control (d) (DBC)	The DBC was used to specify the bank used by all instructions which had direct addressing operation codes. When indirect addressing occurred, the d bank was used for the first memory address.
Indirect Bank Control (i) (IBC)	For instructions using indirect addressing, the IBC specified the bank for selecting the final address, e.g., the effective address. As an exception, jump instructions only used the RBC control.
Buffer Control Bank (b) (BCB)	For I/O instructions, the BCB specified the bank from which information was transferred to or from.

The CDC 169 Auxiliary Memory Unit allowed two CDC 160 computers to be operated in tandem by sharing a common memory and a buffer channel. It provided expansion of the basic in modules of 8K words up to a maximum of 32K words.

2.1.4 INTERRUPTS

An *interrupt* was a program signal that transferred control to some fixed location in memory. The CDC 160A had four interrupt lines: two internal lines and two external lines. The four lines were organized in a priority sequence so that a lower-numbered line was recognized first if concurrent signals occurred. When an interrupt occurred, the contents of the P register were stored at the first memory location and control was transferred to the second memory location for each interrupt as specified in Table 2-5.

Table 2-5. Interrupt Memory Locations

Interrupt Type	Store c(P) at	Load P From
Manual Interrupt from Console	(d) 0010	(r) 0011
Buffer Completion Interrupt	(d) 0020	(r) 0021
Peripheral Device Interrupt	(d) 0030	(r) 0031
Peripheral Device Interrupt	(d) 0040	(r) 0041

Figure 2-5 demonstrates how an interrupt was handled (CDC 1965ad). Letters d, r, and i in the instructions represent storage bank identifiers.

Location	F	E	G	Comments
(d)0010				Return address put here by interrupt's JPR instruction
(r)0011	JFI	01		Jump to interrupt routine
(r)0012	02	00		Interrupt routine begins at (r)0200
………				
(r)0200	STF	05		Save A in (r)0205
(r)0201	LDN	00		Set A <- 0
(r)0202	STM		2100	Set (i)2100 <- 0
(r)0204	LDC			Restore A
(r)0206	CIL			Clear Interrupt Lockout
(r)0207	JPI	10		Return to main program

Figure 2-5. Interrupt Handling Example
Source: Adapted from 1965ad

Multiple devices could be connected to the two external interrupt lines. After the interrupt occurred, these lines were interrogated to determine which device caused the interrupt. The CPU selected the peripheral device by issuing a 75_8 instruction that placed a 12-bit code on the output data lines and activated the function ready signal. The interrupt handling routine set up the data required to process the interrupt. The 12-bit code had the following format.

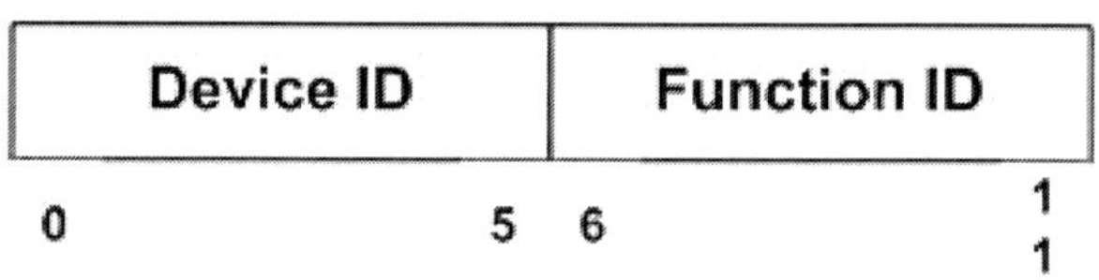

Figure 2-6. CDC 160/160A I/O Code
Source: Adapted from CDC 1965ad

Whenever an interrupt occurred, all further interrupts were locked out until the interrupt being handled was cleared via a CIL operation. Once an interrupt was cleared, all interrupt lines were checked again in priority sequence for activity.

Whenever the console master clear switch was pressed, all interrupt lines were set inactive and the interrupt lockout was removed.

2.1.5 Operator Console

The Operator Console was integrated into a desk-like structure that included a set of drawers for storage of program materials. As depicted in Figure 2-2, a paper tape reader was also mounted on top of the desk, so the drawers often contained rolls of paper tape containing programs and data. Among the paper tape rolls were utility programs and library routines that could be loaded on demand by a program upon notification to the operator. Figure 2-7 depicts the display portion of the console.

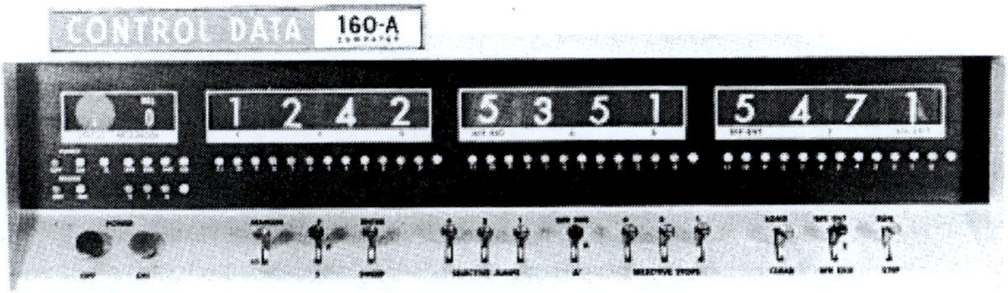

Figure 2-7. CDC 160 Operator Console
Source: CDC 1965ad

At the top of the panel was the register display which could display the contents of nine CDC 160 registers. Centered beneath each display was a three-position switch which selected the register to be displayed in that window. In the following sections, the reader will note that these displays served multiple purposes as alphanumeric symbols were displayed, but the background could be lit to indicate a machine problem.

2.1.5.1 P Register Group

For the leftmost register window - the P Register Group, Table 2-6 presents the registers that could be selected.

Table 2-6. P Register Group Display

Register Selected	Position	Usage
F	UP	Indicated the current effective function code. The most significant digit was lit by a green background.
P	CENTER	Indicated the address of the current instruction being executed.
S	DOWN	Indicated the address of the word about to be transferred to or from storage.

A red background indicated a non-existent storage bank address, which usually resulted from a programming error. This fault was cleared by a control master clear.

2.1.5.2 A Register Group

For the middle register window – the A Register Group, Table 2-7 presents the machine registers that could be selected.

Table 2-7. A Register Group Display

Register Selected	Position	Usage
BFR	UP	Indicated the last word processed during the last buffer operation. The most significant digit was lit by a green background.
A	CENTER	Indicated the current contents of the A register.
A’	DOWN	Indicated the result of the last operation in the adder. The least significant digit was lit by a green background.

A red background indicated a main timing fault, which normally occurred when the computer was first turned on. This fault was cleared by a Master Clear signal. If this condition occurred any time thereafter, the field maintenance team had to be called to investigate the problem. The CDC 160 was initially accompanied by a limited number of diagnostic routines, stored on paper tape, but this number was later increased as multiple machines were delivered to customers.

A blue background in the two center positions indicated an interrupt lockout.

2.1.5.3 Z Register Group

For the right register window – the Z Register Group, Table 2-8 presents the registers that could be selected.

Table 2-8. Z Register Group Display

Register Selected	Position	Usage
BER	UP	Indicated the last word t The most significant digit was lit by a green background.
Z	CENTER	Indicated the current contents of the Z register.
BXR	DOWN	Indicated the last word address + 1 of the last buffer operation. The least significant digit was lit by a green background.

A blue background indicated the presence of an instruction in the Z register rather than a transient data word.

A red background in the two center positions indicated that the High-Speed Punch was low on paper tape.

2.1.5.4 Status Mode Indicator

The leftmost display window was the Status Mode Indicator. If it had a green background, this indicated the computer was in run status, and that instructions were being executed. A red background indicated that the computer was either stopped or operating in step status. Step status was set when the Run/Step switch was set to Step and allowed the operator to step one instruction at a time through a program for debugging purposes. Several alphanumeric symbols were displayed against the colored background, which indicated the computer's current status as described in Table 2-9.

Table 2-9. Status Mode Symbols

Indicator	Meaning
ERR	The computer executed an ERR instruction and was stopped.
SEL	This indicator was displayed each time an EXF or EXC instruction was executed. It remained displayed until the selection was complete. A constant display with no apparent I/O meant the computer had attempted an illegal selection.
OUT	This indicator was displayed during normal output operations. A constant display of OUT with no apparent I/O meant the computer had made an improper unit selection.
IN	This indicator was displayed during normal input operations. A constant display of IN with no apparent I/O meant the computer had made an improper unit selection. It was also displayed when waiting for an external device, such as TTY, to provide data.
IBA	This indicator was displayed during buffer input operations.
OBA	This indicator was displayed during buffer output operations.
A, B, C, or D	These indicators were displayed when the next storage reference cycle was executed during at the next Step.

2.1.5.5 Memory Control Status Indicator

Below the Status Mode Indicator was the Memory Control Status (MCS) Indicator. It displayed the storage bank number that was set for each of the four storage banks. The buttons below the lights allowed the system operator to set the binary value of the storage bank number to the associated storage bank.

2.1.5.6 Switch Panel

The Switch Panel was located below the main indicators for the register groups. From the left, the function of each switch function is described in Table 2-10.

Table 2-10. Switch Panel Functions

Switch	Function
Power On/Off	Blue button turns power on; red button turns it off.
Margin	This switch was for maintenance use to vary the bias on magnetic core storage sense amplifiers.
F, P, S	Three-position switch to choose the register to be displayed in the P register group.
Enter/Sweep	Enter was used to enter data into core storage unit. Sweep was used to display the contents of the core storage unit.
Selective Jump Switches (4,2,1)	UP selects jump conditions for interrogation by the SLS and SLJ instructions.
BFR, A, A'	Three-position switch to choose the register to be displayed in the A register group.
Selective Stop Switches (4,2,1)	UP selects stop conditions for interrogation by the SLS and SLJ instructions.
Load/Clear	LOAD enabled the reading of paper tapes into storage by the paper tape reader. CLEAR performed a computer master clear of registers and indicators, but did not alter core storage.
BFR ENT, Z, BFR EXIT	Three-position switch to choose the register to be displayed in the Z register group.
Run/Step	In RUN position, a program was executed starting at the location specified by the P register. The center position stopped the computer In STEP position, one storage cycle of the instruction was executed each time the switch was set. This was used for debugging purposes.

2.2 CDC 160 Instruction Set

The minimum main memory of the CDC 160 was 4K Words. It was addressed by the 12-bit Storage (S) Register, whose format is depicted in Figure 2-8.

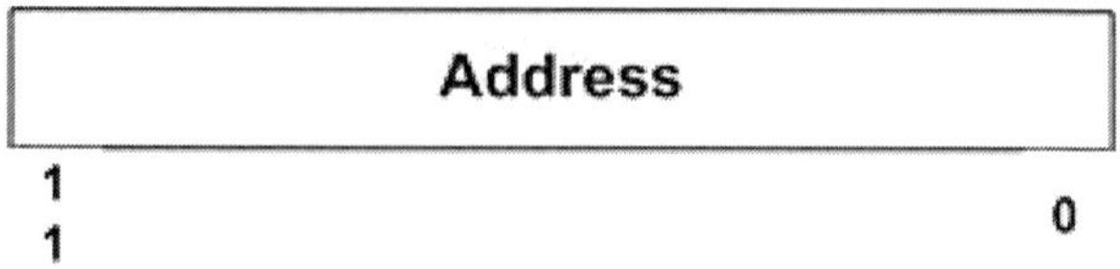

Figure 2-8. CDC 160 S Register Format
Source: Adapted from CDC 1965ad

The Program Counter (PC) for the CDC 160 was also 12 bits and had the format depicted in Figure 2-9.

Figure 2-9 CDC 160 Program Counter Format
Source: Adapted from CDC 1965ad

All arithmetic and logical operations were performed on the 12-bit Accumulator (A), whose format is depicted in Figure 2-10.

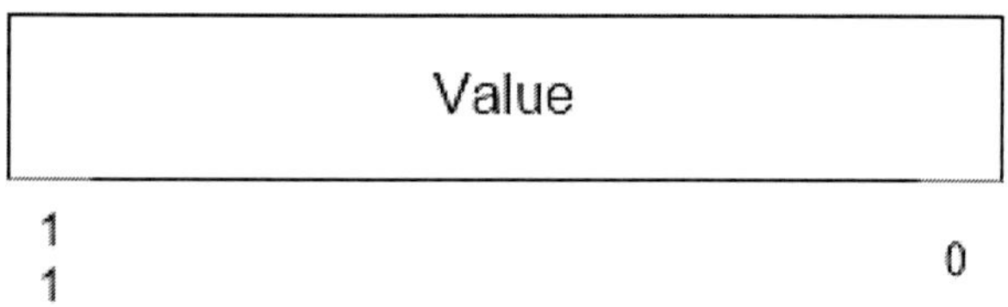

Figure 2-10. CDC 160 Accumulator Format
Source: CDC 1965ad

2.2.1 ADDRESSING MODES

The CDC 160A supported nine addressing modes as described in Table 2-11. The upper 6-bits of a CDC 160A instruction are labeled F, while the lower 6-bits are labeled E. If a second word was used in the instruction, it was labeled G. These are depicted in Figure 2-11.

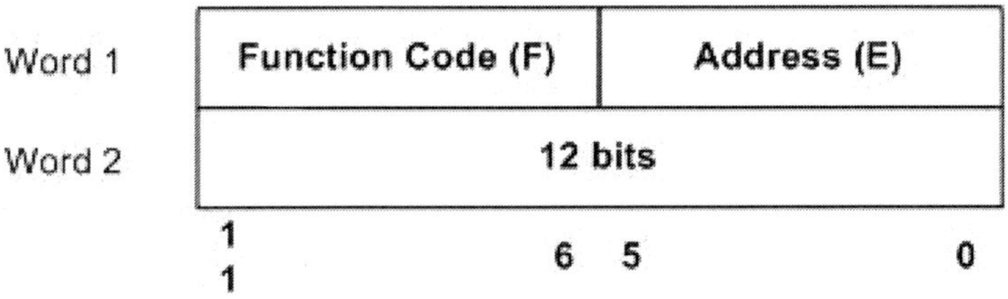

Figure 2-11. CDC 160 Instruction Format
Source: Adapted from Control Data 1963b

Table 2-11. CDC 160A Addressing Modes

Address Mode	Description
No Address (N)	The E portion was used as a 6-bit constant in arithmetic and logical operations. For example, consider this instruction: Location F E 0100 LDN 43 0101 <next instruction> The effective address was 0043_8. Control continues at location 0101.
Direct Address (D)	Refers to a 12-bit operand in the first 64 locations of memory. Location F E 0076 12 34 1075 LDD 76 (Load Data Direct) c(0076) was transferred to the A register. Thus, c(A) = 1234.
Indirect Address (I)	The 6-bit E portion was used as the address of the operand or jump address and referenced the first 64 locations of memory. Location F E 0045 33 65 3365 46 57 4121 LDI 45 4122 <next instruction> c(E) of the Load Indirect instruction references the contents of location 3365, whose contents 4657, will be transferred to the A register.

Relative Address Forward (F)	The E portion was added to c(P) to specify one of 63 addresses immediately following the current address. Location F E 0233 LDF 22 0234 <next instruction> 0255 77 03 E was added to c(P) = 0233 to yield an effective address of 0255. After this instruction was executed, c(A) = 7703. Control continues at location 0234.
Relative Address Backward (B)	The E portion was subtracted from c(P) to specify one of 63 addresses immediately prior to the current address.
Forward Indirect Addressing (FI)	The E portion was added to c(P) to specify an operand or jump address.
Specific Address (S)	The effective address was always (0)7777_8 in storage bank zero. The E portion of the instruction must always be zero. Location F E 0177 LDS 00 0200 <next instruction> 7777 43 21 The fact that E = 00 was used in decoding this instruction was to recognize that the effective address was 7777_8. The value at 7777_8, e.g., 4321, was transferred to the A register. Execution continues at address (r)0200.
Constant Address (C)	The G portion contains the operand. Location F E G 0101 LDC 00 0102 7337 0103 STC 00 0104 2345 0105 <next instruction> When the instruction at 0101 was executed, the quantity 7337 in location 0102 – the operand address, was loaded into the A register. When the instruction at 0103 was executed, c(A) was stored into location 2345.
Memory Address (M)	The G portion contains the address of the operand. E was always zero. Location F E G 3477 LDM 00 3500 1111 3501 STM 00 3502 0024

	3503 <next instruction> 1111 67 66 0024 02 34 When the LDM instruction was executed at location 3477, 1111_8 becomes the effective address and results in 677 being placed in the A register. When the STM instruction was executed, the effective address was 0024_8 into which 6766 was stored.

2.2.2 OPERATE INSTRUCTIONS

The Operate Instructions consisted of six shift instructions and three control instructions. Table 2-12 presents the shift instructions.

Table 2-12. CDC 160 Shift Instructions

Mnemonic	Opcodes$_8$	Operation
LS1	01 02	Shift Left One: A was circularly shifted one place left.
LS2	01 03	Shift Left 2: A was circularly shifted two places left.
LS3	01 10	Shift Left 3: A was circularly shifted three places left.
LS6	01 11	Shift Left 6: A was circularly shifted 6 places left.
Shift Left 10	01 12	A was multiplied by 10. This was a microcoded combination of shifting left one and three times.
Shift Left 100	01 13	A was multiplied by 100.
RS1	01 14	Shift Right One: A was circularly shifted one place right.
RS2	01 15	Shift Right Two: A was circularly shifted two places right.
SRD	44 XX	Shift Replace Direct:
SRM	45 00 XXXX	Shift Replace Memory
SRI	45 XX	Shift Replace Indirect:
SRC	46 00 XXXX	Shift Replace Constant:
SRF	46 XX	Shift Replace Forward:
SRS	47 00	Shift Replace Specific
SRB	47 XX	Shift Replace Backward

In the original design it was planned to expand this group of instructions to multiplication by other small constants, where the constant would appear as the literal in the E field. However, the last opcode seemed to indicate that this planned was abandoned as the last shift left instructions were not replicated in the shift right instructions.

2.2.3 Control Instructions

The Control Instructions performed miscellaneous operations that did not fit into other categories. Perhaps, the key one was Transmit PC to Accumulator, which was used to save the PC during subroutine jumps. Table 2-13 depicts the Control Instructions.

Table 2-13. CDC 160 Control Instructions

Name	Opcodes	Operation
NOP	0000	When the Run switch was in the RUN position, control was passed to the next instruction (while consuming storage cycles).
Halt/Error	7700/7777	Halt and Error instructions operated the same. The CPU stops and could only be halted by pressing the RUN switch on the console.
Transmit PC to Accumulator	0101	Moved the current value of the PC to the Accumulator.

Using the Transmit PC to Accumulator instruction, the CDC 160 could accomplish a subroutine call by linkage through the accumulator.

2.2.4 Jump Instruction Format

Jump instructions consisted of four relative jump instructions and two indirect jump instructions. The relative jump instructions performed jumps relative to the PC based on the value of the accumulator.

Bit 8, the forward/backward (f/b) bit, determined whether the jump was forwards or backwards. When f/b was 0, the contents of the Address were added to the PC; otherwise, they were subtracted from the PC. If the condition succeeded, then the effective address (PC +/- Address) was loaded into the PC. Otherwise, the PC was incremented by one. Figure 2-12 depicts the format of the Relative Jump instructions. Table 2-14 presents the indirect jump instructions.

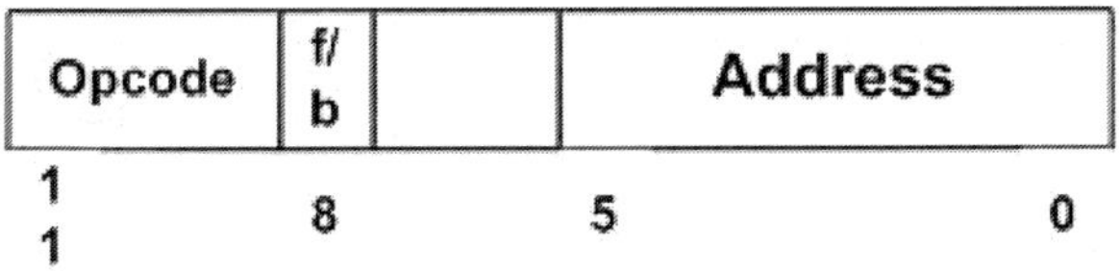

Figure 2-12. CDC 160 Relative Jump Instruction
Source: Adapted from CDC 1963e

Table 2-14 CDC 160 Relative Jump Instructions

Mnemonic	Opcodes$_8$	Operation
ZJF	110x00	Zero Jump Forward: Jump if all bits of A are zero.
NZF	110x01	Non-Zero Jump Forward: Jump if any bit of A was nonzero.
PJF	110x10	Positive Jump Forward: Jump if A was positive.
NJF	110x11	Negative Jump Forward: Jump if A was negative.

The format of the Indirect Jump Instructions was presented in Figure 2-13. The indirect jump address field was used to access one of the first 64 memory locations for its contents. Table 2-15 presents the Indirect Jump Instructions.

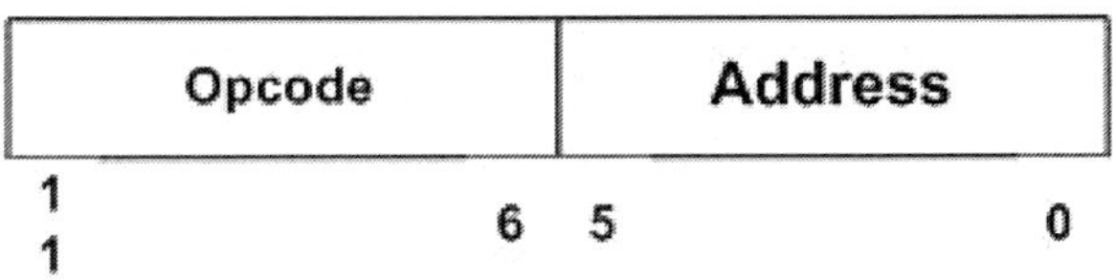

Figure 2-13. CDC 160 Indirect Jump Instruction Format
Source: Adapted from CDC 1963e

Table 2-15. CDC 160 Indirect Jump Instructions

Name	Opcodes$_8$	Operation
JPI	70xx	Jump Indirect: Use Address to address one of the first 64 memory locations, and load the contents of that location into P.
JFI	71xx	Jump Forward Indirect: Use forward relative addressing to fetch the destination address.
JPR	71 00 XXXX	Return Jump to XXXX.

2.2.5 Memory Reference Instructions

The Memory Reference instructions (MRI) moved data between memory and the registers. Each MRI could accommodate any of the four addressing modes described in Table 2-16 (CDC 1963e).

Table 2-16. Addressing Modes

Mode	Bits 7-6$_8$	Description
Direct	00	Direct addressing uses the 6-bit Address, padded with zeros, to directly address the first 64 words of memory. These words are typically used for global variables and pointers. So, S = Address.
Indirect	01	If 6-bit Address was zero, indirect addressing uses the word following the instruction as a pointer to the operand anywhere in memory. The next instruction to be executed will be fetched from the word after this pointer. If the Address was nonzero, indirect addressing uses the Address, padded with zeros, to address the first 64 words of memory. The word fetched was then used to address the operand anywhere in memory. So, if Address = 0 then { S = P; S = M[S]; P = P+1 } else { S = Address; S = M[S] }
Forward Relative	10	If 6-bit Address was zero, the operand was in the next memory location. The next instruction to be executed will be fetched from the word after the operand. If the Address was nonzero, the operand address was computed by adding the Address to the PC. So, if E = 0 then { S = P; P = P+1 } else { S = P + Address }
Backward Relative	11	The operand address was computed by subtracting the Address from the program counter. So, S = c(P)-Address.

The format of the memory reference instructions was depicted in Figure 2-14. The Mode bits were interpreted according to the table above.

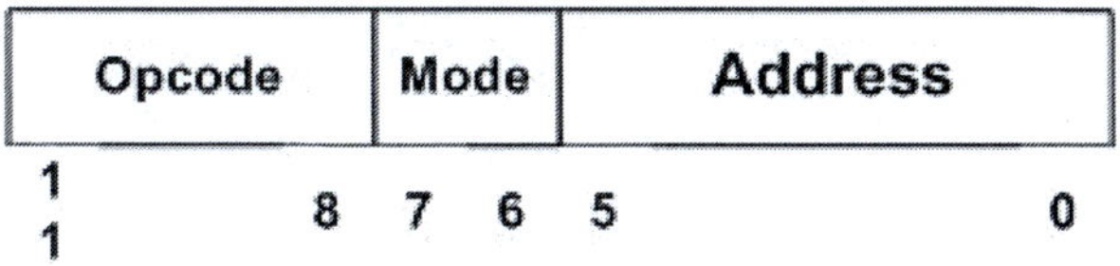

Figure 2-14. CDC 160 Memory Reference Instruction Format
Source: Adapted from CDC 1963e

Table 2-14 presents the memory reference instructions. These included the logical and arithmetic instructions. The notation M[S] means to fetch the operand from the memory address stored in the S register.

Table 2-17. CDC 160 Memory Reference Instructions

Name	Opcodes$_8$	Operation
And	0001	The data from M[S] was logically ANDed with A, bit by bit.
Or	0010	The data from M[S] was logically ORed with A, bit by bit.
Load	0011	The data from M[S] was loaded into A.
Load Complement	0100	The data from M[S] was ones complemented and loaded into A.
Add	0101	The data from M[S] was added to A. One's complement addition was used, i.e., addition with end-around carry.
Subtract	0111	The data from M[S] was subtracted from A, i.e., the data was complemented and then added with end-around carry.
Store	1000	The contents of A are stored in M[S].
Shift and Replace	1001	The data from M[S] are circularly shifted one place left, with the results stored in both A and M[S].
Add and Replace	1010	The data from M[S] are circularly shifted one place left, with the results stored in both A and M[S].
Add One and Replace	1011	The data from M[S] are added to A, with the results stored in both A and M[S]. One's complement addition was used, i.e., addition with end-around carry.

2.2.6 IMMEDIATE INSTRUCTIONS

The Immediate instructions used the 6-bit value in the Immediate Operand field as an operand with the accumulator. These included two logical operations, two arithmetic operations, and two accumulator loading operations. Figure 2-15 depicts the format of the immediate instructions. Table 2-18 presents the immediate instructions.

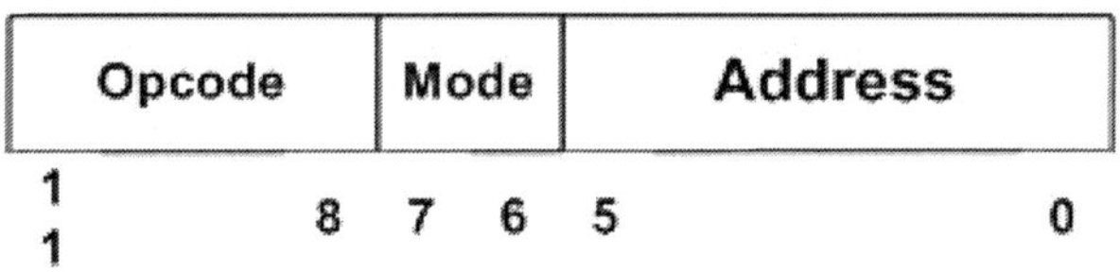

Figure 2-15. CDC 160 Immediate Instruction Format
Source: Adapted from CDC 1963e

In the Immediate instructions, the value in the Immediate Operand field was padded with zeroes before the operation.

Table 2-18. CDC 160 Immediate Instructions

Name	Opcodes$_8$	Operation
And	0001	The Immediate Operand was logically ANDed with A, bit by bit.
Or	0010	The Immediate Operand was logically ORed with A, bit by bit.
Load	0011	The Immediate Operand was loaded into A.
Load Complement	0100	The Immediate Operand was ones complemented and loaded into A.
Add	0101	The Immediate Operand was added to A. One's complement addition was used, i.e., addition with end-around carry.
Subtract	0111	The Immediate Operand was subtracted from A, i.e., the data was complemented and then added with end-around carry.

2.2.7 FUNCTION INVOCATION

The CDC 160 had no instruction that both transferred control to a function and saved the return address. The latter operation had to be performed in the instruction sequence before making the jump. An example of how to do this is shown below (CDC 1963e):

Address	Instruction/Data
X	Load Forward Relative
X+1	<return address>
X+2	Store Indirect
X+3	P <destination return link>
X+4	Jump Forward Indirect
X+5	P+1 <destination address>

and the receiving and return sequences for the function calling sequence could be set as:

Address	Instruction/Data
P-1	Jump Forward Relative
P	<return address>
P+1	<entry point to function>
....	
....	<function body>
....	
P+N	Jump Forward Indirect
P+N+1	<address of return jump>

2.2.8 Data Transmission Instructions

The Data Transmission Instructions transferred data to and from the accumulator within or between storage banks, and between internal registers. Table 2-19 presents these instructions.

Table 2-19. Data Transmission Instructions

Name	Opcodes$_8$	Operation
BLS	01 00 XXXX	Block Store was used to set selected positions of storage to any desired value. BER <- FWA, BXR <- LWA +1. (b) was set to the storage bank. A gets the value to be set into storage. The next instruction was not executed until BLS was completed.
PTA	01 01	Transfer B to A: A <- c(P); P <- 1 + c(P).
ATE	01 05	A to Buffer Entrance Register: BER <- c(A). P <- 2 + c(P).
ATX	01 06	A to Buffer Exit Register BXR <- c(A). P <- 2 + c(P).

ETA	01 07	Buffer Entrance Register to A: A <- c(BER). P <- 1 + c(P).
CTA	01 30	Bank Controls to A: A_{11-9} <- (b). A_{8-6} <- (d). A_{5-3} <- (i). A_{2-0} <- (r). P <- 1 + c(P).
STP	01 5Y	Store P at Location 5Y. (d) 005Y <p c(P). P <- 1 + c(P).
STE	01 6Y	Store BER at Location 006Y
		Load Instructions: The operand from the location specified by the addressing mode was loaded into the A register.
LDN	04 XX	Load No Address
LDD	20 YY	Load Direct
LDM	21 00 XXXX	Load Memory
LDI	21 YY	Load Indirect
LDC	22 00 XXXX	Load Constant
LDF	22 XX	Load Forward
LDS	23 00	Load Specific
LDB	23 XX	Load Backward
LCN	05 XX	Load Complement No Address
LCD	24 XX	Load Complement Direct
LCM	25 00 XXXX	Load Complement Memory
LCI	25 XX	Load Complement Indirect
LCC	26 00 XXXX	Local Complement Constant
LCF	26 XX	Load Complement FORWARD
LCS	27 00	Load Complement Specific
LCB	27 XX	Load Complement Backward
		Store Operations: The value in the A register was transferred to the location specified by the address mode.
STD	40 XX	Store Direct
STM	41 00 XXXX	Store Memory
STI	41 XX	Store Indirect
STC	42 00 XXXX	Store Constant
STF	42 XX	Store Forward
STS	43 00	Store Specific
STB	43 XX	Store Backward
HWI	76 XX	Half Write Indirect

2.2.9 Input/Output Instructions

I/O Instructions performed I/O operations, including (1) reading or writing data and (2) external function constants and status codes, and (3) checking the status of devices. Table 2-20 presents the CDC 160 I/O Instructions. XXXX and YYYY specified addresses relative to the 4K bank.

Table 2-20. CDC 160 I/O Instructions

Name	Opcodes8	Operation
CBC	01 04	Clear Buffer Control
CIL	01 20	Clear Interrupt Lockout
IBI	72 00 XXXX	Initiate Buffer Input
IBO	73 00 XXXX	Initiate Buffer Output
INP	72 XX YYYY	Normal Input
OUT	73 XX YYYY	Normal Output
OTN	74 XX	Output No Address
INA	76 00	Input to A
OTA	76 77	Output From A
EXC	75 00 XXXX	External Function Constant
75 XX	EXF	External Function Forward

2.3 I/O Subsystem

Communications between the central processor and the peripheral devices occurred through two cables – one carrying input signals, the other carrying output signals. Each cable carried 12 data lines plus various control lines.

Every external unit had to be connected to the output cable because the external function code was only carried by the data lines of the output cable. However, the power capacities of the transistors in the output amplifier cards and the maximum cable length limited the number of devices attached to a CDC 160/160A to five.

The paper tape reader and punch, which were directly connected to the CPU, were not included in this count.

The CDC 160A had an I/O bandwidth of 70K words/s. I/O was buffered and operated independently of the CPU.

2.3.1 CHANNELS

The CDC 160A had two I/O channels – a normal channel and a buffer channel. Both channels could operate simultaneously. Devices connected to the normal channel could only be read or written on the normal channel. Devices connected to the buffer channel could be read or written on both channels. An operation on the normal channel required the CPU to wait until it was completed.

All devices were connected to the normal channel in order to transmit external function codes to and from the CPU. When external equipment was selected, all other external devices were logically disconnected from the computer. A device on the buffer channel performing an operation was not disconnected.

The general procedure for performing an I/O operation was:

1. Request the status of the selected unit;
2. Test the status for the capability to perform the required function;
3. Select the unit to perform the I/O function;
4. Select the proper storage bank and initiate the I/O operation on the correct channel; and
5. At the completion of the I/O operation, request the status of the selected unit and check that the operation was completed successfully.

If a device could not perform the requested function, the computer could be indefinitely delayed and SEL would appear in the Status Mode Indicator on the Operator Console. Figure 2-17 depicts a procedure checking the status of the typewriter:

Location	F	E	G	Comments
(r)<addr>	EXC		4240	Request typewriter status
(r)<addr>+2	INA			Read status response into A
(r)<addr>+3	ZJF	03		Select if typewriter ready
(r)<addr>+4	JPR		W	Return jump to determine status trouble
(r)<addr>+6	EXC		4210	Select typewriter
Continue with program				

Figure 2-16. Testing Device Status
Source: CDC 1965ad

If the typewriter was not ready, a jump was performed to the subroutine at W to determine what to do. A status response from the typewriter indicated that it was ready to perform an I/O operation. Although not performed on the typewriter, status checks were performed on some devices such as magnetic tape units to determine if any of several error conditions might have occurred.

The CDC 160A Reference Manual contained several examples of testing devices and performing I/O operations.

2.3.2 CDC 160A Peripheral Devices

The CDC 160/160A supported the following optional equipment:

- CDC 1608 Magnetic Tape Subsystems
- CDC 167/177/1614 Punched Card Readers and CDC 170 Punches
- CDC 1612 High- and CDC 166 Low-Speed Line Printers
- CDC 165 Plotters
- A/D and D/A Equipment
- Up to two CDC 160/160A computers operating as satellite systems
- Two CDC 160A's operating independently, but sharing magnetic core memory
- CDC 168 Auxiliary Arithmetic Unit

The CDC 160A also supported various analog-to-digital and digital-to-analog acquisition and conversion equipment.

2.4 CDC 160 Software

The CDC 160A was oriented towards scientific and engineering programming. The system and applications software was focused on supporting the basic tasks that scientific and engineering practitioners used to process data.

2.4.1 OSAS-A

Source: CDC 1964bd

OSAS-A was a symbolic assembler that supported fully symbolic coding and translated a program into an absolute or relocatable object module. Pseudo operations (e.g., control directives) controlled the assembly process. It performed automatic address assignment, code error checking, and provided y listing of source and object modules. Object code could be generated in absolute or relative format.

OSAS-A was a two- or three-pass assembler depending on the size of the symbolic program. During the first pass, the source code was read, scanned for various fields, and stored in condensed form in a reserved block of storage. When the block was full, it was written onto the output medium specified by an parameter set during the generation of the OSAS-AS assembler. Other steps included assigning values to location symbols, entering symbols into the symbol table, translating operation codes to their numeric equivalents, and managing the location counter.

During the second pass, it analyzed and converted the intermediate representation into binary and wrote it to the output device. If the symbol table was required for assembly of other programs, it was punched to on a separate, non-listable paper tape to be read later. The intermediate form could also be punched to paper tape as a means of assembling separate program elements.

A third pass was required if the listable and binary output were to be written to paper tape.

All programs assembled by OSAS-A were relocatable by specifying a relocation address at load time. Thus the binary output from OSAS-A was relative to an initial location of 0, and, during relocation, the relocation address was added to the storage addresses assigned to variables.

2.4.2 SICOM

SICOM was a general-purpose interpreter used to provide floating point calculations. It effectively converted the CDC 160A from a 12-bit fixed point machine to a 10 decimal digit plus exponent and sign floating-point machine via simulation.

2.4.3 AUTOCOMM

AUTOCOMM provided a commercial data processing capability using English language statements to specify the operations to be performed. It supported BCD arithmetic and comparison operations using numbers having up to 12 decimal digits. It provided editing capabilities and indexing operations provided flexible access to data structures. OSAS-A assembly language code could be intermixed with source code to provide faster computation for complex problems.

2.4.4 FORTRAN II

CDC provided a complete FORTRAN II compiler with an associated subroutine library that included trigonometric routines for the CDC 160A. A library contained I/O routines for all peripherals that could be used with the CDC 160A.

2.4.5 CEPS

A Civil Engineering Programming System (CEPS) provided geometric calculations for highway design, right of way analysis, bridge design and loading, and structures analysis and hydraulics among other applications. A Biomedical Experimentation and Analysis system supported data acquisition and data processing. Coupled with an analog-to-digital converter or digital-to-analog converter, it could operate a wide variety of scientific instrumentation.

2.5 CDC 160G

Source: CDC 1964z

The CDC 160G was an enhanced version of the 160A. The 160G incorporated logic and technology from the CDC 3600 systems. It reduced the cycle time to 1.35 microseconds and the memory access time to 0.7 microseconds. Main memory was expandable to 128K words and it could accommodate up to 8 IO Channels. It was upward compatible from the CDC 160 and 160A and accommodated most of the peripheral devices for those systems.

It incorporated all the CDC 160 and 160A instructions, but also included hardware multiply and divide instruction support. Average instruction execution time was 3 microseconds. Typical fixed point multiply time was 7 microseconds and typical fixed point divide time was 8.5 microseconds. It also added two other instructions: high-low comparison and bit-by-bit jump. Figure 2-17 depicts the CDC 160G. Notice the enhanced operator's console.

Figure 2-17. CDC 160G Computer System
Source: CDC 1963aa

2.6 CDC 160A Assessment

The CDC 160(A) was the first computer to be housed in a standard office disk configuration. This removed some of the concern about using computers because users saw it as a tool like those on their desks that they could use to solve problems even though it was backed up by multiple large cabinets.

As Seymour Cray's "first" computer, it was complex in its architecture as seen in Figure 2-3. As one traces the flow between components, it is difficult to understand how the structure correlates to some of the instructions. The flow of data between registers and to and between components seems to indicate that Cray was trying out some ideas in computing architecture. Some of these later were resolved with the architecture of the CDC 1604 and the CDC 6600.

The CDC 160A and CDC 160G were intended to be used with paper tape as the input and output medium of programs. Later, limited support for. magnetic tape systems were provided for simple storage. Since the system executed one program at a time, it could be viewed as an early personal workstation.

CHAPTER THREE

CDC 1604

Source: CDC 1961ao, Thornton 1980b

Because some of the founders of CDC came from ERA, their first significant computing machine, the CDC 1604, looked a lot like the ERA machines from an architectural standpoint. CDC initiated the CDC 1604 project with the aim of entering the scientific computer market as a target of opportunity. The CDC 1604 was the first fully transistorized computer and was designed by Seymour Cray and Bob Kesl. It was first announced in 1959.

One apocryphal story was that the number 1604 was derived by adding 501 – CDC's first street address – to Cray's last project, the 1103. Another was that 1604 meant 16K memory and 4 tape units (Hawley, p. 21 in Lincoln 1975).

It was one of the first solid-state computers. It had a clock speed of 1.2 microseconds. Peripheral devices included paper and magnetic tape, teletype machines, punched cards, and line printers. It was used for applications that included real-time data processing, weapon-system control, large-scale scientific problems, engineering and commercial applications, and industrial process control. At its introduction, it was the world's most powerful computer (Lincoln 1975).

When the 1604 was announced it had almost no software associated with it, except some diagnostic software written in machine language. CDC's philosophy, at the time, was that the customer knew better what software to write to best utilize the machine. However, once the IBM 7090 started selling with IBSYS, CDC quickly reversed its opinion and started to develop software for the 1604.

The first production CDC 1604 was delivered to the Naval Postgraduate School (NPGS) at Monterey, California in January 1960. Within 10 days, NPGS had put the machine into operation and accepted it for production computing. This machine was used to support the Navy Numerical Weather Prediction (NANWEP) program for predicting meteorological conditions for the Pacific Test Range. It also provided computing support for the NPGS students. Figure 3-1 depicts Professor Elmo Stewart, Director of the NPGS Computer Center, at the console of the CDC 1604.

Figure 3-1. CDC 1604 at Naval Postgraduate School
Source: CDC Ad circa 1961
Courtesy of U.S. Government

Figure 3-2 (a) and 3-2 (b) depict a 1960s era advertisement for the CDC 1604.

Figure 3-2(a) CDC 1604 Advertisement
Source: CDC circa 1960s

CDC early recognized that while customers probably knew what software they had to write to support their business operations and computing requirements, training and maintenance were essential to keeping those customers happy and productive. Thus, their emphasis in 6 of the 9 facts.

Figure 3-2(b) CDC 1604 Advertisement
Source: CDC circa 1960s

Another CDC 1604 was delivered to the Naval Computer System Support Activity (NAVCOSSACT) at the Washington Navy Yard in 1960 to support Fleet Command Center Operations in Hawaii (CINCPACFLT), Norfolk (CINCLANTFLT), and London (CINCUSNAVEUR). Figure 3-3 provides another view of a CDC 1604 computer system showing the entire complement of cabinets.

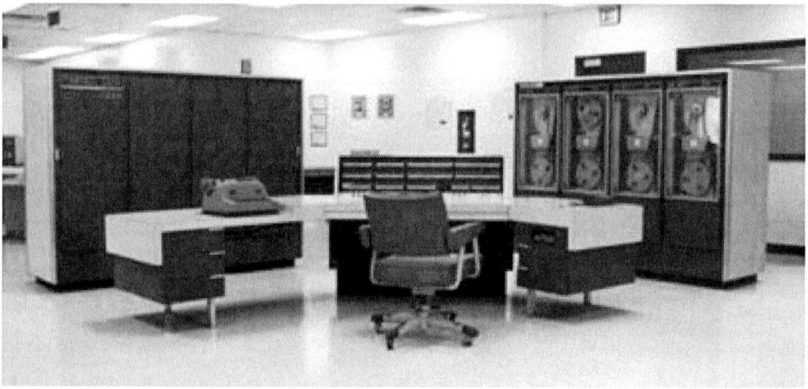

Figure 3-3. CDC 1604 Computer System
Source: CDC circa 1960s

Table 3-1 describes the basic characteristics of the CDC 1604 computer system. Interestingly, it was one of the few 48-bit word machines and one of the first to pack two instructions per word, although this seemed to involve extra circuity. The benefit was that larger floating numbers could be represented without double precision arithmetic.

Table 3-1. CDC 1604 – Basic Characteristics

Characteristic	Value/Explanation
Internal Representation	Fixed Point Binary
# Bits/Word	48
# Instructions/Word	2
# Instructions	62
# Bits/Instruction	24
Instruction Type	One Address
CPU Technology	Transistor-diode logic: cycle time – 4.8 microseconds
CPU Registers	Two 48-bit accumulators, Six 15-bit index registers
Main Memory	Magnetic Core: 32K words, 2.2 microsecond access time
Add Time	Fixed Point: 7.2 microseconds; Floating Point: 18.8 microseconds

Multiply Time	Fixed Point: 25.2 + 8n* microseconds (n = No. of 1's in multiplier) Floating Multiply: 36.0 microseconds
Divide Time	Fixed Point: 65.2 microseconds; Floating Divide: 56.0 microseconds

A basic CDC 1604 system configuration is depicted in Figure 3-4. The CDC 1604 was primarily designed to be a tape-based machine, which limited its overall performance even though it was considered to be (one of) the fastest machines of its era.

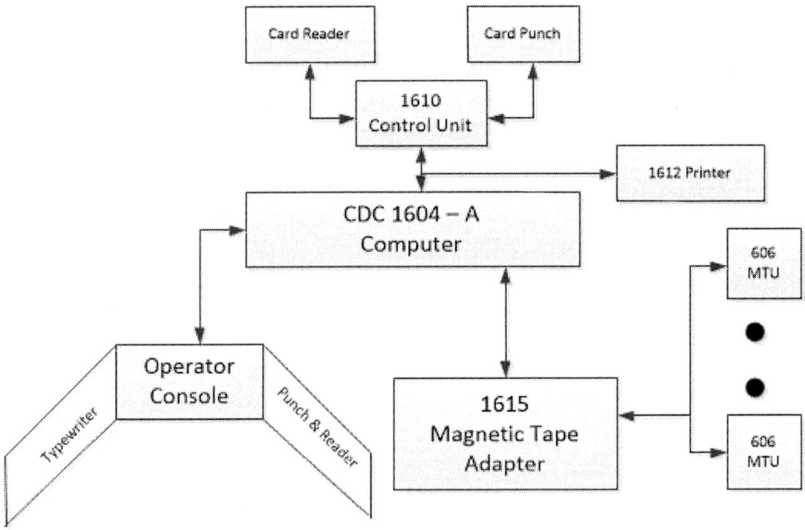

Figure 3-4. CDC 1604 System Configuration
Source: CDC 1963ag

3.1 CDC 1604 System Architecture

Source: CDC 1960 m,n,o

The CDC 1604 had a 48-bit word. Each instruction was 24 bits, so two instructions could be packed into a word. The machine had 62 instructions decoded. The number representation was one's complement for both fixed point and floating-point numbers. Unique to this machine was a *repeat* instruction that acted like a primitive vector operation. It was often used for block data moves within memory.

The CDC 1604 was comprised of four major sections as described below.

3.1.1 Storage Section

The Storage Section provided the memory for storing data and instructions. It provided high-speed random-access storage for 32K words. It was implemented as two banks of 16K words with one bank holding odd addresses and the other bank hold even addresses.

A word was 48 bits in length and contained either a 48-bit data item or two 24-bit instructions. The standard cycle time for accessing a word was 6.4 microseconds. Since the storage accesses of the two banks overlapped each other, the effective access time was 4.8 microseconds while the total cycle time was 6.4 microseconds.

The CDC 1604 supported indirect addressing when the index register B^b value was equal to 7. The value of the address portion of the instruction was used as the address of a memory location which contained the operand address. Indirect addressing required a second storage reference. All instructions except 22, 23, 74, 75 and 76 could use either direct or indirect addressing.

The Storage Section was connected to both the Arithmetic and I/O Sections, but it could only be used by one of these at a time.

3.1.2 Control Section

The Control Section sequences the operations for decoding and executing instructions in a program. It obtained instructions from memory, decoded them to transmit control signals to subcomponents, and fetched the data from memory for use in executing instructions, and stored data in memory that was the result.

The Control Section provided the registers that were used to perform computations and to operate the machine. Table 3-2 presents the CDC 1604 registers.

Table 3-2. Control Section Registers

Register	Bits	Description
A	48	Accumulator: It was used for arithmetic and logical computations. It could be shifted left or right.
Q	48	Auxiliary Arithmetic: It could be coupled with the A register to perform double precision arithmetic (96 bits). Its contents could also be shifted left or right. During logical operation, it held the mask
B1 – B6	15	Index Registers: Used to modify addresses during execution using relative addressing. They were also used to hold the number of words in search and transfer instruction.
P	15	Program Address: It acted as the program counter and held the address of the word whose contents currently resided in U1.
U1	15	Program Control: It held the current program step while the two instructions contained in it were executed. The upper instruction was executed first. Then, the lower instruction was executed unless the upper instruction was a jump instruction or a conditional skip instruction.
U2		Auxiliary Program Control: It was used to modify the operand addresses from the instructions contained in U1.
R		Address Buffer:
CCR, CR1 – CR6		Buffer Control
X		Exchange: An auxiliary register through which all data for I/O passed.
OO		External Function Register: It was used to exchange control information with I/O equipment.
S1, S2		Storage Address Registers: These registers represented even and odd memory addresses, respectively in the 32K word memory. They received instruction addresses from the P-register and operand addresses from the U2 register.
Z1, Z2		Storage Restoration Registers: These registers held a 48-bit word to be written to memory.

3.1.2.1 Real-Time Clock

The CDC 1604 had a real-time clock (RTC) that continuously updated memory location 00000. The 48-bit quantity was advanced by one every 1/60th of a second. The RTC could be started or stopped by an EXF instruction. To get a periodic time interrupt, the program would set an interrupt on arithmetic overflow and set location 00000 to a specified value.

3.1.3 Arithmetic Section

Source: CDC 1965aq

The Arithmetic Section performed arithmetic and logical operations on data stored in the machine's registers. The Accumulator, A, was used for all arithmetic and logical operations. With the Q Register, it could be used as a 96-bit shift register or for double precision arithmetic operations.

The X register was used to move data between sections of the computer as well as for the formulation of logical products with the Q register. The Arithmetic Section executed the standard set of arithmetic and logical functions.

3.1.4 Input/Output Section

Source: CDC 1965aq

The Input/Output Section performed data exchange between the CDC 1604 and its peripherals via six buffered channels. Data exchange was initiated by a program, but performed under control of the I/O channel that was independent of the program.

3.1.4.1 Buffering

Operation of a buffer was initiated by a computer program running on the CDC 1604 CPU via an EXF instruction. It continued at a rate determined by the speed of the external equipment. The CDC 1604 was able to handle three input devices and three output devices concurrently. Each device had its own rate of data transmission and provided its own means of internal control.

Input buffer channels were numbered 1, 3, and 5 while output buffer channels were number 2, 4, and 6. The three input channels transmitted data to the X register. Each output channel was associated with a specific register. Data was held on the line until the external equipment had received it and had acknowledged receipt of the data. Each device had an output register for sending data to one of the input channels.

Data was transmitted in blocks of words by repetitive action at one repetition per word. The next program instruction was executed only after the last word of the block was transmitted. Instruction 62 (INT) performed input while instruction 63 (OUT) performed output. Maximum transfer rate was about one word per 5 microseconds.

3.1.4.2 COMMUNICATING

Communication with external equipment occurred through function signals and data signals. Function signals selected a unit of external equipment while data signals carried the data to be transferred. The number of devices that could be attached to the CDC 1604 was dependent on electrical considerations rather than the number of I/O channels. In fact, the manual referred to attaching devices to the CDC 1604 by "connecting jumper cables from one device to another".

The I/O control translated the channel selection digit and sent one of the following control signals to all the devices on the designated channel:

- Select
  - Input Function Ready
  - Output Function Ready
- Sense
  - Input Sense Ready
  - Output Sense Ready

The selected device sent a select signal and then a *sense signal* to the device. The device sent a *sense response* to the computer if the condition was present. The sense signal caused the device to sample the function line to prepare for the I/O operation. Once the I/O control sensed the device was ready, it sent the words from the data block to the device.

The process for sending a word from the device to the computer operated as follows:

1. The computer, via select and sense signals, selected the device.
2. The computer activated the input buffer active line to signal it was ready to start the data transfer.

3. The device placed a word on the lines and sent an input data ready signal.
4. The computer accepted the input word.
5. The computer sent an input data resume signal to the device.
6. The input data resume signal caused the input data ready signal to drop.
7. The device prepared another input word for transfer.
8. Steps 3 through 7 are repeated until all words have been transferred.
9. Once the device has sent all the words of the data block, it dropped the input data ready signal.

A similar process was used for data output.

3.1.5 Interrupts

A program could be interrupted when certain conditions occurred in external equipment or internal to the computer. When an interrupt occurred, a return jump to memory location 00007 occurred. This location usually contained a jump to an interrupt routine which determined the cause of the interrupt and then jumped to an appropriate interrupt handler. The interrupt handler took the appropriate action and returned to the main program.

3.2 CDC 1604 I/O System

Source: CDC 1965aq

The CDC 1604 contained eight channels – three each for the 48-bit buffered input and output channels and one each for the 48-bit high-speed input and output transfer channels. The I/O channels operated independently of and in parallel with the central processor. An I/O operation was initiated by the CPU by executing an INT or OUT instruction.

To transfer data between a channel and a peripheral device, a protocol was required that sent control signals accompanied by the data.

3.2.1 Buffered I/O

A buffered I/O operation transferred a block of data to or from core storage. The size and location of the data block was specified in the Buffer Control Word (BCW).

Each of the six I/O channels was assigned a BCW whose address was stored in memory locations 1 through 6. Each BCW was stored in the corresponding Control Register 1 through 6. The BCW was divided into two parts: the lower half contained the ending address while the upper half contained the starting address. The upper half was set by the EXF Activate instruction. After each word was transferred, the upper half was incremented by one.

The buffer control continually interrogated the peripheral equipment to determine if any device was ready to send or receive data. When a device was ready to send data, the buffer control acknowledged it and paused so that the data can be entered into the buffer. The buffer control then resumed its interrogation. The buffer asynchronously transferred data to or from memory when the central processor was not making a memory access.

High-speed I/O transfer of Information between 1604's, or between one 1604 and peripheral equipment having comparable speed, was performed under control of the main computer program. Only one instruction was required for a block of input or output data. A 48-bit word was transferred in or out in 4.8 microseconds.

The CDC 1604 often used a CDC 160A computer as a front-end processor for performing unit record equipment I/O operations on low-speed peripheral devices.

3.2.2 EXF INSTRUCTIONS

The EXF instructions initiated a buffer, sensed specific conditions, and selected operations and equipment. The EXF Instruction Format is depicted in Figure 3-5.

OpCode	Designator	Channel	Unit	Condition
23 18	17 15	14 12	11 9	8 0

Figure 3-5. CDC 1604 EXF Instruction Format
Source: CDC 1963ap

The EXF instructions are presented in Table 3-3.

Table 3-3. EXF Instructions

Instruction	$Opcodes_8$	Description
Select	74 0 xxxxx	Selected the external equipment which was to communicate with the computer and selected the channel and specified what conditions may or may not occur. Bits Usage 23-18 Operation Code 17-15 Designator: 0 or 7 14-12 Channel 11-9 Equipment 8 - 0 Condition
Sense	74 7 xxxxx	Sensed the condition of external equipment or the internal condition of the computer. Same as Select
Activate	74 j xxxxx (j = 1 … 6	Activated a buffer on the specified channel. Bits Usage 23-18 Operation Code 17-15 Designator: 1 … 6 14-0 Starting Address of Buffer

The location of a 74_8 instruction in the word determined its interpretation. For example, consider the following (CDC 1963ag):

(00010) 74 7 00010 75 0 40000
(00011) 53 1 00005 16 1 00032

When used in the upper word, the 74 7 instruction was a skip instruction. If channel 1 was active, the next instruction was the upper word of location 11. If it was inactive, the lower word of location 00010 was executed.

3.2.2.1 Internal Select Codes

Internal select codes set or removed interrupt conditions or activated the real-time clock. Table 3-4 presents some internal control select codes.

Table 3-4 Internal Control Select Codes

Select Code	Usage
00010 - 00050	Interrupt on Channels 1-5 inactive, respectively.
00011 - 00051	Remove selection above for Channels 1-5, respectively.
00070	Clear Arithmetic Faults.
01000	Start real-time clock
02000	Stop real-time clock

3.2.2.2 Internal Control Sense Codes

Internal control sense codes caused a program to exit on certain conditions associated with the buffer channels or the arithmetic section. Table 3-5 presents some internal control sense codes.

Table 3-5. Internal Control Sense Codes

Select Code	Usage
00010 - 00050	Exit on Channels 1-5 Active.
00011 – 00051	Exit on Channels 1-5 Inactive.
00110 - 00111	Exit on presence (absence) of divide fault.
00120 – 00121	Exit on presence (absence) of shift fault.
00130 – 00131	Exit on presence (absence) of overflow.
00140 – 00141	Exit on presence (absence) of exponent fault.

3.2.2.3 1605 Adaptor Select Codes

These select codes caused the adaptor to turn or off certain indicators and conditions, select I/O equipment, or initiate I/O processing. Table 3-6 presents

Table 3-6. CDC 1605 Adaptor Select Codes

Select Code	Usage
54000	Begin cycle or start read binary
54005	Rewind
54006	Backspace
54100-54101	Turn On/Off Indicator
544n0	Start read binary, unit n
544n1	Start read coded, unit n
64004	Write end-of-file
64007	Interrupt on end of operation
644n0	Write binary unit n
644n1	Write coded, unit

3.3 Peripheral Equipment

Input-output equipment available with the computer included console input-output equipment and optional input-output equipment. The console equipment was standard with every CDC 1604. It included a 350-character per second transistorized Ferranti 7-level photo-electric paper tape reader, a 60 cps Teletype paper tape punch, and a monitoring electric typewriter for making operator entries and presenting typed copy.

3.3.1 Magnetic Tape System

Optional equipment included the Model 1607 Magnetic Tape System and the Model 1605 Adapter. A CDC 1607 Magnetic Tape System consisted of four Ampex FR307 magnetic tape handlers and a synchronous control system. The system was self-contained in a single cabinet, including data-handling and control circuitry; 48-bit assembly and disassembly registers; parity bit assignment for each written character; parity bit read-check immediately following each character written; longitudinal parity bit generation and recording at end of block; parity bit detection for each character read; and end of tape sensing. A CDC 1607 Magnetic Tape System depicted in Figure 3-6.

Several CDC 1607 Magnetic Tape Systems could be attached to a 1604 computer. Simultaneously among these tape systems, up to three tape handlers could be reading, and up to three tape handlers could be writing on separate systems. Each CDC 1607 system had the facility for simultaneously reading from one tape handler and writing on one tape handler, while the remaining two tape handlers were rewinding. Magnetic tapes created by the

CDC 1607 were compatible electrically and mechanically with IBM Model 727 magnetic tape handlers.

Data was recorded in two formats: binary and binary-coded-decimal (BCD) (referred to as coded). For binary format, the parity bit provided an odd number of ones, while for coded format, it provided an even number of ones. The format was selected by the EXF instruction. The synchronizer generated the appropriate parity bits when writing to a tape. The parity bit was coded in track 6 of a seven-track frame. The system could generate IBM character codes for writing tapes for use with IBM peripheral equipment.

Data was recorded at a density of 200 frames per inch in records of varying length. A ¾-inch gap was used to separate adjacent records. Records could be grouped into a file with an interfile gap using 17_8 as a delimiter spaced 6 inches from the last record.

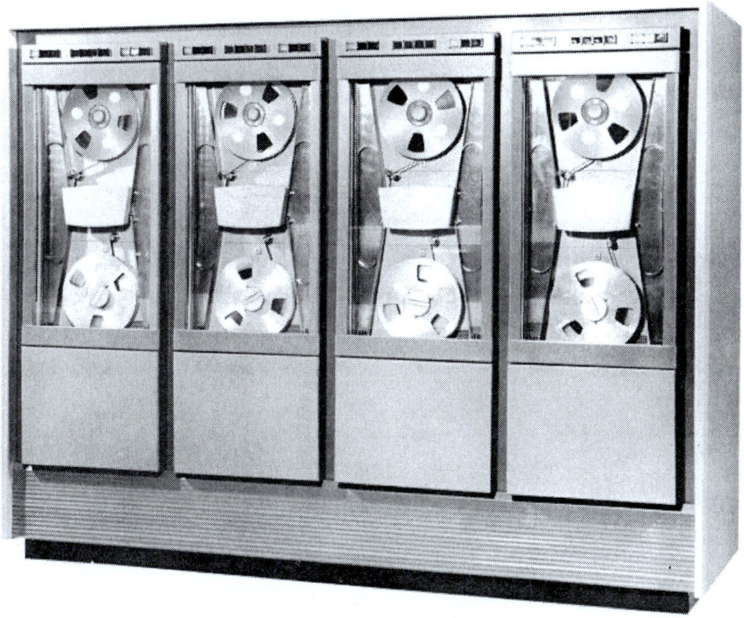

Figure 3-6. CDC 1607 Magnetic Tape System
Source: CDC 1961ar

3.3.2 CDC 1605 Adaptor

The CDC 1605 Adaptor permitted communication between the CDC 1604 computer and any of the following IBM peripheral equipment: 714 Card Reader (via 759 Control Unit), 727 Magnetic Tape Units (via 754 Synchronizer), 717 Line Printer (via 757 Control Unit), 722 Card Punch (via 758 Control Unit). The CDC 1605 selected one of these peripherals as well as the operation to be performed based on an instruction from the central processor. A parity check was made on all information transmitted from the CDC 1605 to peripheral equipment. Each CDC 1605 adaptor could be connected to any of the three buffer input and three buffer output channels, and each CDC 1605 was independently addressable.

The CDC 1605 had the same 48-bit input and output buffer register characteristics as the CDC 1607 magnetic tape system. A number of 1605's together with several CDC 1607 systems could be operated with a single CDC 1604 computer.

3.4 CDC 1604 Instruction Set

CDC 1604/1604A instructions were 24 bits in length. Two of them occupied a 48-bit data word, referred to as a *program step*, and were accessed, respectively, as the upper and lower instructions. Each instruction was composed of three parts: operation code, index designator, and execution address. The instruction format is depicted in Figure 3-7.

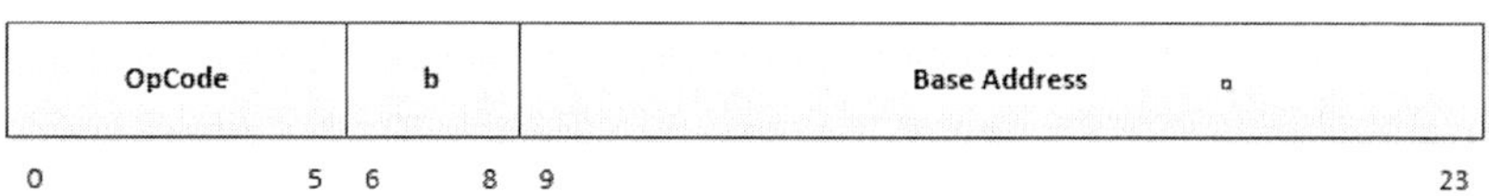

Figure 3-7. CDC 1604 Instruction Format
Source: CDC 1960m

The b designator was interpreted as follows: b = 0, direct addressing, e.g., no address modification; b = 1…6, relative addressing using an index register; and b = 7, indirect addressing.

For a few instructions, these bits would specify the jump or stop condition in those types of instructions. The execution address could be used as a (1) a shift count, k; (2) an operand, y; (3) an address of an operand, m;

or (4) an external function code. Table 3-7 describes how the execution address was modified for uses 1 through 3.

Instruction execution proceeds as follows (CDC 1963ag). Suppose location 00300 holds the following, with $B^1 = (00101)_8$:

(00300)	LDA 0 00310	ADD 1 00210
(00301)	STA 0 00400	SLS 0 00301

The P register holds (00300). The word from 00300 was read into U^1. The upper instruction was retrieved. LDA and the index designator are determined. The contents of location 00310 are loaded into the accumulator. The lower half of U^1 was transferred to the upper half and translated. The contents of (00210 + 00101) = 00311 are added to the accumulator. P was incremented by 1 and the contents of 00301 are fetched into U^1. Again, the upper half was translated and the contents of the accumulator are stored in location 00400.

Table 3-7. Shift Count

Use	Values	Description
Modified Shift Count K	$K = k + c(B^b)$	b = 0, K = k $c(B^b)$, contents of index register b
Modified Operand Y	$Y = y + c(B^b)$	b = 0, Y = y $c(B^b)$, contents of index register b
Modified Operand Address M	$M = m + c(B^b)$	b = 0, M = m $c(B^b)$, contents of index register b

In the following sections, the symbols are used as follows:

A_n	The bit in position in of the A register
A	The A register
Q	The Q register
c(…)	Contents of
M	Memory Location
B^b	Index Register b
Y	Address potion of the instruction

3.4.1 Data Transmission Instructions

The Data Transmission instructions, presented in Table 3-8, moved data between the registers and memory.

Table 3-8. Data Transmission Instructions

Opcode	Format	Description
12	LDA b M	Load A: A <- c(M).
13	LAC b M	Load A Complement: A <- ~ c(M).
16	LDQ b M	Load Q: Q <- c(M).
17	LQC b M	Load Q Complement : Q <- ~ c(M).
20	STA b M	Store A: M <- c(A).
21	STQ b M	Store Q: M <- c(Q).
52	LIU b M	Load Index (Upper): B^b <- $M_{38\text{-}24}$.
53	LIL b M	Load Index (Lower): B^b <- $M_{14\text{-}0}$.
56	SIU b M	Store Index (Upper): $M_{38\text{-}24}$ <- c(B^b).
57	SIL	Store Index (Lower): $M_{14\text{-}0}$ <- c(B^b).

3.4.2 Shift Instructions

Shift instructions shifted the contents of the A, Q or AQ registers to the right or left the number of bits indicated by K. For right shifts, the sign bit was extended and the lowest order bits were discarded. K had a value in the range [0, 127].

For left shifts, the contents of the A, Q, or AQ registers were shifted left the number of bits indicated by K. The low-order bits were replaced by the high order as the shift was performed. K had a value in the range [0, 127].

Table 3-9. Shifting Instructions

Opcode	Format	Description
01	ARS b k	A Right Shift: A <- c(A) right shift K
02	QRS b k	Q Right Shift: Q <- c(Q) right shift K
03	LRS b k	AQ Right Shift: AQ <- c(AQ) right shift K
05	ALS b k	A Left Shift: A <- c(A) left shift K
06	QLS b k	Q Left Shift: Q <- c(Q) left shift K
07	LLS b k	AQ Left Shift: AQ <- c(AQ) left shift K

3.4.3 Address Modification Instructions

The Address Modification instructions either (1) modified the operand address, (2) changed the effect of the index register, or (3) inserted a new value into the P register. Table 3-10 depicts these instructions.

Table 3-10 Address Modification

Opcode	Format	Description
60	SAU b M	Substitute Address (Upper): $M_{38\text{-}24}$ <-$A_{14\text{-}0}$.
61	SAL b M	Substitute Address (Lower): $M_{14\text{-}0}$ <- $A_{14\text{-}0}$.
54	ISK b y	Index Skip: If B^b = y, B^b <- 0, full exit; otherwise, B^b <- c(B^b)-1, half exit.
55	IJP b M	Index Jump: If B^b <- c(B^b)-1, P <- M; otherwise, P <- P+1.

The SAU and SAL instructions replaced the address portion of the instruction at M with the contents of the A register.

The ISK instruction compared c(B^b) to the operand y. If the quantities were equal, B^b <- 0; otherwise, B^b <- c(B^b) +1, and the next instruction was skipped.

The IJP instruction was used to support loops. If c($B^{b)}$ was greater than zero, the c(B^b) was reduced by one and a jump was executed to the base address; otherwise, the next sequential instruction was executed.

3.4.4 Arithmetic Instructions

Arithmetic instructions. Depicted in Table 3-11, operated on the A, Q, or AQ registers for the standard arithmetic operations. Results were either 48 bits or 96 bits depending on the operation.

Table 3-11. Arithmetic Instructions

Opcode	Format	Description
14	ADD b M	Add to Accumulator: A <- c(A) + c(M)
15	SUB b M	Subtract from Accumulator: A <- c(A) - c(M)
24	MUL b M	Multiply Integer: QA <- c(A) * c(M)
25	DVI b M	Divide Integer: A <- c(QA)/c(M); Q <- remainder
26	MUF b M	Multiply Fractional: QA <- c(A) * c(M), operands were assumed to be fractions with binary point immediately to right of sign bit.

27	DVF b M	Divide Fractional: A <- c(QA)/c(M); Q <- remainder, operands were assumed to be fractions with binary point immediately to right of sign bit.
30	FAD b M	Floating Add: A <- c(A) + c(M); operands were assumed to be floating point numbers
31	FSB b M	Floating Subtract: A <- c(A) - c(M); operands were assumed to be floating point numbers
32	FMU b M	Floating Multiply: QA <- c(A) * c(M); operands were assumed to be floating point numbers
33	FDV b M	Floating Divide: A <- c(QA)/c(M); Q <- remainder; operands were assumed to be floating point numbers
34	SCA b K	Scale A: Shift A left circularly until the most significant digit was to the right of the sign bit or until K = 0.
35	SCQ b K	Scale AQ: Shift AQ left circularly until the most significant digit was to the right of the sign bit. The shift continues with K reduced by one each time until normalizing was complete. B^b was set to the number of bits shifted. If K=0, the operation was terminated.

3.4.5 No Address Instructions

The No Address instructions used the address portion of the current instruction as an immediate operand. The value of Y was transferred as a signed 14-bit quantity. The highest order bit of Y was copied into the remaining high-order bits of Q. These instructions are depicted in Table 3-12.

Table 3-12. No Address Instructions

Opcode	Format	Description
04	ENQ Y	Enter Q: Q <- Y; duplicate high-order bit for remaining bits.
10	ENA Y	Enter A: A <- Y; duplicate high-order bit for remaining bits.
11	INA Y	Increase A: A <- c(A) + Y; duplicate high-order bit for remaining bits.
50	ENI b Y	Enter Index: B^b <- Y.
51	INI b Y	Increase Index: B^b <- c(B^b) + Y.

3.4.6 Jump and Stop Instructions

The Jump instructions tested the value of the A or Q registers and jumped to an alternate address based on that value. No address modification was performed on the value of Y. The value of b was used as the jump designator to select one of eight alternative actions for each of these instructions.

Table 3-13. Jump and Stop Instructions

Opcode	Format	Description
22	AJP j Y	A Jump: Selected one of eight alternatives based on the value of j.
23	QJP j Y	Q Jump: Selected one of eight alternatives based on the value of j.
75	SLJ	Selective Jump: Selected one of eight alternatives to jump to based on the value of j.
76	SLS	Selective Stop: Selected of eight alternatives to stop the machine based on the value of j.

The value of j was interpreted as follows:

J	Action
0	Jump if c(A) = 0
1	Jump if c(A) /= 0
2	Jump if c(A) > 0
3	Jump if c(A) < 0
4	Return Jump if c(A) = 0
5	Return Jump if c(A) /= 0
6	Return Jump if c(A) > 0
7	Return Jump if c(A) < 0

Similarly for the Q register.
For SLJ, the value of j was interpreted as follows:

J	Action
0	Jump unconditionally
1	Jump if lever key 1 was set
2	Jump if lever key 2 was set
3	Jump if lever key 3 was set
4	Return Jump unconditionally
5	Return Jump if lever key 1 was set
6	Return Jump if lever key 2 was set
7	Return Jump if lever key 3 was set

For SLS, the value of j was interpreted as for SLJ, except that the machines stopped execution.

3.4.7 Storage Test and Search Instructions

The Storage Test and Search instructions examined the value of the specified memory location to determine the next instruction or to search for a value in a contiguous sequence of values.

Table 3-14. Storage Test and Search Instructions

Opcode	Format	Description
36	SSK Y	Storage Skip: If c(M) < 0, jumped to next word; otherwise, jump to next instruction.
37	SSH Y	Storage Shift: As SSK, but c(M) was shifted left one bit position.
64	EQS b Y	Equality Search: Searched a list of words for a value equal to c(A). The number of words was specified in B^b. The search was performed backwards beginning from $Y + B^b - 1$. If the comparison was unsuccessful, B^b <- B^b-1. The search was terminated upon successful comparison or $B^b = 0$. The address of the successful comparison was $Y + B^b$.
65	THS b Y	Threshold Search: Similar to EQS, but searches for a value in the list that was greater than c(A).
66	MEQ b Y	Masked Equality: Similar to EQS, but the comparison was performed on c(Y + B^b -1) AND c(Q) = c(A).
67	MTH b Y	Masked Threshold: Similar to MEQ, but the comparison was performed on c(Y + B^b -1) AND c(Q) > c(A).

3.4.8 Logical Instructions

The Logical instructions, depicted in Table 3-15, performed bit-by-bit operations on their two operands.

Table 3-15. Logical Instructions

Opcode	Format	Description
40	SST Y	Selective Set: Set the bits of A to one where the bits of c(Y) are also one.
41	SCL Y	Selective Clear: Set the bits of A to zero where the bits of c(Y) are also one.
42	SCM Y	Selective Complement: Complemented A_n where $c(Y)_n = 1$.
43	SSU Y	Selective Substitute: Set $A_n = c(Y)_n$ for $Q_n = 1$.
44	LDL Y	Load Logical: A <- c(Y) AND c(Q).
45	ADL Y	Add Logical: A <-c(A) + (c(Y) AND c(Q)).
46	SBL Y	Subtract Logical: A <-c(A) - (c(Y) AND c(Q)).
47	STL Y	Store Logical: c(Y) <- c(Y) AND c(Q).

3.4.9 Replace Instructions

The Replace instructions replaced the value at Y with the value of the operation M and A.

Table 3-16. Data Transmission Instructions

Opcode	Format	Description
70	RAD Y	Replace Add: Y, A <- c(Y) + c(A).
71	RSB Y	Replace Subtract: Y, A <- c(Y) - c(A).
72	RAO Y	Replace Add One: Y, A <- c(Y) + 1.
73	RSO Y	Replace Subtract One: Y, A <- c(Y) – 1.

3.4.10 Transfer Instructions

The Transfer instructions moved a block of data into memory from external equipment or out to external equipment from memory. The number of words to be transferred was specified by B^b. The data was located in contiguous words beginning at Y. Transfers stored the first word in the list in the last position at address Y + B^b -1. After each word transfer, B^b <- Bb -1. These instructions are depicted in Table 3-17.

Table 3-17. Transfer Instructions

Opcode	Format	Description
62	INT	Input Transfer: Transferred words from the device to memory.
63	OUT	Output Transfer: Transferred words to the device from memory.

3.5 Arbitrary-Precision Floating Point Arithmetic

Source: Stroud and Secrest 1962

The CDC 1604 was oriented to the scientific processing community. This community often desired to carry out scientific computations using arithmetic operations with more significant digits than supported by the physical hardware or the standard programming languages. Section 3.4.4 described single-precision fixed-point and floating-point instructions. Pope and Stein (1960) described an approach for multi-precision fixed-point arithmetic. Stroud and Secrest developed an interpretive program for handling multi-precision floating-point numbers.

An n-precision number was defined as a number which occupied n words of memory. In their scheme, the most significant digits were stored as for single-precision arithmetic, but the fractional part was stored in words at specified intervals. This allowed lists of multi-precision numbers to be operated on using standard indexing techniques. Only 47 bits of the additional words were used with the high-order bit always zero regardless of the number was positive or negative.

Multi-precision arithmetic was carried out using fixed-point arithmetic with the high-order bit used as a carry bit to prevent overflow.

Multi-precision computations were begun by jumping to a subroutine with the address of the following the jump instruction. The interpretive routine examined the words following the jump instruction. The instructions LDA, LAC, STA, FAD. FSB, FMU, FDV, and AJP were performed using a pseudo-accumulator. Before entering the interpretive subroutine, two parameters had to be specified: the degree of precision to be used, and the interval between separate parts of the multi-precision numbers.

A multi-precision number could be written as $P = P_1P_2P_3P_n$ where the P_i represented the parts of the number. As an example, Stroud and Secrest give the following algorithm for computing the quotient $R = P/Q = P_1P_2P_3\ldots P_n/ Q_1Q_2Q_3\ldots Q_n$ of multi-precision numbers P and Q as:

1. Perform the single-precision division $P_1P_2/Q = R_1$.
2. Compute the n-precision number $P\text{-}R_1Q = P' = P'_1P'_2P'_3\ldots P'_n$.

3. Repeat 1 and 2 obtaining:
   $P'_2P'_3/Q = R_2Q$
   $P' - R_2Q = P'_3 \ldots P'_n$ through $P'_{n-1}P'_n$.
4. The quotient R was then $R = R_1R_2R_3 \ldots R_n$.

The interpretive routine, written in FORTRAN, handled accessing the individual digits, and accessing the fractional subparts for steps 2 and 3.

This approach showed that arithmetic operations could be extended beyond the physical limitations of the machine with respect to arithmetic precision.

3.6 NELIAC

Source: Masterson 1960

NELIAC was a compiler for an extended dialect of the ALGOL 60 programming language, which was developed at the U.S. Navy Electronics Laboratory. A compiler for this language was developed for the Remington Rand Univac COUNTESS computer, which generated a version of itself using the machine code for a CDC 1604. The CDC 1604 version was then used to compile itself to provide a native version of the compiler for the CDC 1604. This was an early example of 'bootstrapping' a program from one machine to a machine with a different structure and instruction set.

The compiler translated the input source code directly to machine code without generating an intermediate assembler stage. The input source code was compiled from memory to machine code in memory. As machine code was generated, the source code was erased. The compiler generated machine code from the innermost subroutine outwards. This process was repeated until the main program was compiled at which time the compiler halted. This approach resulted in a simplified compiler.

Machine code generation was based on a current operator (CO) and next operator (NO) concept. A matrix represented the possible combinations of NO-CO, so that code generation was often a simple lookup. An illegal combination resulted in the execution of a routine. Each matrix entry contained a pointer to a subroutine to generate the machine code for that combination.

3.7 CDC 1604 Assessment

The CDC 1604 was delivered at the same time as the IBM 7090 and the early Univac computers. These machines used 6 bits to represent a character, so longer words meant better accuracy. The 48-bit word of the CDC 1604 allowed it to avoid double precision arithmetic. The 1604 had higher performance and competitive pricing when compared to the IBM 7090, which allowed it to claim some of IBM's market share (Lincoln 1975).

The CDC 1604 was the first commercial computer to use transistor logic. The CDC 1604 was also the first machine to implement memory banking. A 32K word machine had two banks. With proper attention to addressing, two memory references could be accomplished in one cycle.

The CDC 1604 had a repeat instruction that operated in a manner similar to a vector instruction, which was often used for block moves of data in memory. It allowed a simulated version of vector operations on the CDC 1604.

The use of the CDC 160A as a separate processor for handling I/O would later be replicated in the CDC 6600 with the PPUs. Early on, Cray had realized that separating I/O handling from the main computational activities significantly improved the performance of the machine.

CHAPTER FOUR

THE CDC 3000 FAMILY

Source: CDC UNKw

The CDC 3000 Series was a larger computing machine, but mostly upwardly compatible with the CDC 1604. The primary machines in this family were the CDC 3400, CDC 3600, and CDC 3800. The first machine in the family was the CDC 3600, which was delivered in June 1963. By 1965, CDC also delivered the CDC 3400 and CDC 3800 systems. These machines used a 48-bit word size. Collectively, they were called the "upper series".

CDC then developed a second series called the "lower series", which was based on the CDC 924 and had a 24-bit word size. Machines in this series included the CDC 3100, CDC 3200, CDC 3300, and the CDC 3500 – the last one, which was released in March 1967. Figure 4-1 depicts the CDC 3100 – the entry level model. Figure 4-2 depicts the CDC 3800 model – the high-end model of the CDC 3000 family.

The I/O subsystem was common to all CDC 3x00 computer systems which allowed different models to be included in a multiprocessor configuration.

The CDC 3x00 series was not designed by Seymour Cray as he had moved on to design the CDC 6600.

Figure 4-1. CDC 3100
Source: CDC 1964q

Figures 4-2. CDC 3800
Source: CDC 1964q

Figure 4-3 depicts an advertisement for the CDC 3600.

Figure 4-3. CDC 3600 Advertisement
Source: CDC circa 1960s

Tables 4-1 and 4-2 present the system characteristics of the Lower and Upper Series of the CDC 3x00 family. Our primary focus in the remainder of this section will be the CDC 3800, which was the most versatile of the CDC 3x00 upper series family members.

Table 4-1. CDC 3000 Lower Series – Basic Characteristics

Characteristic	Value/Explanation
Internal Representation	Fixed Point Binary
# Bits/Word	24
# Instructions/Word	1 or 2
# Instructions	
# Bits/Instruction	24
Instruction Type	One Address
CPU Technology	Semiconductor
CPU Registers	A: Accumulator; Q: Auxiliary Accumulator; E: Optional Floating-Point Arithmetic; P: Program Address Counter; Index Registers: B1 – B3; C: Communication Register for Console; F: Instruction (during execution); S: Storage Address Register; Condition Register
Main Memory	Magnetic Core: 4K - 131K Words; cycle time – ranges from 0.8 to 1.75 microseconds; depending on models (models 3100 – 3300)
Add Time	Model Dependent
Multiply Time	Model Dependent
Divide Time	Model Dependent
Performance	1965: 1 MIPS (CDC 3300)

Table 4-2. CDC 3000 Upper Series – Basic Characteristics

Characteristic	Value/Explanation
Internal Representation	Fixed Point Binary, Floating Point Binary
# Bits/Word	48
# Instructions/Word	1 or 2
# Instructions	
# Bits/Instruction	24 or 48
Instruction Type	One Address
CPU Technology	Solid State Diode Logic w/ Transistor Amplifiers.
CPU Registers	See Table 4-3.
Main Memory	Magnetic Core: 16K – 262K Words; Cycle time: 0.8 to 1.5 microseconds Depending on model (models 3400 – 3800).
Add Time	Model Dependent
Multiply Time	Model Dependent
Divide Time	Model Dependent

The CDC 3600 was the first model of the CDC Upper 3000 series and established the baseline for models in this family. Succeeding models minimized or eliminated some features, and incorporated others. The CDC 3800 – the last model in the series – provided some enhancements as the 3000 series wound down in development.

4.1 CDC 3000 System Architecture

The CDC 3000 system architecture was a model of simplicity, as depicted in Figure 4-4. Note that the central memory was shared by both the central processor and the I/O system. This feature was unique to computer systems of the early 1960s.

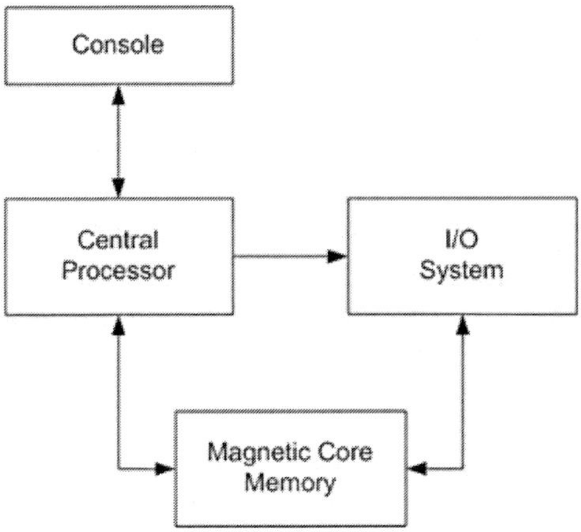

Figure 4-4. CDC 3000 System Architecture
Source: Adapted from CDC 1967g

We will primarily describe the CDC 3600 in this section, while noting differences in other processors where appropriate.

4.1.1 Central Processor

The CDC 3000 Central Processor (CP) was contained in a large frame system about 7 feet high by 18 feet long. The CP was composed of five subsystems: arithmetic, control, memory addressing, I/O, and interrupt processing.

4.1.1.1 Arithmetic Section

The Arithmetic Section performed both fixed point integer and floating-point computations on 48-bit numbers. The range for fixed point integers was $-(2^{-47}-1)$ to $2^{47}-1$. The range for floating point numbers was -10^{308} to 10^{308}.

The Arithmetic section included six 15-bit *index registers* - labeled B1 through B6 – were used to hold quantities that could be added to the address from an instruction. These registers were used for:

- address modifiers for relative addressing: the contents were an offset relative to base address
- as loop control counters: the contents were used to countdown the number of iterations of a loop
- as control quantities for search operations: the contents determined the number of values to compare and which to skip

4.1.1.2 Central Processor Registers

The CP provided multiple registers that were used to handle system operations as described in Table 4-3.

Table 4-3. CP Registers

Register	Bits	Description
A	48	The A register was a 48-bit register used for addition or subtraction using 1's complement arithmetic.
Q	48	The Q register was a 48-bit register used for addition or subtraction using 1's complement arithmetic. Its contents could be shifted left or right separately or in conjunction with the A register. For some arithmetic operations, AQ was treated as a 96-bit register.
U	48	The U register was 48-bits wide. As the Program Control Register, it held the program instruction words while the instruction (s) were being executed. It also was used for address modification.
B1-B6	15	The six B index registers held quantities used for address modification and control data for certain instructions, such as search, locate list element, etc.
D	48	The D register – termed the *flag register* – was used for temporary storage and as a set of flags to indicate conditions in the processor. As a flag register, it could record 48 conditions. A flag test instruction could test any of the 48 bits in the flag register.

E		The (Optional) E register was present when the CDC 3310 Floating Point Module was installed. It consisted of two 24-bit registers, E_U and E_L, ganged together. It was used in floating point arithmetic operations.
P	15	The P register – the *Program Address Counter* - provided a 15-bit offset in the memory bank selected by the 3-bit Instruction Bank Register. It held the address of each program instruction. It was automatically advanced to the next instruction or loaded with a new address if a branch instruction was executed.
IBR	3	The *Instruction Bank Register* was used to form an 18-bit address. Its three bits were used to select the bank to be referenced by the storage address. This storage bank remained selected until explicitly changed.
OBR	3	The 3-bit *Operand Bank Register*, like the IBR, appended 3 bits to the 15-bit address to generate an 18-bit effective address for fetching operands. This storage bank remained selected until explicitly changed.
CIR	3	The 3-bit *Channel Index Register* was logically ORed with the channel designator for several I/O functions.
CR		The *Condition Register* held a set of bits used as flags to record operating conditions and select control actions during Executive mode.
BR	37	The *Bounds Register* was used to specify boundaries for program addressing. It was divided into a 1-bit flag and two 18-bit addresses, which represented the upper (B_U) and lower (B_L) bounds of a program.
Product	48	The *product register* contained a bit-by-bit logical product of the IR and IMR.
SCR	7	The *Shift Count Register* held the shift count whenever a shift operation was performed. On right shifts, it was the true count, while on a left shift it was 140_8 minus the shift count. This arithmetic was required because the shift network could only shift right. It was also used in normalize operations to specify whether normalized or unnormalized arithmetic was selected.
IR	48	The *Interrupt Register* recorded each possible interrupt condition in its own bit. The upper 32 bits were connected to the interrupt lines from the 32 possible communications channels. The lower 16 bits were used to signal internal interrupt conditions.

IMR	48	The *Interrupt Mask Register* had corresponding bits to the 48 bits of the IR. The upper 32 bits were force4d to "1"s to ensure the communication lines were always tested. The lower 16 bits could be set to 0 or 1 by the Inter-Register or Bit Sensing instructions. And interrupt occurred when the corresponding bits in the IR and the IMR were bot set to 1.
MMSR	15	The *Miscellaneous Model Selection Register* held a binary indication of several switches and internal operating conditions of the machine.
Time	27	The *Time register* held the count of the Real Time Clock (RTC). Its contents were incremented by one each millisecond. It could be read, but not written.
TLR	27	The *Time Limit Register* held a value consisting of an RTC count plus a number of milliseconds. When the RTC reached the value held by the TLR, an interrupt occurred.

The A register - the *main arithmetic register* - was used in all arithmetic operations. Quantities in the A register could be shifted left or right, circularly, or off the end. The A register was the only one that could be used in adding the contents of a storage location or another register. The A register held the operand used in conditional jump and search instructions.

The Q register was termed the *auxiliary arithmetic register*. The Q register was often used for masking logical and search operations. It served as a temporary register for the contents of A when the A register was used for another arithmetic operation. It could also be used in shifts in conjunction with the A register to provide the extended AQ register for multiplication and division.

The upper 19 bits of the Bounds Register held a 15-bit storage address, a 3-bit bank address, and the 1-bit Bounds flag specifying the upper bound address. Bounds checking on jump and memory address was performed only if the interrupt system was active and the Bounds flag was set to 1. If these conditions were not met, then:

- A jump to an address out of bounds would not occur and interrupt was signaled. After the interrupt was handled, control returned to the main program to execute the next instruction;
- Writing in an address out of bounds; or
- Reading an instruction from out of bounds.

The only use of an address out of bounds permitted was to read its contents as an operand except when:

- The Bounds Fault bit in the IMR was set;

- The 1604 Mode bit was set in the IMR; and
- The interrupt system was active.

If these three conditions were met, an out of bounds reference interrupt was raised.

Thus, valid addresses were B_L<= S and B_U >S.

The SRC could be used by several non-shifting instructions, such as to govern normalize operations in floating point instructions

Table 4-4 describes the usage of the MMSR bits.

Table 4-4. MMSR Register Bits

Bit(s)	Use	Description
00-05	Console Sense Switches 1 - 6	A program could set any of these six switches, which could then be tested by machine instructions to affect program control flow.
06	Two's Complement Mode	All index arithmetic was performed in two's complement arithmetic, if set to one.
07	I/O Illegal Instruction	If set to 1, the I/O illegal instruction flip flop (FF) was set. If the Illegal Instruction Bit in the IMR was set, an interrupt would occur when an I/O instruction was executed.
08	Interrupt Exit	After an interrupt was processed, control was returned to the main program. If set to 0, the upper instruction was executed; otherwise, the lower instruction was executed.
09	Interrupt Active	If set, the Interrupt system was active. An interrupt occurred if an interrupt condition occurred and the appropriate IMR bit was set.
10-12	Selective Stop Switch 1-3	These bits specified whether the corresponding Selective Stop Switch bit was set to 1.
13	Card Input Mode/Normal Console Switches	If this bit was set to 1, then the card reader was selected for input; otherwise, the console typewriter was selected for input/
14	Negate BCD Conversion	The Negate BCD Conversion flip flop was set, which inhibited BCD conversion.

The console sense switches allowed the operator considerable control over the operations to be performed by the programs as specified by the programmer or user. Setting these switches was often provided with instructions on running the program or through messages printed to the operator console.

The selective stop switches also provided control over program operations, including halting the computer if certain conditions arose within the program. This feature was often used in debugging programs because the operator could then inspect the contents of registers and memory locations. A program could then be resumed by pressing a button the operator console.

4.1.1.3 PROGRAM CONTROL SECTION

The *Program Control Section* was responsible for fetching instructions from memory, decoding them, and executing them, including controlling the sequence of program flow. To determine an address in memory, the Control Section combined the contents of the P register and the *Instruction Bank Register* (IBR) or the *Operand Bank Register* (OBR) to form an 18-bit address. The P register could be incremented by 1, by 2, or gain new contents upon a jump instruction.

When the P register contents reached 777778, it was reset to 000008, but within the same bank. This forced the programmer to be aware of what bank the program was executing in. Program jumps never forced a bank change; the programmer had to explicitly set the IBR to a new bank through the Bank Jump instruction.

The upper instruction in the F register was executed first. Program control then executed the lower instructions without a memory reference. Judicious programming could yield very fast programs using 24-bit instructions.

Once the Operand Bank Register (OBR) was set by the programmer, all succeeding operand references were to that bank. The use of the IBR and the OBR allowed a programmer to separate instructions from data and achieve a modicum of re-entrant programming (assuming other constraints were met).

The CIR permitted programs to be written generically with channel 0, but dynamically assigned at runtime by altering the CIR. The CIR was set from and could be set to the low-order three bits of the A register

Instruction addresses were compared against the upper and lower limits in the BR to determine if they were valid instructions. Attempts to read or write out of bounds caused an interrupt to occur. If the flag bit – bit 37 - was set, upper bounds checking was disabled.

4.1.1.4 Register File

The *Register File* was a 64-word rapid access memory; each word had a length of 24 bits with a cycle time of 0.5 microseconds. The programmer could access all registers in the file with the inter-register transfer operation. Several registers were reserved for special operations, but could be used for temporary storage if that use would not disrupt those operations. The programmer had to be cognizant of when such operations were taking place and plan his program accordingly. Table 4-5 presents the register file assignments (CDC 1968i).

Table 4-5. Register File Assignments

Register (Octal)	Function
00-07	Modified I/O instruction word containing the current character address (channel 0-7 control).
10-18	Modified I/O instruction word containing the last address +/- 1, depending on the instruction (channel 0-7 control).
20	Search instruction word containing the current character address (search control).
21	Move instruction word containing the source character address (move control).
22	Real-time clock, current time.
23	Current character address (typewriter control).
24-27	Temporary Storage.
30	Instruction word containing the last character address + 1 (search control).
31	Instruction word containing the destination character address (move control).
32	Real-time clock, interrupt mask.
33	Last character address + 1 (typewriter control).
34-37	Temporary Storage.

4.1.1.5 Storage Bank Section

A CDC 3600 could be configured with up to eight CDC 3603 Storage Modules, numbered from 0 to 7. Each module was addressed separately using the *Instruction Bank Register* (IBR) and the *Operand Bank Register* (OBR). These registers could be accessed from the console, or using the Inter-Register, Bit Sensing, and Register Jump instructions.

A 3-bit field in each instruction specified the bank to be referenced. An instruction bank remained selected until one of three conditions occurred:

- An Unconditional Bank Jump;
- An Unconditional Bank Jump to Lower; or
- A 48-bit Return Jump.

An operand bank remained selected until one of seven instructions was executed:

- A 48-bit Return Jump;
- Any Bank Jump;
- Execute;
- Search Order;
- Transmit;
- Locate List; or
- Augment.

Programmers writing in assembly language had to be cognizant of the bank the program was running in and how subprocedures and data of the program were allocated to, possibly, different banks. Compilers kept track of allocating program code, data, and subroutines to different banks as necessary to accommodate the size of the program.

4.1.1.6 Operating Modes

The CDC 3600 could be operated in Trace Mode, which was selected by setting the Trace Mode bit in the IMR. In trace mode, all jump instructions where the jump condition was met were trapped by an interrupt before executing the jump.

The contents of the PAR were automatically stored when the interrupt handler was entered. The interrupt routine, written by the programmer, could examines registers and other locations in memory. When the interrupt handler completed its analysis, if any, the jump instruction was interpreted so that the main program resumed control with the next instruction to be executed when the interrupt occurred, unless the interrupt handler determined otherwise (such as jumping to another routine).

The interrupt handler could log each jump instruction, store data relevant to program execution extracted from registers and memory locations, and even set data into registers and memory locations. This latter capability allowed the programmer to correct program errors and continue executing as part of a debugging operation.

The CDC 3600 could also be operated in 1604 Mode using a compatibility package. Except for five instructions – opcodes 00,62, 62, 74, and 77, which designated different instructions, all 1604 programs could be executed on a CDC 3600 computer system. When the CDC 3600 was placed in 1604 mode by setting the 1604 Mode bit in the IMR, the occurrence of any of these instructions was detected and caused an interrupt. The interrupt handler could then interpret the instruction to achieve the expected result. In 1604 mode, a Negate BCD Conversion signal was sent to external equipment, which performed the appropriate operations.

The CDC 3600 normally performed address modification and indexing operations in one's complement. Setting the Two's Complement Mode bit allowed these operations to be performed using two's complement arithmetic. This mode remained in operation until deselected or temporarily disabled by several conditions such as exponent arithmetic or search instruction execution. Two's Complement Mode allowed storage location 77777_8 to be used as an addressable location through address modification.

4.1.1.7 Real Time Clock

The Real Time Clock (RTC) was a free-running, two's complement, 27-bit counter that was incremented each millisecond. The RTC value was held in the 27-bit Time Register (TR). This register could be read by the Inter-Register, Bit Sensing, or Register Jump instructions.

The Time Limit Register (TLR) could be read or set by the three instructions above. A program could specify that an interrupt was to occur when the value in the TR was equal to the value in the TLR. When the time count expired (e.g., the difference reached zero), the Real Time Clock bit was set in the IR and an interrupt occurred on the next clock pulse.

4.1.2 System Bus

The System Bus provided a common path over which data flowed between the central processor, memory, the console typewriter, and the I/O channels. Each component was connected in parallel to the bus. The Main Control determined which component's data transfer path was activated.

A separate Address Bus connected the processor and memory to pass addresses for fetching instructions and data. Addresses were provided by the P and F registers, by Block Control, and the breakpoint circuits.

The Block Control section was an auxiliary processor that handled several operations and devices. It executed search/move instructions. It handled external I/O, the real-time clock, and console typewriter I/O.

Functions in Block Control were divided into three groups as depicted in Table 4-6.

Table 4-6. Block Control Groups

Group 1 Channel Control	Group 2 Channel Control	Group 3
0	4	Real-Time Clock
1	5	Console Typewriter
2	6	Register File Display
3	7	Search/Move

Access to the system bus was shared between the processor and the Block Control circuits. Access was granted through five scanning mechanisms. Program/Buffer Scanning alternately checked between Block Control Requests from Program Control and group requests. Group requests had priority over program requests. When all group requests had been serviced, program requests were serviced.

Another free-running scanner rotated among the three groups checking for an active request in a 3, 2, 1 order. Each group had a four-position scanner which scanned from top to bottom of their groups looking for active Block Control Requests. After an active request was processed, scanning began anew from the top of the group.

This approach to handling requests relieved the central processor of scanning and allowed it to continue to do productive computation while I/O requests were being handled.

4.1.3 MEMORY

The CDC 3600 memory had a maximum capacity of 256K words. A CDC 3803 memory bank consisted of 32K words of 48 bits each. Up to eight of these banks could be configured in a CDC 3800 computer system. Figure 4-5 depicts one memory module (CDC 1967g). To the left was a refrigeration unit for the memory module which pumped Freon through channels in the memory frame to cool the module.

The CP generated an 18-bit address to access a memory location and transmitted it to memory. The upper 3 bits referenced a memory bank and the lower 15 bits referenced a word in the selected memory bank. From 0 to 7 memory banks could be configured in a CDC 3600/3800 system; only one bank could be configured in a CDC 3400.

Figure 4-5. CDC 3803 Memory Bank
Source: CDC 1967g

Three parity bits per word were used for error checking. Three types of parity errors could be detected:

- *Storage Address Parity Error*: This error occurred when the CP generated an address, attached the parity bit, transmitted it to memory, which detected an error in the address. The memory signaled the processor to stop because this error constituted an unrecoverable error.
- *Instruction Parity Error*: This error occurred when the CP read a 48-bit word as an instruction. If the read operation detected a parity error in the 51 bits, the CP stopped because this error constituted an unrecoverable error.
- *Operand Parity Error*: This error occurred when the CP read a 48-bit word as an operand. If the read operation detected a parity error in the 51 bits, the CP continued operating, but generated an interrupt.

4.1.4 I/O Section

Source: CDC 1967aj

The I/O System consisted of a 3802 Communications Module (CM) to which are attached up to eight 3806 bi-directional Data Channels. Each data channel had a hardwired channel number. Each controller also had an identifier, but these could be selected by a dial on the controller panel. Figure 4-6 depicts a CDC 3802 Communications Module.

Up to eight device controllers could be attached to each data channel. Only one physical controller was logically selected at any time. Each controller had a variable number of physical units attached to it, based on the current model.

Data flowed to/from the CP to memory and thence to/from the physical devices through the data channels. The CM received 51 bits from memory, stripped off the three parity bits, and transferred the 48 data bits to the data channel. The data channel divided the word into four 12-bit bytes which it transmitted to the device each with its own parity bit. When receiving data from a data channel, the CM generated three parity bits for each 48-bit word.

CDC provided three types of data channels for use with the 3000 series:

- a standard 12-bit data channel, which assembled four 12-bit bytes into a 48-bit word on input or disassembled a 48-bit word into four 12-bit bytes on output.
- a special 24-bit data channel, which assembled two 24-bit bytes into a 48-bit word on input or disassembled a 48-bit word into two 24-bit bytes on output.
- A 48-bit data channel which transferred 48-bit words directly.

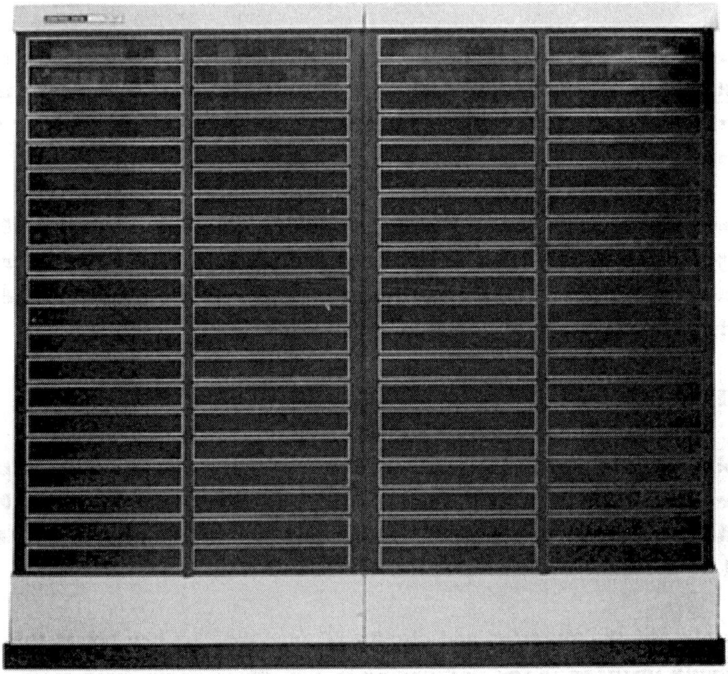

Figure 4-6. CDC 3802 Communications Module
Source: CDC 1967g

4.1.4.1 Standard Data channels

Source: CDC 1964af

The standard data channel for many peripheral devices connected to one or more peripheral devices. This allowed multiple channels to be operation concurrently. However, a data channel could communicate with only of the devices attached to it at a time. Table 4-7 describes the data channel operations.

Table 4-7. Selected Standard Data Channel Operations

Command	Description
Connect	Connected a device controller that was attached to the data channel and allowed it to receive other commands from the data channel. The 12-bit command consisted of a 3-bit device identifier and a 9-bit unit id.
Function	Specified operating conditions and modes to a device unit. When the unit received the 12-bit function code, it initiated the function and returned the Reply signal. If the device unit could not perform the specified function at the time, it returned a Reject signal.
Read	In response to the Read function, the device unit put a word on the data lines and sent the Reply signal to the data channel. If the unit has reached an end of record condition, it returned the End of Record signal.
Write	The data channel placed the word on the write lines and sent the Write function to the device unit. When the device unit has accepted the word, it sent a Reply signal to the data channel.
Master Clear	The CP sent this function to the data channel which sent it to its attached devices. It directed the data channel to return to an initial operating condition, which caused all devices to be disconnected from the channel.
Data	During a Read operation, it indicated that the data channel was ready to receive a word from a device. During a Write operation, it directed the device to write data onto its storage medium. When the Write signal was terminated, the device automatically ended the record.
Negate BCD Conversion	This signal indicated the CP was operating in 1604 mode. During Read operations, data was not converted from BCD by the device to the CDC internal format. During a Write operation, data was not converted from CDC internal format to BCD.
Suppress Assembly/ Disassembly	Many devices handled data s 8-bit bytes. These devices had logic circuitry to convert an 8-bit byte into two 6-bit CDC bytes that fit into a 12-bit word. Alternatively, to convert a 12-bit word to two 8-bit bytes.
Word Mark	A Word Mark signal identified the low-order 6-bit byte of every addressed word.

Status Bits	External devices indicated their operating conditions by placing data on the 12 status lines. Standard status response codes in which the bit was set to 1 included: Bit Meaning 00 Ready to receive a Read or Write signal. 01 Busy – the device was performed an operation. 10 Error – the device has detected an error. 11 Reserved for multi-channel devices. Status bits 7 to 9 indicated a device had reached a certain pre-selected interrupt condition and was generating an interrupt. Magnetic Tape Controllers used these bits for other purposes.

Once a unit was connected to a channel, function codes could be sent to the device to initiate reading or writing as appropriate. On a magnetic tape unit, the density and format had to be sent to the device before any I/O operations could be performed.

An I/O operation specified a Control Word Address, which contained a predefined control word. The control word determined where in memory the data was to be read from or written to and how large a block of data was to be transferred between the memory and the peripheral device. The control word also specified special features such as chaining, end-of-record termination handling, and scatter reading and writing operations.

When the data channel was busy, no other operation could be initiated. However, status checks on channel operation could be requested at any time, using the COPY instruction.

A channel status response could indicate whether a parity error had occurred or if the channel was currently reading or writing. A variety of device status responses could also be obtained.

4.1.4.2 Multi-channel Controller

A multi-channel controller could be connected to multiple data channels and could handle I/O operations from multiple data channels. Figure 4-7 depicts a multi-channel controller. The CDC 3659 Line Printer Controller was an example of this type of controller. Each half of the controller had its own separate write controls, which allowed either channel to transmit data to the line printer.

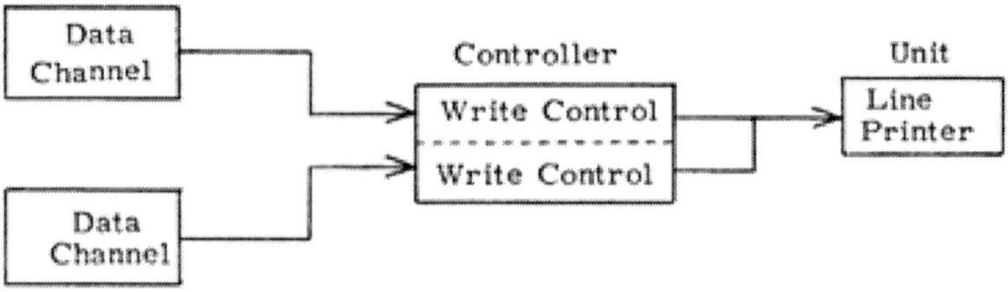

Figure 4-7. A Multi-channel Controller Configuration
Source: Adapted from CDC 1967g

The largest multi-channel controller was the CDC 362x Magnetic Tape Controller, which could attach 8 (x=3) or 16 (x=4) magnetic tape units. An example is depicted in Figure 4-8.

Figure 4-8. CDC 362x Magnetic Tape Controller
Source: CDC 1967g

With four separate read/write controls, up to four magnetic tape operations could be performed concurrently.

4.1.4.3 I/O Chaining

Data could be transmitted to or received from several block locations in memory using I/O Chaining. If I/O chaining was selected, the programmer had to prepare a sequence of control words in consecutive storage locations in the same storage bank.

After performing the first block I/O specified by the first control word , the second control word was read from storage and the I/O operation continued without interruption. The number of words to be transferred in or out was specified by the word count in the control word. The last control word in the sequence indicated termination by specifying a word count of zero.

This was similar to scatter/gather operations in other computer systems.

4.1.4.4 Auto-Load

The auto-load feature allowed instructions or data stored on an external device to be automatically loaded into storage. To do so, the operator pressed the Auto-Load switch on the operator console, which initiated a sequence of operations:

- Performed internal and external Master Clear;
- Connected the channel, equipment, and device unit as specified by the Auto-Load switches on the CDC 3604 chassis;
- Performed the function specified in the Function switches;
- Initiated a Read operation with starting address 0 00000 and word count 40000_8. Data was read until word count or an EOR was reached.
- Begins execution at 0 00000.

The external equipment that could load data included magnetic tape, magnetic disc, or punched card reader. In effect, this procedure booted an operating system into the CDC 3000.

4.1.5 Interrupt Processing

The interrupt processing section on the 3600/3800 differed significantly from that on the 3400. Here we will describe the interrupt processing section for the 3600/3800.

The CDC 3600/3800 supported 48 different interrupts. The interrupts are presented in Table 4-8.

Table 4-8. CDC 3600/3800 Interrupts

Bit(s)	Type	Description
1	Shift Fault – Lowest	Occurred during one of the six shift instructions when an attempt was made to overshift a register more than 48/96 bits.
2	Divide Fault	Occurred in the DVI, DVF, and FDV instructions if the divisor was zero or the quotient exceeded the capacity of the answer register.
3	Exponent Overflow Fault	Occurred in floating point instructions when the exponent exceeds 2^{1777_8}.
4	Exponent Underflow Fault	Occurred in floating point instructions when the exponent exceeds 2^{-1777_8}
5	Arithmetic Overflow Fault	Occurred in add or subtract instructions when the absolute value exceeded 2^{47}-1.
6	Interrupt #1	An interrupt from an external device was raised.
7	Interrupt #2	An interrupt from an external device was raised.
8	Internal Reject	Occurred when a program attempted I/O on a device not attached to the computer.
9	Real Time Clock	Occurred when the RTC reached a preset value.
10	Storage Reference Fault	Occurred when processor attempts to reference a non-existent memory bank.
11	1604 Mode	Occurred when a 1604 incompatible instruction was attempted; allowed the 3600 to trap it and emulate it.
12	Trace Mode	Occurred when jump instructions were successful; allowed trapping jumps before they occurred.
13	Bounds Fault	Occurred when either of the bounds in the Bounds Register was violated.
14	Illegal Instruction Fault	Occurred if illegal parameters were used in an instruction.

15	Operand Parity Error	Occurred if an operand read from memory had a parity error.
16	Manual Interrupt	Occurred when the manual interrupt switch on the console was depressed.
17-48	Data Channels	Data Channels 00 – 31. Occurred when the indicated channel completed an operation or detected an error.

4.1.5.1 Interrupt Masking

An interrupt occurred when the specific condition was met and the bit in the 48-bit Interrupt Mask Register (IMR) corresponding to that interrupt was set. The high order bit of the IMR corresponded to Data Channel 31. The leftmost 32 bits of the IMR were called *external interrupts* and were non-programmable. The 16 low-order bits were called *internal interrupts* and were programmable

A 48-bit Interrupt Register (IR) had a bit set when an interrupt actually occurred. Since multiple interrupts could occur at once, the Interrupt Register recorded all interrupts that occurred.

When an interrupt occurred, control was transferred to bank 0, address 00001. A return address was placed in instruction 00000 of bank 0. The instruction at address 00001 transferred to an interrupt handler which saved the registers and determined which interrupt had occurred. After the interrupt handler processed the interrupt, it could return to the previous program by jumping indirect to the address in location 00000.

4.2 CDC 3300/3500

The CDC 3300 was the primary member of the low-end series of the CDC 3000 family. It implemented the basic 3000 series instruction set. The CDC 3300 included an expanded set of instructions to support business data processing, including the efficient execution of COBOL (CDC 1968i). Figure 4-9 depicts an advertisement for the CDC 3300/3500.

Figure 4-9. CDC 3300/3500 Advertisement
Source: CDC circa 1960s

4.2.1 MAIN MEMORY

Memory capacity was 8K to 256K words. Expansion beyond 128K words was provided by an optional CDC 3311 Multiprogramming Module. The 3311 supported the memory page system, memory protection, and extended addressing to 256K words. Memory was implemented using magnetic core storage.

The upper 32 locations of configured memory were always reserved for autoload and autodump programs when executing in user mode. These addresses were protected by a special storage protection circuit so that these programs could always be initiate din the event of a failure.

Other portions of memory could be protected through operator action. The power console had fifteen 3-position switches which were used to designate protected addresses. Single addresses or blocks of address could be protected depending on the switch settings.

To protect all addresses in memory, all switches were set into the neutral or middle position. Protection could be set dynamically during program execution by setting the switches. Otherwise, two areas could be protected. Switches 0-5 selected an area in upper memory in 512-word blocks while switch 9-14 selected an area in lower memory. In this case, switches 6-8 were set to the neutral position.

4.2.2 I/O SYSTEM

The CDC 3300 used two types of I/O modules. The CDC 3306 bidirectional, 12-bit parallel data channel, which could accommodate up to eight peripheral controllers. Up to eight 3306 data channels could be connected to a 3300.

The CDC 3307 bidirectional 24-bit parallel data channel included assembly/disassembly support. A maximum of four CDC 3307 data channels could be attached to a CDC 3300 with a maximum of four CDC 3306 data channels. Twelve status lines ran between each controller and its I/O channel. Each line monitored one condition within the controller. Each controller had a unique set of line definitions.

The CDC 3300 supported hardware floating point operations through the attachment of an optional CDC 3310 Floating Point Module. It executed 48-bit floating point arithmetic operations. A CDC 3300 computer system is depicted in Figure 4-10.

Figure 4-10. CDC 3300 Computer System
Source CDC circa 1960s
Note that the CDC 3300 had a simplified operator console.

4.2.3 Business Data Processor

The CDC 3300 supported an optional Business Data Processor (BDP) that directly executed business-oriented instructions. The CP signaled the BDP to execute a business instruction when it encountered an instruction in the expanded business data processing set. All business-oriented instructions required three words stored consecutively at P through P+2.

After executing the instruction, the BDP relinquished control to the CP to continue program execution. If an interrupt occurred during BDP execution, it gave control to the CP to handle the interrupt after the current character operation was completed. When the interrupt handling was completed, the BDP read the instruction again from memory and restarted processing at the point of interrupt. Two instructions, CVDB and CVBD, restarted from the beginning. Index register B3 recorded the point in the BDP operation that the execution was interrupted so that a restart could be performed.

Within the BDP, the 2-bit BDP Condition Register (BCR) recorded the result of the completed operation. Result indicators varied with the type of instruction. The BCR could be read by the CP and used in conditional jump instructions.

Table 4-9 presents the BDP instructions (CDC 1965az).

Table 4-9. Business Data Processor Instructions

Opcode	Mnemonic	Description
64,0	MVE r,B_r,\$1,s,B_s,\$2 MVE dc	Moved characters from field 1 in r to field 2 in s. Move characters from field 1 in r to field 2 in s with delimiting.
64,1	MVBF r,B_r,\$1,s,B_s,\$2	Moved characters with Blank Fill.
64,2	MVZF r,B_r,\$1,s,B_s,\$2	Moved characters with Zero Fill.
64,3	MVZS r,B_r,\$1,s,B_s,\$2 MVZS dc	Moved characters with suppression of leading zeros. Move characters with delimiting and suppression of leading zeros.
64,4	EDIT r,B_r,\$1,s,B_s,\$2	Edit according to COBOL picture stored in field C.
64,4	FRMT r,B_r,\$1,s,B_s,\$2	Performed limited according to COBOL Picture stored in field c.
65,4 65,2 65,1 65,3	SCAN,LR,EQ SCAN,LR,NE SCAN,RL,EQ SCAN,RL,NE	Scan Left to Right – Equal or Not Equal Scan Right to Left – Equal or Not Equal

66,0	CVDB r,B_r,\$1,m,B_m	Convert BCD to Binary.
66,1	CVBD r,B_r,\$1,m,B_m	Convert Binary to BCD.
66,2	DTA r,B_r,\$1,m,B_m	Translated BCD to ASCII.
66,3	ATD r,B_r,\$1,m,B_m	Translated ASCII to BCD.
66,4	PAK r,B_r,\$1,m,B_m	Pack 6-bit BCD into 4-bit BCD
66,5	UPAK r,B_r,\$1,m,B_m	Unpack 4-bit BCD into 6-bit BCD.
67,0	ADM r,B_r,\$1,s,B_s,\$2	Add field a to field C, sum in field C.
67,1	SBM r,B_r,\$1,m,B_m	Subtract field a from field c, difference in field C.
67,2	ZADM r,B_r,\$1,m,B_m	Move characters from right to left , from field a to field C with zero fill.
67,3	CMP r,B_r,\$1,m,B_m	Compare field A to field C, terminate upon unequal comparison.
67,4	TST r,B_r,\$1	Test field A for +, -, 0.
70,6	LBR m	Load BDP conditions from c(m).
70,7	SBM m	Store BDP conditions at m.

4.2.4 Time-sharing and Multiprogramming

Multiprogramming in the CDC 3300/3500 systems enabled the instructions of many programs to be executed concurrently using time-sharing operations that shared the CP among the multiple programs and the operating system in time slices.

The system operated in two modes:

- *Monitor State*: A privileged state for the Executive, which was the default state when the system was booted or when a Master Clear of the processor was initiated. The processor reverted to this state during interrupt processing. All instructions could be executed in this state.
- *Program State*: In this state, user programs, and most system utilities were executed. Several instructions could not be executed: Halt, the block transfer instructions (71_8-77_8), or any interregister transfer instruction attempting to modify locations 00 through 37_8 of the register file.

Interrupts or attempts to execute the prohibited instructions in program state caused a transfer to an interrupt handler in the Monitor State. Control was transferred back to Program State after the interrupt handler completed its task.

4.2.4.1 Relocation Hardware

The relocation hardware allowed a CP program, to up to 256K words of memory using an 18-bit address consisting of a three-bit state number and a 15-bit address in P.

The relocation hardware supported a paging system. Memory page size was 2K words. There were 128 of these pages contained in a 3300/3500 maximally configured memory system. A page could be subdivided as four subpages of 512 words each. Programs could be allocated full pages, ½ pages, ¾, ½, or ¼ pages. Partial pages could be allocated to a program, The assembler/compiler noted the page size when constructing the executable program code.

4.2.4.2 Page Index File

Page allocation was facilitated using a word core matrix, called the Page Index File (PIF), that was referenced by a program making a memory reference to obtain a physical page address or a partial page address. Figure 4-11 depicts the translation of a program page reference to a physical page.

Programs issued memory reference as 15-bit addresses, which defined an address relative to the maximum size oof the program, e.g. 32K words. However, the actual memory size was larger, so the program addresses could be mapped to different locations within the physical memory. To map, the program relative addresses to the absolute physical addresses, the relative addresses had to be converted to physical addresses via address relocation.

User programs were also divided into pages16 of which formed a Program Address Group which were mapped to 16 Page Index File registers. One user program could be mapped to a physical page in memory on a page boundary. The entries in the PIF referenced the beginning address of memory pages. The PIF was divided into eight distinct reference areas. The three bits of the ISR and OSR each referenced one of these areas.

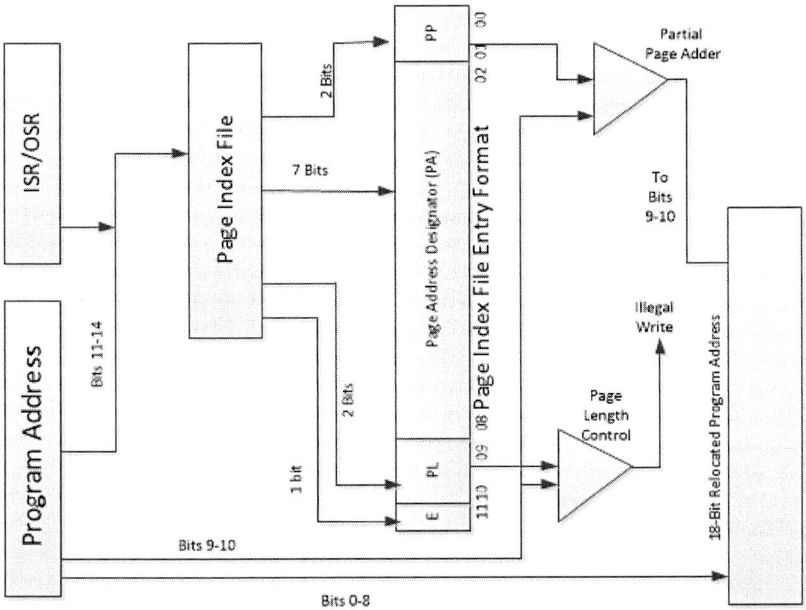

Figure 4-11. CDC 3300 Program Page Reference to Physical Page Translation
Source: Adapted from CDC 1965az

Figure 4-12 depicts the program address and the PIF Entry format.

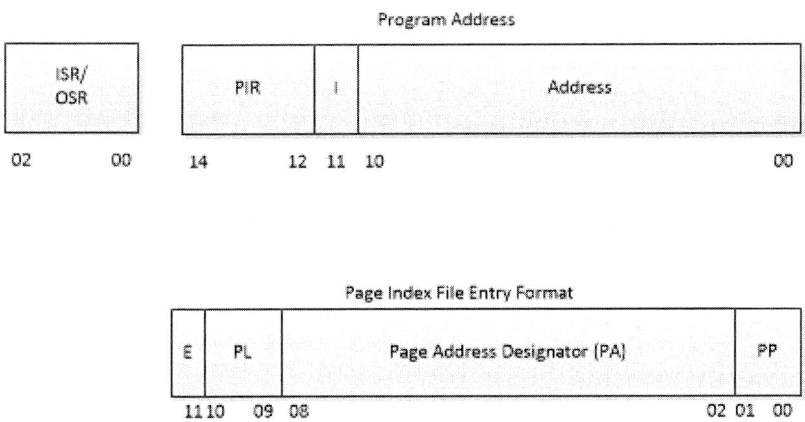

Figure 4-12. Program Address and PIF Entry Format
Source: Adapted from CDC 1965az

The program address consisted of three fields:

- The PIR indicated the index of one of the eight index registers of the even or odd banks;
- I indicated the even or odd bank; and
- PA specified the address within the bank.

Each PIF Entry consisted of 12 bits whose fields indicated:

- E was an exclusion bit, which could have three values:
  - 0, which allowed reading or writing to the page specified by PA;
  - 1, with PA, PL, and PP > 0, which allowed reading of the page; or
  - 1, with PA = PL = PP = 0, which specified an unaddressable page, which generated an Illegal Write interrupt.

Bits 11-0 of PA selected one of the left or right entries of the 24-bit PIF entry, where:

- PL, was the Program Length, defining the number of program quarters required to store the program, where a quarter was ¼ of the page indexes;
- PA, was the Page address (0 to 127 for the pages in memory); and
- P, the partial page designator (e.g., ¼, ½, ¾, or full) page.

From the PIF, the base address of a physical memory page was extracted and combined with the 3 bits of ISR or OSR, depending on the type of reference – instruction or operand – to generate the absolute memory address.

If the value of bits 9 and 10 specified a quarter greater than that allocated by P<= 3, an Illegal Write interrupt was generated.

4.3 CDC 3600

Source: CDC 1964af

The CDC 3600 was the upward compatible successor to the CDC 1604. CDC made the machine aesthetically pleasing with smoked glass panels covering the main cabinets. Since it cost several million dollars to purchase, CDC apparently felt the customer should get something that looked solid and stunning. Figure 4-13 presents an advertisement for the CDC 3600.

Figure 4-13. CDC 3600 Advertisement
Source: CDC circa 1964

4.3.1 SYSTEM CONFIGURATION

Source: CDC 1964af

The CDC 3600 was a stored-program general purpose computer with the configuration depicted in Figure 4-14.

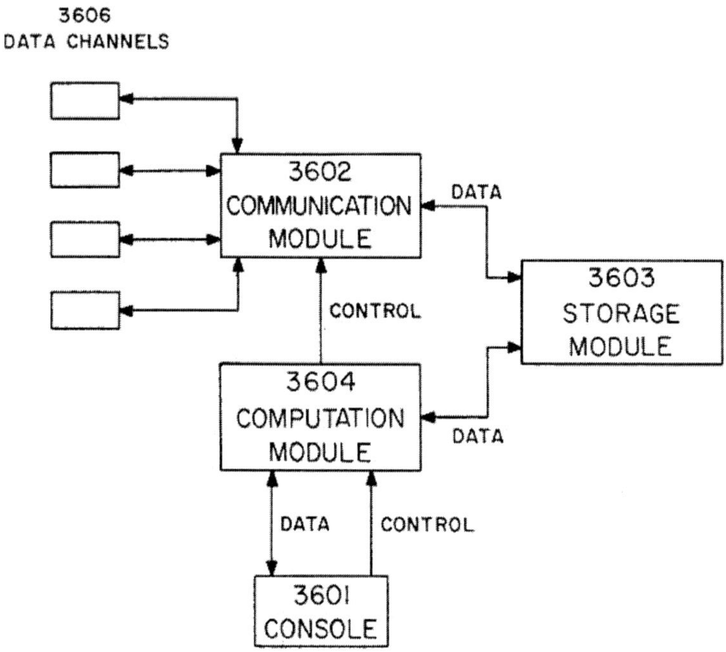

Figure 4-14. CDC 3600 System Configuration
Source: Adapted from CDC 1964af

The basic 3600 consisted of the CDC 3604 computation module, the I/O section consisting of the CDC 3602 communications module and CDC 3606 data channels, a magnetic core storage module consisting of one or two CDC 3603 core storage units, and the CDC 3601 operator's console. The CDC 3602 provided the path between the computation module, the data channels, and the magnetic core storage units.

4.3.1.1 Computation Module

The 3604 Computation Module performed the arithmetic and logical operations and generated the commands to initiate I/O operations in the communication module. A second 3604 computation module could be added to the configuration to provide additional computing capability.

Up to 14 CDC 3609 core storage units could be added to provide the maximum capacity of 256K words of memory. Up to three additional CDC 3602 communication modules could be added to the system configuration to facilitate parallel transfers of data between the other system components. With two CDC 3604s and multiple CDC 3609s, each CDC 3604 could address memory concurrently with the other system as long as they were not referencing the same CDC 3609 storage unit.

The Computation Module (CM) could operate in several special modes. In Trace Mode, which was selected by setting the Trace Mode bit in the IMR, all jump instructions were trapped before being executed. The PAR was automatically stored when the interrupt handler was entered in order to facilitate a return to the main program. The interrupt handler could record data bout the jump and other aspects of CPU state, then interpret the jump and return to the main program with the instruction which was about to be executed. This feature facilitated debugging programs as they were executed.

Another mode was 1604 Mode in which programs written for the CDC 1604 could be executed on a CDC 300 using the 1604 compatibility package. Except for five cases, the instruction opcodes for the 16-4 and 36-4 were identical. Codes 00, 62, 63, 74, and 77 specified different instructions in the CDC 3604 CM. When these codes were detected in 1604 Mode, an interrupt was generated to interpretively execute the instruction. While in 1604 Mode, BCD conversion was inhibited.

A third special mode was Two's Complement Mode. Normally, one's complement was used for addressing and indexing instructions. Selecting Two's Complement Mode specified two's complement arithmetic to be used for all arithmetic instructions.

4.3.1.2 Storage Module

The CDC 3600 directly addressed up to 32K words of memory organized into two banks of 16K words each. Each word was 51 bits consisting of 48 data bits and three parity bits.

The 3609 Storage Units provided random access magnetic core store of up to 16K words. Two 3609 storage units were combined into a CDC 3603 Storage Module, each of which was independently addressable.

Each CDC 3609 Storage Module had five access channels which allowed storage requests from five sources. Each access channel was assigned a number using four binary switches associated with that channel on its operator panel. Up to five CDC 3602 communication modules could be attached to each storage module.

Each CDC 3609 storage module contained a priority section which scanned the five access channels for storage requests. Each was scanned to ensure that it had access to the storage module once per scan cycle, which prevented simultaneous storage requests. If the channel examined by the scanner had an active memory request, the scanner halted and a memory reference for that channel was initiated. Other channels that had active memory requests had to wait their turn.

A unit that had requested memory access transmitted a parity bit along with the storage address. The transmitted parity bit was checked against the parity bit associated with the word at the requested storage address. If a parity error occurred, a Parity Error signal was raised to the requesting unit.

A storage word could contain two 24-bit instructions, a 48-bit instruction, a 48-bit data word, or half of a 96-bit data word.

A storage word was divided into three portions: (1) a 15-bit lower address; (2) a 15-bit upper address, and (3) an 18-bit function specification. Three bits (P3, P2, P1) at the front of the storage word as represented in memory contained the parity bits for each portion, respectively. The format of a storage word is depicted in Figure 4-15.

P3	P2	P1	Function	Upper Address	Function	Lower Address
50	49	48	47 … 39	38 … 24	23 … 15	14 … 0

Figure 4-15. CDC 3600 Storage Word
Source: Adapted from CDC 1964af

For a single instruction word, the two parts of the function were combined into an 18-bit function code, while a two-instruction word used the 9-bit function part to represent the function code.

A memory location was addressed by an 18-bit word whose format is depicted in Figure 4-16.

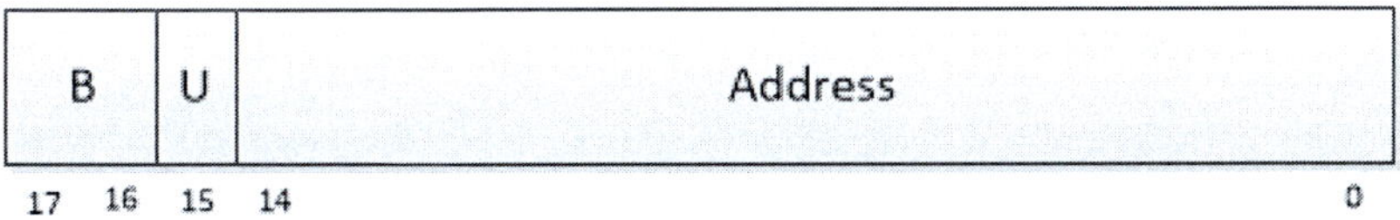

Figure 4-16. CDC 3600 Addressing
Source: Adapted from CDC 1964af

The components of the storage address were:

- B: specified a CDC 3603 storage module;
- U: specified a CDC 3609 unit in a storage module; and
- Address: a 15-bit address within a storage unit.

Each 18-bit address could access one of the four banks in a storage module. The upper four bits (e.g., fields B and U) selected a particular CDC 3609 module. Only the 3609 unit whose channel switch designation matched the upper four bits recognized the memory request. The lower 14 bits specified a particular address within the 3609 storage unit. The specific storage unit was selected by combining the U bit with the 14 address bits.

4.3.1.3 Communications Module

The 3602 Communications Module handled the I/O operations in the CDC 3600 system. The 3606 Data Channel connected the system peripherals to the Communication Module which acted as the data path to the Computation Module.

Three types of Data channels could be attached to the CDC 3602 Communications Module:

- A standard 12-bit data channel which transmitted 12-bits serial and assembled four of these into s 48-bit word.
- A 24-bit special channel transmitted 24 bits of data, but was used for special applications only.
- A 48-bit data channel, which transmitted a 48-bit word, but was used for special applications only.

Information generated by the CDC 3604 as commands and data to initiate I/O operations was conveyed by the CDC 3602 to the data channels. The CDC 3602 sequentially scanned the data channels for storage requests, incremented the storage addresses as storage references were made, and generated or checked parity on data transferred.

The data channels handled the I/O operations requested by the CDC 3604. All controls and registers necessary to effect I/O to and from the peripheral equipment was contained within the data channels.

4.3.1.4 Console

The CDC 3601 Console served as both the Operator Console and the Maintenance Console. It contained switches and indicator lights that allowed the operator to assess the status of the system and set the optional parameters for system operation. An electric typewriter connected to the console served as a direct-entry keyboard for commands and data and provided an output printer capability. It was connected to both the CDC 3604 Computation Module and the CDC 3606 Data Channel. It was divided into two panels – one for operations and one for maintenance.

The CDC 3601 operator's console is depicted in Figure 4-17.

Figure 4-17. CDC 3601 Operator's Console
Source: CDC 1964af, CDC 1967g

The Operator Section is depicted in Figure 4-18.

As seen in Figure 4-18, the lower left section of the panel contains the six Sense switches and the three Selective Jump switches. Their role was discussed previously. Similarly, on the lower right of the panel, the Auto-Load, Interrupt, Type-In buttons are implemented. Of these, Type In indicated that data was to be input to the A register from the console typewriter. On the upper left side of the panel, the Emergency Off removes all power from the computer system when pressed. The Interlock Bypassed was used to bypass any high temperature warnings.

The System Status block contains a set of indicators are lit when the corresponding condition has occurred. Table 4-9 presents a description of these lights from the upper left of the matrix.

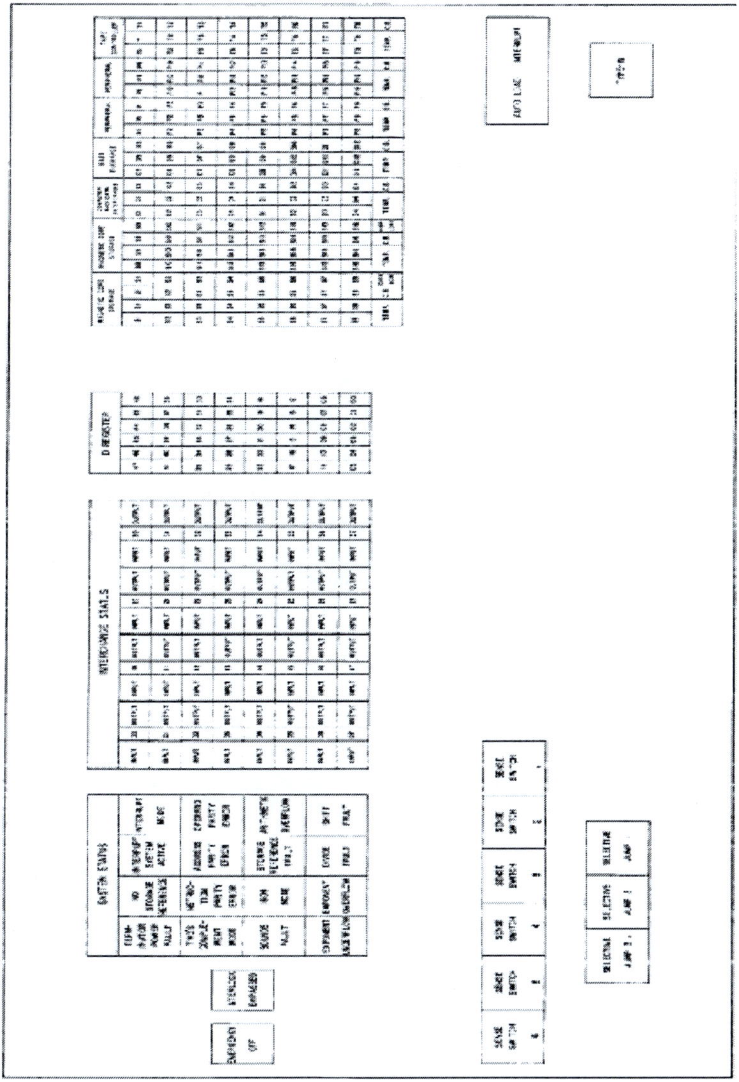

Figure 4-18. CDC 3601 – Operator Section
Source: CDC 1964af

Table 4-9. System Status Indicators

Indicator	Description
Terminator Power Fault	Terminator power was lost or one side of the power line has been shorted to ground.
No Storage Reference	An attempt was made to access a non-existent storage bank.
Interrupt Active	The interrupt system was enabled, allowing interrupt conditions to be examined in an interrupt handler.
Interrupt Mode	The CP was operating in an interrupt handler.
Two's Complement	The computer was operating in two's complement mode.
Instruction Parity Error	A parity error was discovered in reading an instruction from storage by the CDC 1604.
Address Parity Error	A parity error was discovered in writing an address to storage from the CP.
Operand Parity Error	A parity error was discovered in reading an operand from storage by the CDC 1604.
Bounds Fault	A storage reference was attempted outside the bounds specified by the Bounds register.
1604 Mode	The CP was operating in 1604 mode.
Storage Reference Fault	An error occurred in making a reference to a storage location.
Arithmetic Overflow	An add or subtract result exceeded the capacity of the A register.
Exponent Underflow	A floating point instruction generated an exponent underflow, where the exponent was $<= 2^{-10}-1$.
Exponent Overflow	A floating point instruction generated an exponent overflow, where the exponent was $<= 2^{10}-1$.
Divide Fault	An attempt to execute an improper divide instruction was detected.
Shift Fault	A shift count $> 60_8$ or 140_8 was detected using 48 (96) bits.

The D register matrix had indicator lights that were lit when the corresponding bit in the D register was set. The Peripheral matrix had indicator lights that were lit when the corresponding peripheral unit was active.

The Maintenance Section of the CDC 3601 is depicted in Figure 4-19. It was used by CDC Field Engineers (FEs) to diagnose and correct conditions in the computer system. It could also be used by users to debug programs.

The two rows at the top of the panel provided register displays. Each display was comprised of lamp modules each of which displayed a single octal digit only when the computer was stopped.

On the next row, the Display Selector allowed the FE/user to select which of the CDC 3604 arithmetic or index registers to display while debugging or analyzing the system's operation. Their contents were display on the two rows of indicator lights at the bottom of the main panel. The contents of the IBR, OBR, PAR and IR were always displayed during system operation.

The Instruction Format Display (IFD) displayed words or phrases interpreting the values in the instruction that was displayed in the IR. For example, the value 10_8 in the upper two digits of the IR would cause the phrase "Operation Code" to be displayed in the IFD.

The bottom section of the panel contained push buttons for testing system function which are described in Table 4-10.

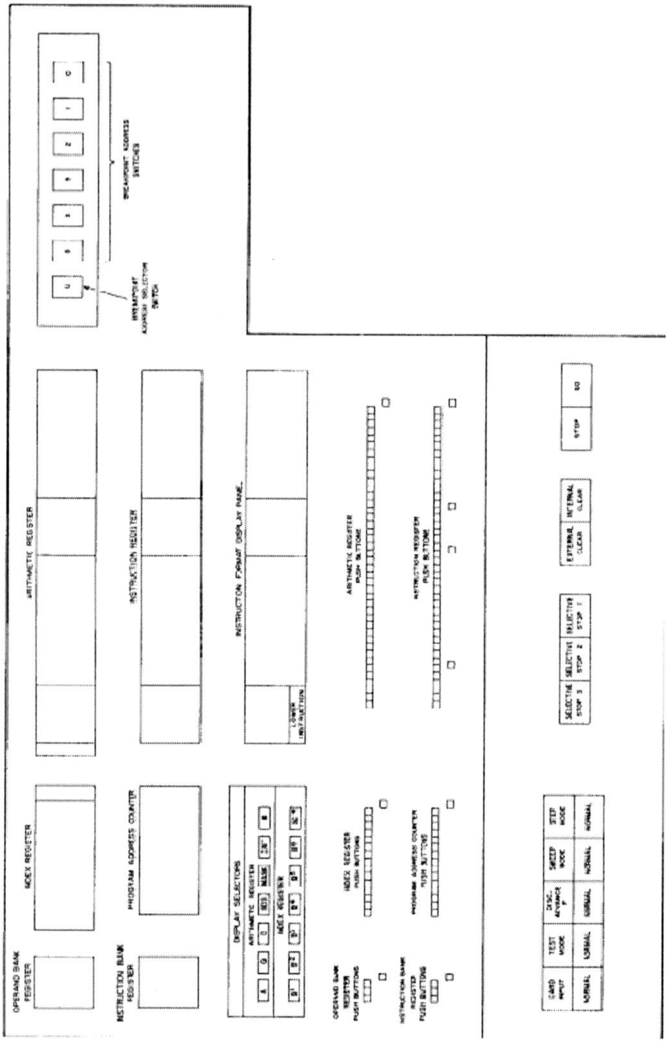

Figure 4-19. CDC 3601 – Maintenance Section
Source: CDC 1964af

Table 4-10. Maintenance Panel Push Buttons

Push Button	Usage
Card Input	This button selected the card reader for an Input To A operation in which a 12-bit character was loaded into the lower 12 bits of the A register.
Normal	This button paired with the Card Input button selected the console typewriter for an Input To A operation. Each 6-bit character was loaded into the lower 6 bits of the A register as each character was typed.
Test Mode	This button placed the CDC 3604 in test mode where: 1. Instructions were executed normally 2. After 300 microseconds, the computer stopped. 3. After another 50 microseconds, a Master clear was issued. 4. After another 50 microseconds, instruction execution began normally at storage location 0 0000. Steps 2 through 4 were repeated while the computer remained in test mode.
Disconnect Advance P	This button disabled incrementing the PAR. When the Go button was pressed, the same instruction was repeated.
Sweep Mode	This button placed the computer in sweep mode. When the Go button was pressed, instructions were read from consecutive storage locations, but were not executed. This allowed the user to step through a program inspecting the instructions.
Step Mode	This button placed the computer in Step Mode, which allowed an FE/user to execute a program instruction by instruction each time the Go button was pressed.

Pressing the Normal button after the last four entries above caused the computer system to resume normal operation. This allowed the FE/user to examine portions of the program to determine where problems might be that caused errors in computation.

The External Clear button issued a Master Clear to all peripheral equipment to reset to their default initial value. Similarly, the Internal Clear button reset all registers and control flip-flops in the CDC 3604 to their default initial value.

4.3.2 Dual CDC 3600 Configuration

Two CDC 3600 computer systems could be coupled together to share both memory and access to a suite of peripheral devices. Figure 4-20 depicts a configuration.

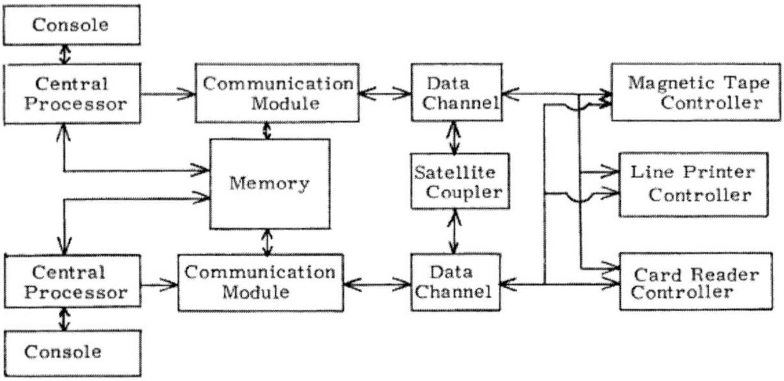

Figure 4-20. CDC 3600 Dual CP Configuration
Source: Adapted from CDC 1967g

The dual CDC 3600 systems communicate through the shared memory, which required some form of synchronization to prevent either CDC 3600 from stepping on the other's data. They also shared access to two data channels and their attached peripherals through a CDC 3682 Satellite Coupler.

4.3.3 Real-Time Clock

Source: CDC 1964af

The CDC 3604 Computation Module provided a Real-Time Clock (RTC) that was two's complement, 27-bit counter that advanced each millisecond. The clock count was held in the Time Register (TR). A 27-bit Time Limit Register (TLR) generated an interrupt when the value in the TLR was equal to the value in the TR. The bit sensing and register jump could set and test the TLR, and read the TR.

4.3.4 Optional Modules

The CDC 3600 could be expanded to provide enhanced performance in several ways:

- A second CDC 3604 Computation Module could be coupled with the initial Computation Module to provide a multiprocessing capability.
- Up to fourteen additional 3609 Storage Modules each with 16K words of magnetic core could be attached to the system yielding a maximum memory of 256K words.
- The 3602 Communication Module could be expanded by four additional Data Channels.

4.4 CDC 3400

Some customers balked at the price of the CDC 3600 as a replacement for the CDC 1604, so CDC developed the CDC 3400 as a cheaper, slower version. The CDC 3400 was primarily oriented towards scientific computation, but was also adapted by many organizations for business data processing because of its speed. Unlike the 3600 and 3800, the CDC 3400 did not have a Communication Module. Its data channels were directly attached to memory and controlled by the CP (CDC 1964b, 1964c). The CDC 3400 console with the processor cabinet in the background is depicted in Figure 4-21.

Figure 4-21. CDC 3400 Advertisement
Source: CDC UNK

4.4.1 CDC 3400 System Configuration

The basic system configuration for the CDC 3400 consisted of a Model 3404 Central Processor with 16K words of storage, a Model 3401 Control Console, and a Model 3406 Standard Input/Output Channel (SIOC). The SIOC could handle up to eight external devices. Up to three additional SIOCs could be configured in a CDC 3400 system configuration. An optional 16K word CDC 3409 Storage Unit could increase total memory to 32K words. An optional CDC 3410 Floating Point Option could be configured for scientific computing.

As an option, a CDC 3407 Special I/O Channel, which handled 24-bit devices, could be configured. Magnetic Tape Controllers, providing 1 to 4 channels, could handle up to 8 magnetic tape transports. A standard set of unit record devices, compatible with the CDC 1604, could also be configured in a CDC 3400 system.

A CDC 3417 Direct Access Data Channel could be used to couple a CDC 3600 to a CDC 3400 whereby the CDC 3400 was treated as an extra memory bank.

However, CDC often recommended that customers configure a CDC 160 with unit record devices in offline mode, thus allowing the CDC 3400 to operate at high-speed using magnetic tape.

4.4.2 3400 System Architecture

The CDC 3400 supported only one bank of memory (32K words). Its arithmetic section only had a P register that served as the program address counter. It had no Instruction Bank Register since it only issued 15-bit addresses. The accumulator (A register) was 48 bits. It provided six 15-bit index registers. The Program Control U register held an instruction while it was being executed.

4.5 CDC 3800

The CDC 3800 was an enhanced version of the CDC 3600. Figure 4-22 depicts the CDC 3800 console displayed at the Smithsonian Air and Space Museum – Udvar-Hazy Center in Chantilly, Virginia. Figure 4-23 depicts a plaque describing it.

Figure 4-22. CDC 3800 Console
Source: Photo by S.H. Kaisler, 2016

Figure 4-23. CDC 3800 at Smithsonian Air & Space Museum
Source: Photo by S.H. Kaisler, 2016

4.6 CDC 3000 Instruction Set

Source: CDC 1964af

The 3x00 instruction set consisted of 24-bit and 48-bit instructions divided into three classes. The 24-bit instructions had a fixed format, but 48-bit instructions had variable formats. The format for the Class I 24-bit instructions is depicted in Figure 4-24. Two of these instruction words were stored in each 48-bit word.

6 bits	3 bits	15 bits
f	b or j	m, y, or k

where:

f	function code
b or j	index register or jump designator
m, y, k	where m represents the execution address, y represents an immediate operand, and k represents the shift count

Figure 4-24. CDC 3x00 24-Bit Instruction Format
Source: Adapted from CDC 1964af

The index designator, b, designated one of six index registers when b was equal to 1 … 6. If b = 0, no index register was used. If b = 7, indirect addressing was used. Class II 24-bit instructions had 9-bit function codes and a 15-bit operand. Class III 48-bit instructions had the format depicted in Figure 4-25.

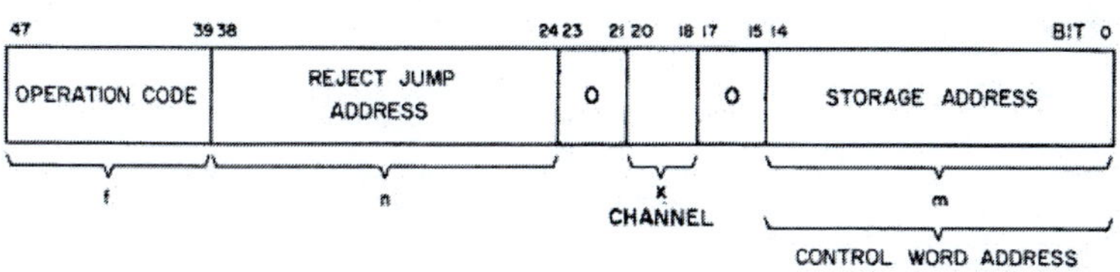

Figure 4-25. CDC 3x00 Class III Instruction Format
Source: Adapted from CDC 1964af

Sign extension replicated the sign of the source register to the remaining bits.

A storage address had consisted of 18 bits as depicted in Figure 4-26.

Figure 4-26. CDC 3600 Storage Address
Source: Adapted from CDC 1964af

The bit assignments for the 18-bit storage address were:

- Bits 15-17 selected a 3609 Storage Module;
- Bit 14-selected one of two 3604 computation Modules;
- Bits 13-0 provided an address in the selected storage module.

4.6.1 Inter-Register Transfer Instructions

The Inter-Register Transfer Instructions exchanged the contents of the A and Q registers. When the floating-point module was installed the E register could be loaded to/from AQ and the E_L and E_U registers could be loaded to/from other registers. These instructions are presented in Table 4-11 (Source: CDC 1964af).

Table 4-11. Inter-Register Transmission Instructions

Opcode	Bits 12-14	Mnemonic	Description
53,0 (b = 0)	4	AQA	Add Q to A: A <- c(A) + c(Q)
53,0	4	AIA b	Add Index to A: A <- c(Bb) + c(A)
53,1	4	IAI b	Add Index + A to Bb: Bb <- c(Bb) + c(A)
53,0	0	TIA b	Transfer Index to A: A <- c(Bb)
53,1	0	TAI b	Transfer A to Bb: Bb <- c(A)
53,0	1	TMQ v	Transfer v to Q: Q <- v
53,1	1	TQM v	Transfer Q to v: v <- c(Q)
53,0	2	TMA v	Transfer v to A: A <- v
53,1	2	TAM v	Transfer A to v: v <- c(A)
53,0	3	TMI b,v	Transfer v to Bb: Bb <- v
53,1	3	TIM b,v	Transfer Bb to v: v <- c(Bb)
55,1	0	ELQ	Transfer E_L to Q: Q <- c(E_L)
55.2	0	EUA	Transfer E_U to A: A <- c(E_U)

55,3	0	EAQ	Transfer E to AQ: AQ <- c(E)
55,5	0	QEL	Transfer Q to E_L: E_L <- c(Q)
55,6	0	AEU	Transfer A to E_U: E_U <- c(A)
55,7	0	AQE	Transfer AQ to E: E <- c(AQ)
77,66	0	AIS	Transfer A to ISR: ISR <- c(A_{00-02})
77,67	1	ISA	Transfer ISR to A: A_{00-02} <- c(ISR)
77,66	0	AOS	Transfer A to OSR: OSR <- c(A_{00-02})
77,67	1	OSA	Transfer OSR to A: A_{00-02} <- c(OSR)
77,54	0	ACI	Transfer A to CIR: CIR <- c(A_{00-02})
77,55	0	CIA	Transfer CIR to A: A_{00-02} <- c(CIR)
77,64	0	APF	Transfer A to PIF: PIF <- c(A_{00-11}). If bit 11 was one, B2 was used for address modification.
77,65	0	PFA	Transfer PIF to A: A_{00-11} <- c(PIF). If bit 11 was one, B2 was used for address modification.
77-63 Bits 0-11 are zero	0	CRA	Transfer Cr to A: A_{00-05} <- c(CR)
77,63 Bits 9-11 are 4	0	ACR	Transfer A to CR: CR <- c(A_{00-05})
77,56	0	JAA	Transfer Jump Address to A: A_{00-14} <- c(P)

4.6.2 Load and Store Instructions

The Load and Store Instructions, described in Table 4-12, transferred a full word of 48 bits between memory address m and the A and Q registers. Both indirect and indexed addressing may be used. If b = 0, no operation was performed (Source: CDC 1964af).

Table 4-12. Load and Store Instructions

Opcode	Mnemonic	Description
20	LDA m,b	Load A: A<- c(m)
21	LDQ m,b	Load Q: Q<- c(m)
22	LACH r,b	Load A, Character: A_{00-05} <- c(r)
23	LQCH r,b	Load Q, Character: Q_{00-05} <- c(r)
24	LCA m,b	Load A, Complement: A <- ~c(m)
25	LDAQ m,b	Load AQ: AQ <- c(m), c(m+1)
26	LCAQ m,b	Load AQ, Complement: AQ <- ~c(m), ~c(m+1)
27	LDL m,b	Load A, Logical: A <- c(Q) AND c(m)
54	LDI m,b	Load Index: Bb <- $c(m)_{00-14}$
40	STA m	Store A: m<- c(A)
41	STQ m	Store Q: m <- c(Q)
42	SACH r,b	Store A, Character: r <- A_{00-05}; if b = 1, r = r + c(B2)
43	SQCH r,b	Store Q, Character: r <- Q_{00-05}; if b = 1, r = r + c(B1)
44	SWA m,b	Store 15-bit Word Address:
45	STAQ m,b	Store AQ: m, m+1 <- c(AQ)
46	SCHA m,b	Store 17-bit Character Address: m <- A_{00-16}
47	STI m,b	Store Index: m_{00-14} <- c(Bb)

Note: ~ means « one's complement »

4.6.3 Fixed-Point Arithmetic Instructions

The Fixed-Point Arithmetic Instructions operated on 24-bit scalar quantities for A or Q and 48-bit quantities for the AQ register. The Floating-Point instructions operate on 96-bit quantities using the AQ register. In on all cases, M <- m + c(Bb) to yield the effective address. These instructions are presented in Table 4-13 (Source: CDC 1964af).

Table 4-13. Fixed Point Instructions

Opcode	Mnemonic	Description
30	ADA m,b	Add Memory to A: A <- c(A) + c(M).
31	SBA m,b	Subtract Memory from A: A<- c(A) – c(M).
32	ADAQ mb	Add to AQ: AQ <- c(AQ) + c(M).
33	SBAQ m,b	Subtract from AQ: AQ <- c(AQ) - c(M).
34	RAD m,b	Replace Add: M <- c(M) + c(A).
50	MUA m,b	Multiply A by M: QA <- c(A) * c(M); QA was a 48-bit quantity.
51	DVA m.b	Divide A by M: QA <- dividend; A <- c(QA)/c(M); Q <- remainder.
56	MUAQ m,b	Multiply AQ: AQE <- c(AQ) * c(M), c(M+1) yielding 96 bits.
57	DVAQ m,b	Divide AQ : AQ <- c(AQ)/c(M),c(M+1); E <- remainder.
60	FAD m,b	Floating Point Add Memory to AQ: AQ <- c(AQ) + c(M), c(M+1) normalized and rounded.
61	FSB m,b	Floating Point Subtract Memory from AQ: AQ<- c(AQ) – c(M), c(M+1) normalized and rounded.
62	FMU m,b	Floating Point Multiply AQ by M: AQ <- c(AQ) * c(M), c(M+1); AQ was a 48-bit quantity.
63	FVQ m,b	Floating Point Divide AQ by M: A <- c(QA)/c(M),c(M+1); AQ <- quotient rounded and normalized; E <- remainder.
67	ADM r,s	Add BCD Field A to BCD Field C: r was address of lowest character in field A; s was the address of lowest character in field C; in c(P)+2, fields S1 and S2 contain lengths of fields A and C, respectively.
67	SBM r,s	Subtract BCD Field A to BCD Field C: r was address of lowest character in field A; s was the address of lowest character in field C; in c(P)+2, fields S1 and S2 contain lengths of fields A and C, respectively.

Field A could be shorter than field C. Addition terminated when field A was exhausted. The upper two bits of the lowest character in A and C respectively contained their sign. The BDP condition register recorded the sign of the result.

4.6.4 Address Arithmetic Instructions

Address Arithmetic Instructions increment the specified register by the immediate operand given in the instruction. These instructions are presented in Table 4-14 (Source: CDC 1964af).

Table 4-14. Address Arithmetic Instructions

Opcode	Mnemonic	Description
15,0	INI y,b	Increase Index Register: Bb <- c(Bb) + y
15,6	INA y	Increase A by y: A <- c(A) + operand y
15,4	INA,S y	Increase A by y: A <- c(A) + operand y, sign extended
15,7	INQ y	Increase Q by y: Q <- c(Q) + operand y
15,5	INA,S y	Increase Q by y: Q <- c(Q) + operand y, sign extended
54	ISK y	Compare Bb with y: If equal, Bb <- 0; skip lower instruction If not, Bb <- c(Bb) + 1; execute lower instruction.

4.6.5 Control Instructions

Control instructions, as depicted in Table 4-15, halted program execution (Source: CDC 1964af).

Table 4-15. Control Instructions

Opcode	Mnemonic	Description
00	HLT m	Halt: Unconditionally halt the processor at the instruction at address m. Restart via an RNI instruction at address m.
7770	SLS	Selective Stop: Halt the processor if the SELECT STOP switch on the operator console was depressed. Restart via RNI from address c(P)+1.
7777	UCS	Unconditional Stop: Halt the processor. Restart via RNI from address c(P)+1.

4.6.6 Enter Instructions

Enter instructions, which are depicted in Table 4-16, loaded immediate values into registers A, Q, or one of the index registers (Source: CDC 1964af).

Table 4-16. Enter Instructions

Opcode	Mnemonic	Description
14,0	ENI y,b	Enter Index with y: Bb <- y
14,6	ENA y	Enter A with y: A <- y
14,4	ENA,S y	Enter A with y, sign extended
14,7	ENQ,S y	Enter Q: Q <- y, upper bits sign extended
14,5	ENQ y	Enter Q: Q <- y
11,0	ECHA z	Enter Character Address in A: A <- z
11,1	ECHA,S z	Enter Character Address in A, sign extended: A <- 0; A <- z

4.6.7 Skip Instructions

The Skip Instructions, depicted in Table 4-17, tested the value in the A, Q, or an index register against a supplied immediate value and skipped an instruction if the specified condition was met (Source: CDC 1964af).

Table 4-17. Skip Instructions

Opcode	Mnemonic	Description
04,0	ISE y	Index Skip Equal: if y = 0, P = c(P) + 1
04.1-3	ISE y,b	Index Skip Equal: if c(B_b) = y, P = c(P) + 1
04,6	ASE y	Accumulator Skip Equal: if c(A) = y, P = c(P) + 1
04,4	ASE,S y	Accumulator Skip Equal, Sign Extended: if c(A) = y, P = c(P) + 1
04,7	QSE y	Q Skip Equal: if c(Q) = y, P = c(P) + 1
04,5	QSE,S y	Q Skip Equal, Sign Extended: if c(Q) = y, P = c(P) + 1
05,0	ISG y	Index Skip Greater Than: if y >= 0, P = c(P) + 1
05.1-3	ISG y,b	Index Skip Greater Than: if c(B_b) >= y, P = c(P) + 1
05,6	ASG y	Accumulator Skip Greater Than: if c(A) >= y, P = c(P) + 1

05,4	ASG,S y	Accumulator Skip Greater Than, Sign Extended: if c(A) >= y, P = c(P) + 1
05,7	QSQ y	Q Skip Greater Than: if c(Q) >= y, P = c(P) + 1
05,5	QSQ,S y	Q Skip Greater Than, Sign Extended: if c(Q) >= y, P = c(P) + 1
10,0	ISI y,b	Index Skip Incremental: if c(B_b) = y then B_b <- 0, P = c(P) + 2; else B_b = c(B_b) + 1, RNI from c(P) +1
10,1	ISD y,b	Index Skip Decremental: if c(B_b) = y; then B_b <- 0, P = c(P) + 2 else B_b = c(B_b) - 1, RNI from c(P) +1

4.6.8 Jump Instructions

The Jump Instructions, depicted in Table 4-18, transferred program control to other program sections based on the specified test criteria. The operator could selectively cause jumps by setting one of the six switch keys on the console (Source: CDC 1964af).

Table 4-18. Jump Instructions

Opcode	Mnemonic	Description
00	SJ1-6 m	Jump If Switch Key 1-6 was set: Jump to m else RNI from c(P)+1
01	UJP m	Unconditional Jump: P <- m
70	JMP,HI m	Jump on Positive Result: if BDP operation result > 0, P<- m
70	JMP,ZRO m	Jump on Zero Result: if BDP operation result = 0, P<- m
70	JMP, LOW m	Jump on Negative Result: if BDP operation result < 0, P<- m
02	IJI m,b	Index Jump, Increment Index: if B_b = 0, RNI from c(P) +1; else B_b = c(B_b)+1, then RNI. If b = 0, no operation
02	IJD m,b	Index Jump, Decrement Index: if B_b = 0, RNI from c(P) -1; else B_b = c(B_b)+1, then RNI. If b = 0, no operation

03	AZJ m	Compare A w/ Zero for Jump Condition: c(A) compared w/ zero based on bits 15-16, the jump designator. J Test 0 c(A) = 0 1 c(A) /= 0 2 c(A) > 0 3 c(A) < 0
03	AQJ m	Compare A w/ Q for Jump Condition: Compare c(A) w/ c(Q) jump designator. J Test 0 c(A) = 0 1 c(A) /= 0 2 c(A) > 0 3 c(A) < 0
00	RTJ m	Return Jump: m <- c(P) + 1; P <- m+1

4.6.9 SHIFT INSTRUCTIONS

The Shift instructions, depicted in Table 4-19, shifted the contents of a memory location, or the A or Q or index registers left or right by the indicated number of bits. All shifts were end around meaning that bits moved out of one end were entered at the opposite end.

The Scale Instruction was used during normalization of floating-point numbers (Source: CDC 1964af).

Table 4-19. Shift and Scale Instructions

Opcode	Mnemonic	Description
10	SSH m	Storage Shift: m <- m shift one bit left, end around; if bit 32 = 0, RNI c(P)+1, else RNI c(P)+2
11	SHA k,b	Shift A: K <- c(B_b) k; if K > 0, left shift A by $K_{00\text{-}0}5$ bits; else right shift A by ~$K_{00\text{-}05}$ bits; bits are carried end around
12	SHQ k,b	Shift Q: K <- c(B_b) k; if K > 0, left shift Q by $K_{00\text{-}0}5$ bits; else right shift Q by ~$K_{00\text{-}05}$ bits; bits are carried end around
13	SHAQ k,b	Shift AQ: K <- c(B_b) k; if K > 0, left shift AQ by $K_{00\text{-}0}5$ bits; else right shift AQ by ~$K_{00\text{-}05}$ bits; bits are carried end around

14	SCAQ k,b	Scale AQ: shift AQ left end around until bit 46 /= bit 47; Bb (for b > 0) <- K, the number of bits shifted

4.6.10 Logical Instructions

The Logical instructions, depicted in Table 4-20, performed Boolean operations on the A, or Q or an index register (Source: CDC 1964af).

Table 4-20. Logical Instructions

Opcode	Mnemonic	Description
16,0	XOI y,b	Exclusive OR of Index and y: B_b <- c(Bb) XOR y
16,6	XOA y	Exclusive OR of A and y: A <- c(A) XOR y
16,4	XOA,S y	Exclusive OR of A and y, sign extended: A <- c(A) XOR y
16,7	XOQ y	Exclusive OR of Q and y: Q <- c(Q) XOR y
16,5	XOQ,S y	Exclusive OR of Q and y, sign extended: Q <- c(Q) XOR y
17,0	ANI y,b	AND of Index and y: B_b <- c(B_b) AND y
17,6	ANA y	AND of A and y: A <- c(A) AND y
17,4	ANA,S y	AND of A and y, sign extended: A <- c(A) AND y
17,7	ANQ y	AND of Q and y: Q <- c(Q) AND y
17,5	ANQ,S y	AND of Q and y, sign extended: Q <- c(Q) AND y
35	SSA m,b	Selectively Set A: Set bits of A to 1 for corresponding bits in c(M) that are 1
36	SCA m,b	Selectively Complement A: Set complement the bits of A for corresponding bits in c(M) that are 1
37	LPA m,b	Logical Product A: A <- c(A) and c(M)

Note: Effective address M = m +c(B_b) for b = 1,2,3

4.6.11 Masked Search and Compare Instructions

The Masked Search and Compare instructions, depicted in Table 4-21, performed bit comparisons between the contents of A and Q where Q 's contents are masked by the contents of a memory location (Source: CDC 1964af).

Table 4-21. Masked Search and Compare Instructions

Opcode	Mnemonic	Description
06	MEQ m,i	Masked Equality Search: Compare c(A) with the logical product of c(Q) and c(M). Do as follows: 1. Decrement B1 by i 2. If B1 changed sign, RNI from c(P+1) 3. M = m + c(B1) 4. If c(A) = c(Q) dot c(M), RNI from c(P+2) 5. go to 1
07	MTH m,i	Masked Threshold Search: Compare c(A) with the logical product of c(Q) and c(M). Do as follows: 1. Decrement B1 by i 2. If B1 changed sign, RNI from c(P+1) 3. M = m + c(B1) 4. If c(A) >= c(Q) dot c(M), RNI from c(P+2) 5. go to 1
52	CPR m,b	Compare (with limits test): Do as follows: 1. If c(M) > c(A), RNI from c(P)+1 2. If c(Q) > c(M), RNI from c(P)+2 3. RNI from C(P)+3
67	CMP r,s	Compare Field A to Field C: Compare the characters in field A to corresponding characters in field C. r and s are addresses of lowest characters in each field. Br and Bs are contained in c(P+1). Terminate when an unequal character comparison occurs.
67	CMP,DC r,s	Compare Fields w/ Delimiting: Compare the characters in field A to corresponding characters in field C. r and s are addresses of lowest characters in each field. Br and Bs are contained in c(P+1) Terminate when an unequal character comparison occurs, one of the fields was exhausted or a character in either field equals the delimiting character DC.

Note: i was represented by 3 bits which allowed a decrement interval of 1 to 8 bits.

4.6.12 Condition Test Instructions

The Condition Test Instructions, depicted in Table 4-2, tested memory and a field within a word (Source: CDC 1964af).

Table 4-22. Condition Test Instructions

Opcode	Mnemonic	Description
77	TMAV	Test Memory Availability: test core storage for the presence of a specific address; used to determine amount of memory configured in a system. If yes, RNI from c(P+2); else RNI from c(P+1)
67,0	TST r	Test Field A for Sign: scan characters in field A for a sign character in the upper 2 bits. Set the BDP condition register if found.
67,1	TSTN r	Test Field A for Numeric: scan characters in field A for numeric codes for BCD numbers. Set the BDP condition register if found.

4.6.13 Sensing Instructions

The Sensing Instructions, depicted in Table 4-23, tested interrupt status (Source: CDC 1964af).

Table 4-23. Sensing Instructions

Opcode	Mnemonic	Description
77,2 Bits 00-11 = 0	EXS x, ch	Sense External Status: set 1 in x, the sensing status mask, for each status to be tested. RNI from c(P+1) if any status was 1 when instruction was executed for channel ch (ch = 0 to 7).
77,2	COPY x, ch	Copy External Status: do the following 1. A_{00-11} <- external status from channel ch 2. A_{12-23} <- c(IMR) 3. RNI from c(P+1).
77,4	INTS x, ch	Sense Interrupt: RNI from c(P+1) if an interrupt line was active and a sensing bit was 1 for channel ch; otherwise, RNI from c(P+2).

77,3	INS x, ch	Sense Internal Status: RNI from c(P+1) if 1 bit in the sensing mask x correspond to 1 bit in the channel status; otherwise, RNI from c(P+2).
77,3 Bits 00-11 = 0	CINS x, ch	Copy Internal Status: do the following: 1. A_{00-11} <- internal status code 2. A_{12-23} <- c(IMR) 3. RNI from c(P+1).

4.6.14 Pause Instructions

The Pause Instructions, depicted in Table 4-24, temporarily halted the operation of the processor (Source: CDC 1964af).

Table 4-24. Pause Instructions

Opcode	Mnemonic	Description
77, 60	PAUS x	Pause: Halt processor operation for a maximum of 40 msecs if a condition defined by the Pause Sensing Mask x exists. If no lines are active, RNI from c(P)+2.
77,61	PRP x	Priority Pause: Same as PAUS, except that the real-time clock does not advance.

Note: The Pause Sensing Mask had bits for sensing different I/O conditions, such as I/O Channel readiness and Console Typewriter busy.

4.6.15 Interrupt Instructions

The Interrupt Instructions, depicted in Table 4-25, handled the enabling and disabling of interrupts (Source: CDC 1964af).

Table 4-25. Interrupt Instructions

Opcode	Mnemonic	Description
77,74	EINT	Enable Interrupt Control: Enable interrupts; the instruction at P+1 will execute before interrupts can occur.
77,73	DINT	Disable Interrupt Control: disable interrupts.
77,50	INCL x	Clear Interrupt: clear the interrupts specified in the interrupt mask code x.

77,52	SSIM	Selectively Set Interrupt Mask: set Interrupt Mask Register according to interrupt mask code x.
77,53	SCIM x	Selectively Clear Interrupt Mask: clear Interrupt Mask Register according to interrupt mask code x.
77,51	CILO x	Channel Interrupt Lockout: disable all interrupts on channels specified by the channel mask x.
77,71	SFPF	Set Floating Point Fault: when optional floating-point arithmetic installed, enable floating point interrupts.
77,72	SBCD	Set BCD Fault: enable BCD faults

4.6.16 Program and Relocation Control

The Program and Relocation Control Instructions supported the multiprogramming capability of the CDC 3300/3500 systems. Table 4-26 depicts these instructions. These instructions were no-operation instructions in non-monitor mode.

Table 4-26. Program and Relocation Control Instructions

Opcode	Mnemonic	Description
55.0	RIS	Relocate to Instruction State.
55.4	ROS	Relocate to Operand State.
77.56	JAA	Transfer Last Jump Instruction Address to A.
77.610	TMAV	Send Storage Request: RNI to c(P) +2, if no reply in 5 microseconds.
77.62	SBJP	Enable transfer from monitor to program state at next jump instruction.
77.624	SDL	Set destructive load A condition in the CR.
77.63	CRA	Transfer c(CR) to lower 6 bits of A.
77.634	ACR	Transfer $A_{00\text{-}05}$ to CR.
77.64	APF w,2	Store $A_{00\text{-}11}$ to page file index w. B_2 was used for indexing.
77.65	PFA w,2	Load $A_{00\text{-}11}$ from page file index w. B_2 was used for indexing.
77.66	AOS	Transfer $A_{00\text{-}02}$ to the OSR.
77.664	AIS	Transfer $A_{00\text{-}02}$ to the ISR.
77.67	OSA	Transfer OSR to $A_{00\text{-}02}$.
77.674	ISA	Transfer ISR to $A_{00\text{-}02}$.

4.6.17 I/O INSTRUCTIONS

The Input/Output Instructions were used to manage data channels and to move data between registers and peripheral equipment. Table 4-27 presents the I/O instructions. In the following 'ch' specified the data channel.

Table 4-27. I/O Instructions

Opcode	Mnemonic	Description
73.0-3	INPC ch,r,s	Transferred the character addressed to storage.
74.4-7	INAC ch	Transferred the character addressed to A.
74.0-3	INPW ch,m,n	Transferred the word addressed to storage.
74.4-7	INAW ch	Transferred the word addressed to A.
75.0-3	OUTC ch,r,s	Transferred character from storage to equipment.
75.4-7	OTAC ch	Transferred character from storage to equipment.
76.0-3	OUTW ch,m,n	Transferred word from storage to equipment
76.4-7	OTAW ch	Transferred word from storage to equipment.
77,0	CON x,ch	Connected to data channel.
77,1	SEL x,ch	Selected the function to be performed on the data channel.
77,51	IOCL x	Cleared I/O channel, typewriter, S/M control.
77,51	CLCA cm	Cleared channels specified by mask 'cm'.
77,54	ACI	Transferred $A_{00\text{-}02}$ to CIR
77,55	CIA	Transferred CIR to $A_{00\text{-}02}$.
72,75	CTI	Set console typewriter input.
72,76	CTO	Set console typewriter output.

ACI and CIA were treated as no-operations if the system was running in non-monitor mode.

4.7 PROGRAMMING SYSTEMS

The CDC 3000 series supported multiple programming languages – primarily COMPASS assembly and FORTRAN IV – because it was oriented the scientific and engineering community.

4.7.1 Assembly Language Example

This program provides an example of the use of CDC 1604 instructions for solving the following problem, which was extracted from CDC 1967g.

A random set of integers ranging from 1-100 and starting at address SCORES was to be separated into groups according to the following patterns:

1. scores less than 70 stored beginning at address UNSAT
2. scores greater than or equal to 70 but less than 76 stored beginning at address POOR
3. scores greater than or equal to 76 but less than 91 stored beginning at address FAIR
4. scores greater than or equal to 91but less than 96 stored beginning at address GOOD
5. scores greater than or equal to 96 stored beginning at address EXCELENT

The program for performing this separation is given in Figure 4-27.

```
Location
Operation      Address            Comments

IDENT          SEPARATE
ENTRY          SEPARATE
SCORES         BSS     100
UNSAT          BSS     100        Reserve 100 words for this category
POOR           BSS     100
FAIR           BSS     100
GOOD           BSS     100
EXCELENT       BSS     100        Identifiers can only have eight
                                  characters
SEPARATE       BSS     1          Start of program
               ENI                0,1
               ENI                0,2
               ENI                0,3
               ENI                0,4
               ENI                0,5
               ENI                0,6
NEXT           LDA                SCORES,6
               RGJP,LT A,70,LT70  (A) LT70
               RGJP,LT A,76,LT76  (A) LT76
               RGJP,LT A,91,LT91  (A) LT91
               RGJP,LT A96,LT96   (A) LT96
```

```
GE96        STA    EXCELENT, 5
            INI    1,5
TEST        ISK    99,6        100 scores Tested
            SLJ    NEXT        No
            SLJ    SEPARATE          Yes (contains the return address)
LT70        STA    UNSAT,2
            INI    1,2
            SLJ    TEST
LT76        STA    POOR,2
            INI    1,2
            SLJ    TEST
LT91        STA    FAIR,2
            INI    1,2
            SLJ    TEST
LT96        STA    GOOD,2
            INI    1,2
            SLJ    TEST
            END
```

Figure 4-27. Sample CDC 3000 Assembly Language Program
Source: Adapted from CDC 1967g

Note that 100 locations were reserved for each of the categories because it was possible for all scores to fall solely within that category.

4.7.2 FORTRAN IV

The FORTRAN IV compiler and run-time support was a superset of that initially provided for the CDC 1604, but enhanced to work with enhanced SCOOPE operating system.

4.7.3 Library Functions

Source: CDC 1966be

The system library consisted of functions were written to be called with both an assembly language interface and as FORTRAN functions. These functions included single- and double-precision version of the commonly used arithmetic and trigonometric functions, complex arithmetic functions, arithmetic conversion functions, and various utility routines. They were read from paper tape and linked into assembly language and FORTRAN IV programs.

4.8 CDC 3000 Assessment

The CDC 3000 series was a very successful product for CDC. At the time of its introduction, this series had very few competitors. It was one of the first superminicomputers (although the term had not yet been invented) which delivered performance at an attractive price for many organizations. The series allowed CDC to expand into several markets - small and large scientific and commercial. The CDC 3600 was a high-performance machine that filled a gap in product revenues while delays in delivering the CDC 6600 were resolved. The CDC 3600 was one of the first machines to implement a modular architecture which made it easy to manufacture, assemble, and test and maintain.

CHAPTER FIVE

THE SCOPE OPERATING SYSTEM

Source: CDC 1966ah, CDC 1965ax

The Supervisory Control of Program Execution (SCOPE) operating system operated on several CDC models: the 1604, the 3000 series, the 6600/7600 series, and the Cyber 70/170 series. SCOPE was a batch operating system that loaded user programs and supervised their execution. It also provided mapping and debugging utilities, including dump utilities, and recovery utilities. SCOPE was often referred to as the Monitor.

While the basic concepts were the same, SCOPE was reimplemented for each machine due to instruction set and architectural differences and an improved understanding of the operating systems role in high-speed computers.

This chapter will focus on the SCOPE operating system as developed and used on the CDC 1604 and CDC 3000 computer systems.

5.1 SCOPE CONCEPTS

Source: CDC 1967c

A user task was called a *job*. A job included all statements between a JOB card and an end-of-file card. End-of-file cards also separated runs within a job. Within a job, control cards determined what actions were performed or initiated by the Monitor.

SCOPE sequenced through a set of user jobs under operator control. Each job was introduced by a JOB statement. Jobs were separated from other jobs by a SEQUENCE statement. A sample SCOPE job deck to compile and run a COMPASS program is depicted in Figure 5-1.

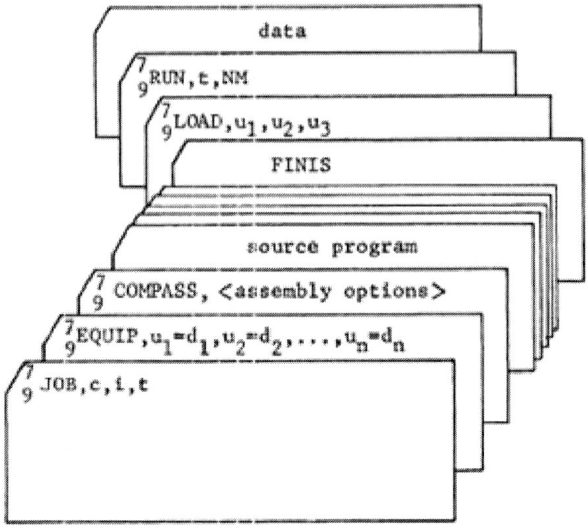

Figure 5-1. Sample SCOPE Job Deck
Source: CDC 1964g

5.2 SCOPE CONTROL CARDS

Control cards specified the actions to be performed by the computer under control of SCOPE. A control card was a binary card with a 7,9 punch in column 1 and the statement name beginning in column 2. Table 5-1 presents the control cards (CDC 1965at).

Table 5-1. SCOPE Control Cards

Statement	Description
JOB,<c>, <i>, <t>	All jobs started with a JOB card. The parameters are: c: the charge number of the account i: the user identification t: the maximum time limit for the job A single job card could be used for the execution of multiple independent programs, but the time specified was the maximum allowed for execution of all the programs.
SEQUENCE,<n>	This statement assigned a job sequence number, n, to the following job, which was used for all scheduling requests. When this statement was encountered, all resources for the previous job are released.
COMPASS, I,P,X,L,B,R,M	This statement invokes the Assembler to assemble a program consisting of machine language statements whose cards follow it. The parameters are: I = u:the logical input unit number P = u: the logical punch unit number X= u: the load-and-go logical unit number L = u: the lister logical unit number B = u: the binary output logical unit number R = u: the cross-reference symbol table listing logical unit number M = u: the programmer macros listing logical unit number
SCOPE	This statement terminates an assembly or compilation process.
LOAD,<u>	This statement loads a relocatable binary subprogram into storage from a programmer unit or load-and-go unit.
RUN,<t>,p><r>,<m>,<d>	This statement initiates program execution by transferring control to an object program in storage. The parameters are: t: the execution time limit in minutes p: the maximum number or print or write operations which may be requested on the standard output unit

	r: specified an area to be dumped if the program did not proceed to normal completion m: if blank, the memory map will be listed on the standard output unit after loading d: if not blank, a memory dump was taken after normal termination
FILE,<u> FILE END	This statement transferred binary records from the standard input unit to another logical unit <u>. All records up to a FILE END statement were transferred to logical unit <u>, whose value had to lie in the range 1 to 59, 69 specifying the load-and-go unit. The FILE END statement caused SCOPE to write an end-of-file mark and then backspace over it.
EQUIP, <u>=<d1>,…,<dn>	The EQUIP statement had to precede the RUN statement to declare programmer or scratch units which were standard density, labeled magnetic tapes. Parameters were: <u> was the logical unit number. <di> were declarations that are described in Table 5-2. Scratch units were available for a single execution, while programmer unit declarations were valid for all executions in a job, unless changed by other EQUIP statements.
LIBRARY,<u>	Specified an auxiliary library unit to be used during the job. The table of contents of the tape was transferred to core memory. Program requests for undefined entry points caused those routines to be loaded from the library tape. <u> was a logical number in the range 70 to 79.
END	End of file cards were used to separate jobs in a job stack or separate programs within a job.
END REEL	This statement terminated the current reel on the standard input unit and caused SCOPE to load the next reel if there was one.
END SCOPE	This statement signaled to SCOPE that the job stack was completed. It appeared on the unit following the set of jobs to be processed.

The declarations for the EQUIP statement are described in the following table. The EQUIP statement took the form EQUIP, <u>= <hhn>, where <hhn> specified the hardware type and physical unit number (CDC 1965at).

Table 5-2. EQUIP Declarations

Declaration	Description
Hardware, <u>=<hhn>	hh was one of the following: MT Magnetic Tape CR Card Reader PT Paper Tape Station CP Card Punch DF Disk File LF On-line Printer DR Magnetic Drum TY Typewriter TV Display PL Plotter n indicated an available physical unit.
Usage,<u>=<hh>	Usage declarations were made for equipment types for which they were appropriate. <hh> was one of: RW read/write operations BY bypass; all operations to this unit except MODE and STATUS were treated as no operations. RO read only; any write operations attempted caused the job to be terminated.
Density,<u>=<hh>	Density declarations were allowed for appropriate device types. <hh> was one of: LO low density (200 bpi) HI high density (556 bpi) HY hyper density (800 bpi)
Equivalence, <u>=<u'>	Unit u' was made equivalent to unit <u>, e.g., it referred to the same physical unit.
Unlabeled Tape,<u>=<**>	Any logical tape unit could be declared unlabeled. <**> was one of: READ The program had to specify the operator the tape to be mounted. WRITE SCOPE looked for any available unit.

An example of a job specification might appear as (CDC 1965at):

```
JOB, xxxx,STEVE,15
EQUIP,10=CR2
EQUIP,9=CP1
<object program 1>
RUN,7,300,7,1
<end of file>
EQUIP,11=CR3
<object program 2>
RUN,6,250
<end  of file>
```

This job was submitted by STEVE. It required both the card reader, CR2, and the card punch, CP1. It ran and <object program> that was submitted in-line. It required a second card reader, CR3, and then ran second object program. Output was sent to the card punch.

5.3 REQUESTS

A *request* was written as a macro instruction and assembled into a calling sequence to a SCOPE routine or invoked through a programming language interface to SCOPE. Requests could be made through a COMPASS program. Table 5-3 presents the programmer requests.

The following parameters could appear on a request statement:

u	A logical unit number
cwa	An address of an I/O control word
ra	A reject address to which control as transferred if the unit was unavailable.
ia	A program's interrupt subroutine to which control was transferred when an interrupt condition was sensed.

Table 5-3. Programmer Requests

Request	Description
READ/WRITE (u, cwa, ra, ia)	Requested that data be read from or written to the specified unit. For example: READ(INP, CONTROLA, SAM, INTRPT).
REOT/WEOT (u, cwa, ra, ia)	Magnetic tape controls that allowed reading and/or writing after the physical end-of-tape. Used to transfer to a continuation reel on a multireel application.
Tape Control (u, ra, ia)	Provided tape control functions as: BSPF: backspace a tape file BSPR: backspace one record REWIND: rewind the tape to the load point SKIP: skip to an end-of-file or end-of-tape record. ERASE: Erases 6 inches of tape. MARKEF: mark an end-of-file
UNLOAD (u, ra, ia, c)	Rewound a tape to its load point and signaled the operator to unload the physical tape. 'c' indicated the disposition of the tape: 0 release the unit. Other do not release the unit.
RELEASE (u, ra, c)	Released the assignment of a physical unit. 'c' indicated the disposition of the tape: 0 dispose of tape after release. Other rewind the tape and release, but do not dispose of the tape.

I/O statements within the programming language were translated into the appropriate SCOPE requests.

5.4 Logical Units

In CDC 3000 SCOPE, a *logical unit* designated a reference to a piece of equipment managed by SCOPE. Logical units were designated by integers in the range 1 to 80. There were three classes of logical units as presented in Table 5-4.

Table 5-4. SCOPE Logical Units

Logical units	Range	Description
Programmer Units	1-49	These units were assigned during a job for reference by a program. When a magnetic tape was released at the end of a job, it could be unloaded or saved for use by a later job.
Scratch Units	50-59	These were magnetic tapes that could be used at any time during a job by a program, but they were released at the end of a program execution.
System Units	60-80	These units were assigned by the Monitor during initialization, and were released at the end of a job stack.

5.4.1 System Units

Table 5-5 describes the system units available to a job and programs within the job. The logical unit number (LUN) and mnemonic by which the unit could be referenced in a program are presented.

Table 5-5. SCOPE System Units

System Unit	LUN	Description
STANDARD INPUT	60	INP: All control cards for all jobs were placed on this unit. Also placed here were programs and data.
STANDARD OUTPUT	61	OUT: All control cards, diagnostics, and loader control cards were written in BCD on this unit. Usually, program output was also written here.
STANDARD PUNCH OUTPUT	62	PUN: Program data – source code, binary object programs, and data for punching onto cards were placed on this unit.
INPUT COMMENT	63	ICM: Comments from the operator to the Monitor were made on this unit. The programmer could include directions for handling input.
OUTPUT COMMENT	64	OCM: Messages from the Monitor to the operator were placed on this unit. Messages from a program, to the operator were also placed on this unit.

ACCOUNTING INFORMATION	65	ACC: Job cards, date, time on and off the machine, and elapsed job time were written to this unit for installation records.
SATELLITES	66-68	Satellite units were assigned by the operator to remote computers which communicated with the 3600. These units were used exclusively by SCOPE.
LOAD-AND-GO	69	LGO: Binary object programs loaded from INP or produced from compilation or assembly were stored here prior to loading and execution.
SCOPE LIBRARY	70	LIB: This unit contained the Monitor and all programs and subroutines that operated under SCOPE, such as compilers and utilities.
AUXILIARY LIBRARIES	71-79	These units were used for library preparation including editing and organizing as well as for additional system libraries.
SYSTEM SCRATCH RECORD	80	Equipment data tables, accounting data, and recovery dump information were stored in the first record of this unit. If the monitor was destroyed in part by a running program, it could be recovered from data on this unit. User programs could not access this unit.

From the descriptions above, it was clear that the system units were associated with multiple magnetic tapes attached to the CDC 3600.

5.5 File System

SCOPE maintained a directory of all known files in the File Name Table (FNT). Files consisted of a set of logical records. For unit record devices, the logical record size was equivalent to the physical record size. For magnetic disks and magnetic tapes, it could vary depending on the device. Files could be transferred from one device to another, such as from a disk file to the card punch resulting in a card deck.

I/O operations were performed on files or devices by naming the files or devices on job control cards. Five file names were reserved for each job as described in Table 5-6.

Table 5-6. Reserved SCOPE File Names

File Name	Description
INPUT	The file from which job input will be read. Its name was specified on the job card.
OUTPUT	The file which will be printed when the job was complete. All job output was directed to the named file.
DAYFILE	A file which contains the system history, e.g., messages for the job.
PUNCH	A file which was punched in Hollerith when the job was completed.
PUNCHB	A file which was punched in binary when the job was completed.

5.6 Loading Programs

A binary object program on the standard input unit was loaded directly into memory as the cards were read.

Relocatable binary subprograms were loaded into memory from programmer and scratch units or from the (Load-and-Go) LGO unit.

When a LOAD statement was encountered, SCOPE backspaced the unit one file. It then loaded subprograms until an end-of-file card or two SCOPE control cards were encountered.

5.7 Executing Object Programs

The RUN control card-initiated program execution by transferring control to the object program in storage.

The last executable statement in a program should return control to SCOPE. Usually, this was accomplished through an EXIT request or via an END card in programming languages which caused the generation of an EXIT request in the binary object. Programs that terminated with no abnormal conditions terminated normally. Programs terminating under all other conditions terminated abnormally. Upon abnormal termination, a recovery dump could be taken if specified on the RUN control card.

5.8 Real-Time SCOPE

Source: CDC 1965x, CDC 1969aa

Real-Time SCOPE (RTS) for the lower level 3000 series machines supported multiprogramming of two independent programs. High-priority interrupts were recognized on channels reserved for real-time applications. These channels were used for programs needing immediate access where data transfer had to keep pace with physical processes during a given time period. Real-time I/O was handled outside of the centralized I/O handling.

RTS was based on magnetic tape to hold programs and system and user program libraries. It provided support for mass storage devices, but these were optional in the system configuration.

5.8.1 Stacked Jobs

A *stacked job* was comprised of one or more programs to be executed, which could be a library program such as a compiler or a user program loaded from a system logical unit. Job sequencing, program loading, and program execution were determined by control cards inserted in the job deck.

A stacked job consisted of foreground and background programs. A *foreground program* was a normally executed program such as compilations, system utilities, or user programs. Large foreground programs could be divided into overlays that were dynamically loaded as needed. A *background program* was one that either required control at discrete time intervals or based on certain I/O -dependent conditions. The background program was memory-resident and did not have overlays.

5.8.2 Loading Relocatable Programs

The RTS Loader was invoked by the RTS executive whenever programs needed to be loaded. The Loader loaded relocatable binary information, including the background program after linking independently compiled subprograms from user and system libraries. It determined the I/O drivers required for program execution and loaded them from the library tape. It assigned logical units to physical units for both programs, and prepared overlay segments for foreground programs. It assigned storage areas and loaded data and instructions into specified storage areas. It linked symbols to entry points. Once loading of the programs was completed, control was transferred to the background program for initialization.

5.8.3 Time-sharing

RTS provided time-sharing between the foreground and background programs. Time-sharing was controlled by the background program. Once programs were loaded, the background program received control for initialization. The background program set the interrupt masks to ensure that it would receive control under interrupt conditions. It then transferred control to the foreground program.

If a real-time interrupt occurred, the background program would receive control, which ensured that time-critical interrupts were properly handled.

If the CDC 3300/3500 Multiprogramming Option was installed, then memory protection between the foreground program(s), background program, and RTS ensured that each was independent of the others. No direct I/O was allowed by foreground program(s):

- Use of privileged instructions such as HLT and DINT were not allowed by foreground or background programs; and
- All modifications of RTS tables and the IMR were performed by RTS routines.

5.8.4 I/O Control

RTS allowed one or two data channels to be declared as real-time channels, which could be used for equipment requiring special handling of interrupts or I/O operations. I/O for the real-time channels had to be provided by the user's background program.

When a system I/O request was made, RTS performed the following operations:

- Saved all the necessary registers;
- Determined the availability of the unit and channel; if either or both was unavailable, rejected the request;
- Connected the unit to the available channel;
- Ensured the operation on the specified unit was legal; if not, the request was rejected and the job terminated.
- Initiated the requested operation; and
- Restored the saved registers.

Data channels could be shared between the foreground and background programs without equipment status conflicts or loss of information. Up to eight devices per channel could be active. However, foreground and background programs could not share mass storage devices.

5.8.5 Interrupt Control

The central interrupt control (part of the RTS kernel) gave priority to the background program. Interrupts were handled as previously described. High priority interrupts on real-time channels were processed before all other interrupts were considered.

5.8.6 RTS Utilities

RTS provided support for debugging foreground and background programs, including making octal corrections to loaded binary programs; and performing recovery or snap dumps as part of the debugging support.

RTS provided support for library tape preparation, including editing and library preparation for both system libraries and user library tapes. Library preparation included origin addresses for routines, and records to be destroyed, replaced, or added to the library tape. Library preparation included preparing an index of the name and record number for each element to be added or updated for the library tape.

5.9 Drum SCOPE

Source: CDC 1967r, CDC 1967au

Drum SCOPE was a variant of the SCOPE operating system for the CDC 3600 machines that used the drum storage system as the primary I/O device. Jobs were read from a card reader and placed on the magnetic drum. Drum SCOPE retrieved the jobs and executed them according to the SCOPE scheduling algorithm.

Drum SCOPE used the Mass Storage I/O subsystem to manage files on the CDC disk drives.

5.9.1 Logical Records

Logical Records could be either fixed or variable length. A file must have all records of the same type. Variable length records could be defined in four ways as described in Table 5-7.

Table 5-7. Variable Length Record Definition

Type	Description
Simple	Each record had a key field which specified its length and was in the same position in each record. The key field had to be set before the record was written.
Fixed Length with Trailer	A record consisted of a fixed length base and a variable number of fixed length trailer items. A key field in the fixed length portion specified the number of trailer items
Record Mark	A variable length record terminated by a record mark (72_8) supplied by the user as part of the record the record mark had to occupy the last six bits (0-5) of the last word of the record.
Universal	The user specified an address containing the length of the record at the time it was to be written. MSIO added a 48-bit prefix with the number of 6-bit characters in the record. MSIO removed the prefix when the record was read and returned the number of six-bit bytes.

5.9.2 Physical Records

Physical record size was determined by the mass storage device used. The CDC 828 disk had a physical record size of 32-words or one sector. It was recommended that a user define a record length that was a multiple of the block size so as not to waste space.

5.9.3 Buffers and Record Areas

The Mass Storage I/O system (MSIO) used two types of intermediate storage to move data between mass storage and the computer:

- A buffer consisted of one block;
- A record area consisted of one logical record.

For variable length records, the record area had to be large enough to contain the largest possible logical record within a file. Buffer areas were defined by the user with a FILEDESC macro and the READFILE and RITEFILE requests. Table 5-8 specifies the variations on buffers (B) and record areas (RA).

Table 5-8. Variations in Buffers and Record Areas

Variant	Description
2 B/1 RA	Data was transferred from one buffer to the record area or device while the other buffer was being filled. Records were blocked/deblocks as they moved to the device or record area.
2 B	Data was transferred into/from one buffer while the other was being filled. Records were blocked/deblocked. If they spanned blocks, parts might be inaccessible.
1 B/1 RA	Records were blocked/deblocks as they moved to the device or record area. The buffer had to be emptied before it could be refilled leading to inefficiency in I/O operations.
1 B	The user reserved space for one buffer block, but no I/O buffering can occur. Records larger than one block were not available to the user.
1 RA	No blocking/deblocking was performed. Data transfer to/from device was limited to the size of one block. Record larger than one block had data beyond the first block inaccessible.

These variations were on a per file basis, not a system or job basis. Users had to be fully cognizant of the record structure of their files before declaring buffers and records areas prior to beginning I/O operations.

Random-access files were not buffered as MSIO could not predict the next block address.

5.9.4 Device Labels

Each mass storage device had a device label which uniquely identified the device in the system. This label was written to the device by a utility program when the system was installed. A device label contained the fields described in Table 5-9.

Table 5-9. Device Label Fields

Field	Description
Device Name	Name assigned to the device at installation time.
Device Address	Hardware address of device label.
Directory Address	Hardware address of label directory file.
HI Limit	Highest absolute address for each of 18 areas on the device
LO Limit	Lowest absolute address for each of 18 areas on the device
Next Available Sector	Relative address of next available sector for each of 18 areas on the device.
Unused Sectors	Number of released (e.g., unallocated) sectors for each of 18 areas on the device.

The location of the device label was fixed for each type of device. The device label pointed to the label directory and record allocation information.

Before any records could be processed, file space had to be allocated on the device. The device label was searched for the smallest amount of contiguous space which could accommodate the ALLOCATE request. If no area existed, the largest available area was reserved as the first file segment, followed by the next available area until the request was satisfied or the number of segments allocated exceeds the number requested. File segments were allocated a s number of blocks on the device. Each device had 18 allocatable areas.

5.9.5 File Label

A File Label identified a file that was allocated space on the device so that it could be referred to by I/O requests. When an OPENFILE requests was issued, MSIO used the file label to locate the file and make it ready for I/O operations. File labels were not attached to file, but were stored in the label directory.

A file label consisted of 32 words of which the first 14 were accessible by the user. The remainder were used by MSIO administrative purposes such as security keys and segment location information. The first ten words were used to describe magnetic tape files, while the first fourteen words were used for mass storage files. Table 5-10 presents the user accessible fields of the file label.

Table 5-10. File Label Fields by User

Field	Word	Bits	Description
d	0	47-42	Magnetic Tape Density: 2=200 bpi; 5=556 bpi; 8=800 bpi.
()	0	41-30	Unique Label Identifier.
nn	0	29-18	Logical Unit Number.
rtn	0	17-0	Retention Period: number of days file was to be saved after written.
file	1	47-0	File Name: 14 alphanumeric characters.
name	2	47-12	Rest of file name.
rr	2	11-0	Reel Number, if magnetic tape: 0-99.
mmddyy	3	47-12	Date written.
ee	3	11-0	Edition number: 01 – 99, or blank.
any information	4-9	47-0	Used by applications.
file usage	10	47-24	# times the file has been opened.
file condition	10	23-0	# record linkages.
First eof block #	11	47-24	Relative block position of the EOF, or zero.
# OPENs	11	23-15	# FETs which indicate the file was currently open.
Linkage Location	11	14-0	Location in logical record of linkage data.
Unused	12	47-39	
Trailer size	12	38-24	Trailer size for record type 2 in 6-bit bytes.
s	12	23-21	Key field size.
m	12	20-18	Key mode (not used).
Unused	12	17-15	
Key position	12	14-0	Key field position in logical record.
Record type	13	47-43	Logical record type.
Unused	13	42-39	
Fixed record size	13	38-24	Fixed Portion size of logical record.
File format	13	23-15	Not Used.
Block size	13	14-0	Physical record size (block) in 6-bit bytes.

A File Environment Table (FET) was constructed by MSIO at program assembly time for each file submitted by the user from file description macros.

5.9.6 Seek Address Key

When a file was opened for reading or writing, MSIO set up several Seek Address Keys (SAK) fields in the FET. These fields identified the record currently being processed, the next available record for writing, the previous record processed, and the first and last records in the file. Each SAK field consisted of:

- a relative block address of 24 bits, which specified the block position relative to the beginning of the file; and
- a word count field of 24 bits relative to the beginning of the block.

The SAK field was used to access records in the block in an order determined by the access type: sequential, linked sequential, random, and sequentially indexed.

5.9.7 File Descriptor

A File Descriptor was used to specify information about a file to be used by a user program. MSIO used the file descriptor macros to construct the FET. Selected macros are described in the following sections. The reader was referred to the MSIO Reference Manual for the structure of the FET and other macro descriptions.

5.9.7.1 FILEDESC

The FILEDESC macro specified information about a file that was to be used by the user program. It had the following format:

- Column 1: File name of up to 9 characters;
- Column 10-72: FILEDESC(p1, …, p13)

where p1 to p13 were parameters describing the file as shown in Table 5-11.

Table 5-11. FILEDESC Parameters

Parameter	Usage
p1	Logical Record Length: Based on record type, values could be 17 to 32,760, or blank.
p2	Record Area: memory address of an area into which each logical record was to be moved for I/O.
P3	Record Block Length: buffer length in words.
P4	Buffer Address: beginning address of the buffer in memory.
P5	Alternate Buffer Address: memory address for an alternate buffer that was assigned to the field.
P6	Mass Storage or Logical Unit Number (LUN); 828 or 814 indicated a disk drive model, or LUN of magnetic tape drive.
P7	If p6 indicated a disk drive, the device name of 1-8 characters; otherwise the density of a magnetic tape drive.
P8	Internal File Number: used by MSIO for disk drives; otherwise, recording mode for tape drives.
P9	If p6 indicated a disk drive, the logical record type; otherwise, the file position on a multi-file reel for magnetic tapes.
P10	If p6 indicated a disk drive, a blank entry indicated that standard error recovery procedures were to be used; otherwise, they were inhibited, in which case, the user was responsible for providing error recover procedures in their programs.
P11	If p6 indicated a disk drive, this entry specified a file security key of 1-8 characters; otherwise, blank.
P12	Optional File Indicator: if blank, indicated a mandatory file; otherwise, optional.
P13	If p6 indicated a disk drive, the memory address of a routine used to locate a record in the file; otherwise, for magnetic tapes, indicated whether records were to be written one at a time or blocked to the buffer capacity.

5.9.7.2 LABELING

The LABELING macro was required for all mass storage files and for magnetic tape files. Its format began in column 10 with the LABELING macro name followed by a list of five parameters. Table 5-12 describes the parameters.

Table 5-12. LABELING Parameters

Parameter	Usage
p1	Label Identification Address: The memory address of the file identification. It was compared against the file identification field in input files. It was written for output files. It was assumed to contain 14 characters, left justified.
p2	Edition Number Address: Two BCD digits, left justified with blank fill. (Optional)
p3	Reel Number Address: Two BCD digits, left justified with blank fill. (Magnetic Tape Only)
p4	Date Written Address: mmddyy format, left justified with blank fill. It was used in locating the correct input file.
p5	Retention Location: : memory address for an alternate buffer that was assigned to the field. Three BCD digits, left justified with blank fill. Written in the output file label. On input, indicated whether the file was permanent or scratch.

Label processing was initiated when a file was opened by the OPENFILE request macro. Data provided here was used to access the FET and, thus, locate the correct file for processing.

5.9.7.3 VARIABLE

The VARIABLE macro specified information for variable-length logical records. Its format began in column 10 with the VARIABLE macro name followed by a list of four parameters. Table 5-13 describes the parameters.

Table 5-13. VARIABLE Parameters

Parameter	Usage
p1	Record Type: blank indicated simple variable or fixed-length with variable trailer. Any other value indicated a variable-length record terminated by record marks.
p2	Key Field Size: an entry from 0-7 where 0 indicated a full-word binary key and 1-7 indicated the number of 6-bytes in the key field.
p3	Byte position of the first character of the key field within the logical record , which must be a multiple of 8 plus 1.
p4	Trailer Size: The number of 6-bit bytes for each occurrence of a trailer item.

Fields p2 – p4 were ignored for records that were to be terminated by record marks.

For records with trailer items, p2 and p3 referred to a field specifying the number of trailer items in the record.

5.9.7.4 LINKMODE

The LINKMODE macro specified information for the linkage fields to process records using a linked sequential or random-access format. . Its format began in column 10 with the LINKMODE macro name followed by a list of two parameters. Table 5-14 describes the parameters.

Table 5-14. LINKMODE Parameters

Parameter	Usage
p1	Linked Key Address: The linkage key first character position in the record.
p2	Linkage Type: The type of linkage: F Forward linkage only B Backward linkage only FB Forward and backward linkage Linkage words were 48 bits in length

5.9.8 Request Macros

When using the MSIO subsystem, the user program issued request macros to open, read, write, and close files on mass storage devices among other operations. Table 5-15 briefly describes a few of these macros. The reader is referred to referred to the MSIO Reference Manual for a complete description of the macros.

Table 5-15. Selected Request Macros

Macro	Brief Description
ALLOCATE	Allocates space on a mass storage device for a file.
OPENFILE	Initiated processing of a file in preparation for I/O operations. This macro had to precede any I/O request.
READFILE	Requested that a logical record be transferred to the designated record area or the buffer area.
RITEFILE	Requested that a logical record be transferred from the record from the designated record area or buffer area to the specified device.
CLOSFILE	Terminated the processing of a file that prevented any further I/O operations until it was opened again.
CLOSREEL	Closed a reel of a magnetic tape file.
POSITION	Altered the SAK fields in the FET in accordance with the specified parameters.
LOOK	Searched for a logical record according to the specified parameters.
INSERTM	Wrote a logical record according to the parameters on the RITEFILE request and adjusted the linkage to cause it to be logically inserted just before the record recently retrieved from the file.
DELETEM	Adjusted the linkage to delete the logical record that was most recently retrieved from the file.
INDXFILE	Created an index for a file, if one did not exist, that was to be accessed by random requests.
SPACEM	Provided the user with remaining space available to the system for allocation of files.
ATTACH	Requested linkage of the FETs for two files such that one could be used as the index for the other.
READBLOC/ RITEBLOC	Transmitted one block according to the control word chain provided in the request.
REWINDM	Manipulated the SAK fields of the file to make the next logical record in the file be the first logical record in the file.
BSP(FM,RM)	Backspaced one file (FM) or record (RM) to adjust the SAK fields to the next logical record.
SKIPM	Positioned the file at the first record after the next user-supplied end-of-file.
MARKFM	Marks the end-of-file for files using sequential processing.

5.10 SCOPE Assessment

SCOPE was originally written for the CDC 1604 as a batch system. The CDC 1604 operated with magnetic tapes for on-line or offline storage. When the CDC 3000 series was developed as the successor to the CDC 1604, SCOPE was modified to use new instructions, the greater memory capacity of certain models, and the different features of certain models. The latter included Real-Time SCOPE and Drum SCOPE.

With SCOPE, CDC had realized that it needed to provide an operating system and utilities and compilers for those users who did not have the expertise, opportunity, or staff to create their own system software. In part, as noted, this was in direct response to IBM's announcement of the IBM 7090 and provision of the IBJOB system.

However, CDC was constrained by its scientific and engineering background and focus on that environment. The features of SCOPE were sparse and CDC was a definite latecomer to the development of timesharing and interactive use of the computer.

CHAPTER SIX

THE MASTER OPERATING SYSTEM

Source: CDC 1966ca

The MASTER (Multiple Access Shared Time Executive Routine) operating system was used for the CDC 3300/3500 models. It supported multitasking and multiprocessing at a time when the IBM System/360 was struggling to handle multiple programs concurrently. The benefits of multiprocessing quickly became apparent to many customers.

MASTER consisted of an operating system and a system executive. The operating system accepted jobs from the input devices and translated them into executable tasks. The operating system operated in problem state. The system executive administered requests from tasks for system services and assigning tasks to processors when they became idle. The system executive was entered from a task via an interrupt. The system executive operated in monitor state.

Major features of MASTER were:

- Concurrent execution of computing tasks and I/O operations to obtain greater throughput;
- Provided a centralized, file-oriented I/O control system supporting multiple peripheral devices;
- Provided system protection of tasks through hardware and software mechanisms;
- Loaded and linked executable tasks from libraries and user-defined files;
- Segmented programs into non-contiguous pages in memory; and
- Provided a rich set of library and system programs for updating libraries, debugging programs, maintaining files, and performing data transfer operations among devices.

MASTER required the CDC 3300/3500 models to have installed the executive mode and relocation hardware implemented by the Multiprogramming Option.

6.1 Typical Configuration

A typical CDC 3300 configuration, which is depicted in Figure 6-1, included:

- 32K words of magnetic core memory;
- A 3304 o 3504 CPU;
- A 3311 or 35121 Multiprogramming Options;
- One CDC 405 Card Reader and buffered controller;
- One Model 501 or 505 Line Printer and buffered controller;
- One CDC 415 Card Punch and buffered controller;
- Two CDC 3306/3307 or CDC 3506/3507 Data Channels;
- 2.5M words of mass storage from several different types of disk drives; and
- Four to eight magnetic tape drives.

This configuration would cost several million dollars.

6.2 Operating Modes

MASTER operated in two states:

- Monitor State, which allowed execution of all instructions, and
- Program State, which prohibited execution of reserved instructions (such as for I/O)

Program state was entered by a boundary jump by the EXEC while operating in Monitor state. Several instructions, if attempted execution while in program state, caused an interrupt to monitor state:

- Halt and Pause;
- I/O initiation;
- I/I status interrogation;
- Interrupt selection; and
- Inter-register transfers that might alter the contents of register location 30-37.

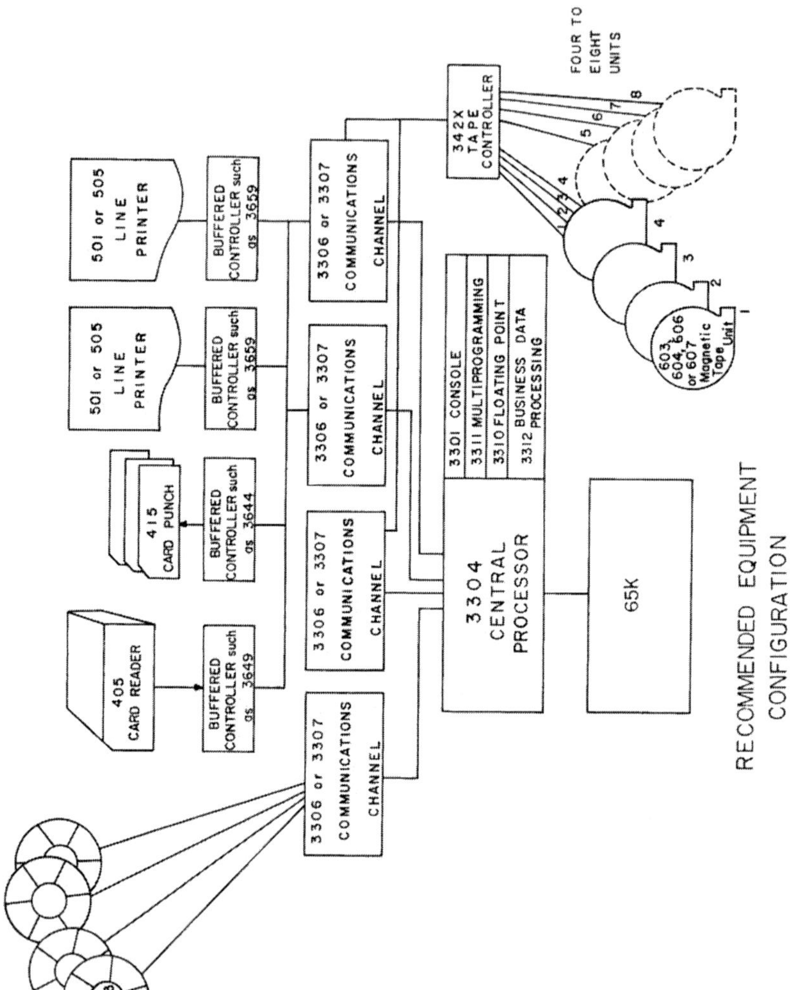

Figure 6-1. MASTER Configuration
Source: CDC 1966ca

6.2.1 INTERRUPTS

All interrupts caused the CPU to enter the EXEC in Monitor State to handle them. Interrupts were handled by the External Interrupt Control (EIC) system. The EIC saved registers, decoded the interrupt code, and transferred control to the EXEC routine to handle it. After the EXEC processed the interrupt, it transferred control to Assign A Processor, a routine which selected a user program task in ready mode to execute. The EXEC recognized eight types of interrupts as described in Table 6-1.

Table 6-1. MASTER Interrupt Handling

Interrupt Type	Description
Internal Faults	The User Interrupt Control (UIC) processed all internal faults such as arithmetic overflow, memory violations, etc.
Floating Point	When floating point hard ware was not configured in the system, floating point instructions could be simulated as an installation option by FDPBOXS.
Clock	When EXEC placed a task into execution, it set a time limit on its execution. When this limit expired, the clock generated an interrupt to determine the status of the job. The time limit was determined as: • The time remaining in job time limit; • The time remaining in the LIMIT request; or • The time of the execution cycle, which was the maximum time the task was allowed to execute without an interrupt.
EXEC Requests	All EXEC request were initiated through an illegal instruction, which transferred control to an EXEC routine to handle the request.
I/O	An I/O interrupt was routed to the appropriate MIOCS routine for handling.
Dedicated Channel	A dedicated channel handled special equipment usually for real-time operations. This interrupt was routed to a user-provided real-time routine that was integrated as an extension to the EXEC.
Manual	The operator could generate an interrupt from the console to initiate a request for service.
Other	An illegal instruction (except for EXEC requests) interrupt terminated the job being processed.

6.3 MASTER Initialization

MASTER was initialized by autoloading a version of MASTER from the system library, typically on magnetic tape. The modules loaded included the system initialization routine and resident portions of the system EXEC, its tables, and the Master Input/Output Control System (MIOCS).

Once loaded, MASTER automatically began executing the system initialization routine. This allowed the operator to set the date and time and modify any installation parameters through the SET command. The initialization routine then established system files and tables. Finally, it transferred control to the Input Backgrounder, which prepared job files.

6.4 Job Flow

User *jobs*, which consisted of control cards, and program and data cards, were ingested serially by MASTER through the card reader. The Input Backgrounder (IB) read card images and wrote them to the job INP file on disk. Jobs were read into the INP file until the card reader hopper was empty.

After the IB transferred a job to its INP file, it invoked the Job Scheduler, an operating system task, and passed it information extracted from the DIRECT, JOB, and SCHED cards in the job deck.

6.4.1 Job Classes

Each job submitted to MASTER was assigned to a class by the Job Scheduler. A job's class determined when it would be initiated into execution by the Job Initiator. MASTER maintained five job classes as presented in Table 6-2.

Table 6-2. MASTER Job Classes

Job Class	Description
Emergency	A job was classified as emergency if: (1) the user declared it class E on the SCHED card; (2) the job deck was preceded by a DIRECT card.
Background	A job that generally used slow-speed peripherals and use little compute time, but needed attention quickly to drive their devices at full speed. Declared as class B on the SCHED card.

Special Job	MASTER declared a job as special if: (1) an I/O or computer job with an estimated time 'te' on the SCHED card, and (2) Tmin <= te < Tmax. It provided a fast turnaround capability for small jobs.
Input/Output	Job was classified as I/O if the user specified I on the SCHED card and it was not a special job.
Compute	A job was classified as a compute if the user specified C on the SCHED card and it was not a special job.

6.4.2 Job Initiation

When MASTER sought a new job, it considered several variables including job class, peripheral equipment needed, core requirements, and wait time. All resources required by a job had to be available before the job was initiated into execution.

MASTER first examined emergency jobs waiting for initiation. If one was found with its equipment requirements satisfied, MASTER initiated the job and typed "B i" (i was the job identifier from the JOB card) on the operator console.

If no emergency jobs were active or waiting, then MASTER tried to keep at least one job from the other four categories active. Another job from the same class was initiated if no jobs from any other class were waiting. Within a class, jobs were initiated on a FIFO basis, but only if core and I/O requirements were met. However, no job could be refused initiation more than a <installation parameter> times due to lack of equipment availability. When this limit was reached, the job's class was changed to emergency and no other non-emergency job was initiated until that job was complete.

6.4.3 Job Processing

After a job was initiated, the Job Monitor processed control statements from the job's INP file. These statements directly or indirectly caused loading and execution of program tasks.

A *task* was a part of a job that either (1) was initiated by a control card, or (2) initiated by the operating system to service a program. Tasks inherited the priority assigned to their job. Tasks, such as the Job Monitor and the Relocatable Loader, were loaded into core allocated to the job. A task of a job was to be loaded by the Relocatable Loader (RL). The RL was loaded and then loads the task appropriately. When finished, the RL returned to the Job Monitor, which released the core associated with the RL and transfers control to the task.

When all tasks in a job were completed, control returned to the Job Monitor. If an abnormal condition was detected, the Job Monitor aborted the job. If the INP file was empty, the Job Monitor closed all open files, and released scratch files, the INP file, allocated core, and any allocated devices. The Output Backgrounder was requested to process the OUT and PUN files. The Job Monitor returns control to MASTER, which types "T i" on the operator console.

6.4.3 Job Postprocessing

The Output Backgrounder (OB) drove all available printers and punches at full speed if there were OUT and PUN files to be processed.

OUT files were processed in FIFO order. If all available printers were occupied, an OUT file was placed in a FIFO queue.

When an OUT file was processed by OB, a standard header was printed, followed by accounting information, the job's output, and a standard trailer. If the job abnormally terminated, then additional information was printed under the heading JOB ABORTED. Such information might include the register file contents and a memory dump.

When a PUN file was processed by OB, it was placed in a FIFO queue if no card punch was available. The punch queue was processed in FIFO order.

6.5 Memory

The CDC 3300/3500 systems supported both automatic relocation and paging features.

Physical memory was based on magnetic cores with a minimum of 32K words and a maximum of 256K words.

A page was a block of 2048 words. A fully populated system contained 128 pages. Individual pages could be subdivided into four partial pages of 512 words each.

6.5.1 The Page Map

The Page Map recorded the active pages in memory. When EXEC loaded a program task, one of the MASTER loaders – either relocatable or absolute - loaded the task into available pages in memory. The task remained in memory until completed or its memory was released by the job or MASTER.

During task loading, generated one page map for both program and common areas, or two maps – one for each of program area and common area. When a task's memory was released, its page maps were erased.

A page map consisted of 16-page indexes having the structure depicted in Figure 6-2. Table 6-3 describes the Page Map fields.

Figure 6-2. MASTER Page Map Structure
Source: Adapted from CDC 1966ca

Table 6-3. MASTER Page Map Fields

Fields	Bits	Description
Exclusion Bit (e)	1	Access rights to page: 0 – Page can be read/written by a task 1 – Page can only be read
Page Length	2	Task Usage of Page: 0 – uses all of page 1 – task uses 1/4th of page. 2 – task uses ½ of page 3 – task uses ¾ of page
Page Address	7	The number of the physical memory page used by the task from 0 to maximum number of pages configured.
Partial Page Bits	2	Specified part of page used by address: # Physical Logical 0 0 0 1 0 01000 2 512 02000 3 1024 03000

When a task required fewer than 16 page indexes, the remaining page indexes each had the Exclusion Bit set to one. References to excluded pages resulted in an interrupt and termination of the job associated with the task. A message on the job's OUT file noted the system action.

6.5.2 Program Addressing

A task could not reference any physical memory location that was not assigned to it by MASTER. A program address of a task the structure depicted in Figure 6-3.

Page Index	Logical Address
14 11	10 00

Figure 6-3. Task Program Address
Source: Adapted from CDC 1966ca

The Page Index was the octal location in the page map specifying the physical page containing the logical address. The Logical Address was the offset location in the specified page relative to zero.

6.5.3 Chapters

MASTER provided a simplified view for users. MASTER memory consisted of two blocks each with 32K logical addresses, which were called *chapters*. All binary programs and program listings and memory maps used chapter addressing.

A user writing a one-chapter task could use 30K of memory for program instructions, common, and data areas. For a two-chapter task, the user could use 30K for the program and data areas, and a second 32K for common areas. Different combinations of assigning common areas to the two chapters facilitated intertask communication for multiple tasks within a job that were loaded into memory.

6.5.4 States

Each time a task was placed into execution, its page map was loaded into an area, called a *state*, of the Page Index File (PIF), so that the CDC 3300/3500 hardware could access the physical page assignments. The PIF consisted of eight states. At most, MASTER could accommodate eight running one-chapter tasks. But, one of these was reserved for MASTER itself. Two-chapter tasks required two states. When a task was loaded, MASTER assigned states to its chapters. The state assigned to chapter one was loaded into the Instruction State Register (ISR). If a second chapter was included, it was loaded into the Operand State Register (OSR). One-chapter tasks set OSR to the single chapter.

A user task required a state only when it was active, at which time the hardware was using the map and could not be disturbed. When a task was inactive, its state was inactive. Thus, the page map could be overwritten with a new map of a task to be executed.

Figure 6-3 depicts the mapping of a logical address to a physical memory address.

Assuming a two-chapter task, the state was determined by the ISR or the OSR and the type of access required. The four-bit page index was extracted from the program address to access the PIF to select a page map entry. The physical memory address was created by concatenating the page address form the page map, the partial page designator, and the logical address into an 18-bit entry.

6.6 Tasks

MASTER scheduled tasks to use the hardware resources of the CDC 3300/3500 systems. Two types of tasks were supported.

A *program task* consisted of one or more subprograms and associated routines. Program tasks were relocatable binary files produced by assemblers and compilers, or absolute format after having undergone relocation processing. Program tasks could be loaded from user files, system libraries, or upon request by a job. Program tasks could be permanently allocated. Tasks that were not permanently allocated had their memory released once they finished their processing. MASTER program tasks included the scheduler, the monitor, the loader, and selected utilities.

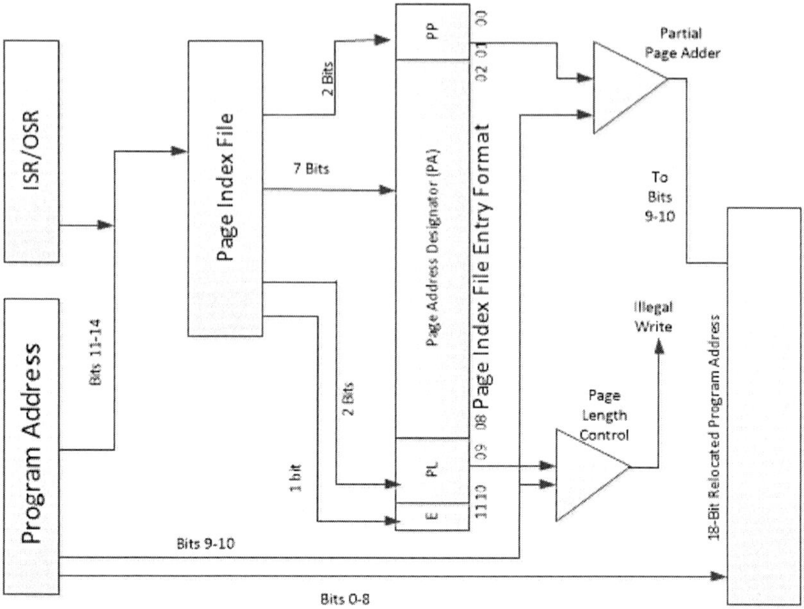

Figure 6-4. Physical Address Creation
Source: Adapted from CDC 1966ca

Jobs were divided into program tasks via control statements.

I/O tasks handled the transfer of data between the computer system and the peripheral devices.

6.6.1 Task Management

Active program and I/O tasks are contained in a task list. Tasks have a priority associated with them. MASTER assigned I/O tasks to data channels and program tasks to the CPU on a priority basis with the objective of maximizing the workload processed.

When the EXEC was entered via an interrupt, it processed the interrupt, updated the accounting information, initiated as many I/O tasks as possible, and transferred control to the highest priority program task ready for execution.

A program task could request execution of another program task or I/O task via an EXEC call. Control was transferred to the called task. When the tasks completed, it relinquished control by returning to the EXEC, which notified the calling task. Both the call and the return were accomplished through EXEC services by generation of an interrupt.

Program task initiation by means of control cards were accomplished by the job monitor issuing a call to the EXEC. When the called task completed and returned to the EXEC, which returned control to the job monitor. Library tasks were placed in the system library file at system generation. Some library tasks were reserved for operating system use only. Library tasks could be permanently allocated and loaded during MASTER initialization and remained resident in memory for the duration of MASTER operation.

User-defined program tasks did not have a permanent name. A name was assigned by the user the first time the task was called in a job via a Task Name card. The name existed for the duration of the job.

A task with a name not beginning with '*' was copiable. Each job that called a copiable task mean that a distinct instance of the task was loaded for the job in its allocated memory. Each time the task was called, an existing copy in memory was re-used. If the task was busy when called, subsequent calls were queued and executed as the task became available.

A task with a name that began with '*" was not copiable. When it was called, if the task was busy, subsequent calls were queued on a priority basis.

6.6.2 Intertask Communication

Tasks within a job could communicate with each other by passing parameters, transferring common areas, and using the register file.

6.6.2.1 Parameter Passing

A calling task can pass up to 511 parameters to its callee. The callee may return parameters to its caller via the RETURN statement. However, a caller cannot pass more parameters than the callee was prepared to accept. A callee cannot return more parameters to its caller than the caller was able to receive. A caller may pass parameters through the console registers, but the callee may not return parameters in the same manner.

6.6.2.2 Via Registers

All tasks of a job could pass parameters through locations $40_8 - 77_8$ of the Register File. If register file usage was declared on the SCHED card, the contents of the registers will be maintained for the job.

6.6.2.3 VIA COMMON

Two-chapter tasks can communicate with each other through Chapter Two common. MASTER passes it as a single contiguous block of logical addresses starting at address 00000. There was no symbolic linking when common was passed. The user was responsible for providing code to link common addresses.

Suppose Task A passes to Task B a beginning address in common as a parameter. In the CALL to task B, a parameter specified whether common was read-only or read-writable by Task B. Another parameter specified whether the caller was passing its own common or the common of its caller.

6.6.3 TASK MULTIPROGRAMMING

A job could be segmented into multiple tasks to effect parallel execution among several tasks (perhaps just a subset of the total number of tasks). For example, Task A may call Task B and assume ready status. The two tasks could share the processor with one task executing instructions while the other waited for I/O to complete.

A job that was too large for the available memory would be segmented into tasks to enable it to run. The user has several options for executing the tasks, some of which could be executed in parallel. One was a straight pipeline where a task A performs its functions, then calls task B, and then removes itself from memory. Another was to use an overlay scheme in which two or more tasks can occupy the same area of memory, but only one of which can occupy it at any time. Depending on the complexity of the computations to be performed and the size of the job, other schemes may be used.

6.6.4 TASK ENTRY & EXIT

Every task was required to incorporate a library module, User Interrupt Control (UIC), which provided the task with:

- An entrance routine;
- An exit routine;
- A reserved area for parameter passing; and
- Internal fault selection.

A task began at *tpep* - the task's primary entry point - which was a label for a jump instruction, UJP, to **. tpep appeared in column 4-8 of a punched card. A call to a task connected with a UIC routine which contained a return jump to tpep. The return address was inserted into ** as a normal function of return jump execution. The return address in ** + 1 was the address of the first word of the parameters passed in the call.

A task could return to its caller through a jump to tpep or through a RETURN macro coded in the program.

There were two forms of UIC – standard and nonstandard. The nonstandard version did not include a parameter passing area and the RETURN had no parameters. The nonstandard form was a macro taking three arguments:

- N: the maximum number of parameters the task could receive from or return to its caller;
- F: indicated the task required a fault selection routine;
- NR: the task was not to be released from memory after execution.

6.6.5 Task Status

Task could have any one of multiple statuses during its execution and residence in the system. Table 6-4 presents the task statuses.

Table 6-4. Task Status Codes

Codes	Status	Description
00	Inactive	The task has completed its processing and returned to its caller. It remained in an inactive state until it was called again.
01	Wait	The task has called another task. As a parameter of the call, it indicated it not be resumed until the callee has returned to it.
02	Deferred Wait	The task called other tasks and then resumed execution. It then requested it not resume execution until at least one of the called tasks has returned to it.
03	Wait I/O	The task called an I/O task. As a parameter of the call, it indicated it not be resumed until the I/O task has returned to it.
04	Deferred Wait I/O	The task called I/O tasks and then resumed execution. It then requested it not resume execution until at least one of the I/O tasks has returned to it.
05	Table Wait	The task was waiting for access to a table being used by another task.
06	File Wait	The task was waiting for access to a file being used by another task.

07	Read Lockout	The task has called the job copy of the deblocking routine while another task was using it.
10	Write Lockout	The task has called the job copy of the blocking routine while another task was using it.
11	Call	The task has called another task. Until the call can be connected, the caller was in call status and cannot resume execution.
12	Finish	The task has finished its processing and was waiting to return to the caller.
13	Select	The task has been called and was waiting to be loaded.
14	Ready	The task can begin or resume execution or was in execution.
15	Busy I/O	The task was not in execution, but has I/O going on.

6.7 Mass Storage

MASTER supported disk-based and drum-based mass storage. The efficiency of its time-sharing and multiprogramming operations depended on efficiently managing its mass storage assets. Mass storage was divided into two levels: devices and units of allocatable storage.

6.7.1 Devices

Devices were divided into Class A devices which were logically or physically associated with disk/drum drives and Class B devices which were removable, typically magnetic tapes. Class A devices were always on-line. All mass storage devices were identified by a device label.

Files could extend over multiple mass storage units, some of which may not be on-line. If a call to access a file referenced a device not on-line, MASTER issued a request to the operator to mount the device on a specified drive.

6.7.2 Files

Files were logical entities that contained data. Each file was divided into *blocks* of identical size. A logical block size was the number of 6-bit characters in each block. File could vary in the number of blocks and the block sizes. Each logical block started at the beginning of a hardware record and could not exceed 128K characters.

Files had labels which were used to identify and describe the mass storage space allocated to it. A user requested MASTER to create a file label providing data such as name, security codes, block size, block count, etc. MASTER used this data to create an entry in a system file.

A file identifier was a concatenation of the owner, file name, and edition number. The user could supply an access security code, a modification security code, or both in the file label definition call.

The access security code protected a file from unauthorized use. When opening a file, the proper security code had to be provided by the task to allow access to the file. Modification security codes handled calls to release, expand, and modify a file.

6.7.3 File Environment

When MASTER was booted, it established a file environment by generating nine mass storage files that it needed to process jobs. These are described in Table 6-5. Each of these files was maintained on Class A on-line mass storage.

Table 6-5. MASTER File Environment

File Name	Description
MSIO MSDFILE	Contained copies of all device labels for all mass storage system devices configured in the system.
MSIO LABEL FILE	Contained labels of all files resident in the mass storage system.
MSIO IDFILE	Contained the file identification and security codes for all files resident in the mass storage system
MASTER LIBRARY	Contained all the library files for MASTER.
MASTER LIBRARY DIRECTORY	Contained a directory of the MASTER LIBRARY.
MASTER SYSTEM INPUT MASTER SYSTEM OUTPUT MASTER SYSTEM PUNCH MASTER SYSTEM SCRATCH	A pool of permanently allocated contiguous mass storage that was managed by the EXEC for each hob in the system.

The first three files were used for the management of the mass storage system and were accessible only by the EXEC.

6.7.4 Managing Job Scratch Files

OCARE was a set of file management routines for managing and manipulating the file pool files. The user program managed the scratch file by making call to the OCARE routines. Table 6-6 presents the basic functions of OCARE.

Table 6-6. OCARE Routines

Routine	Description
SALOCATE(dsi, block size, block count)	Allocated space for a scratch file from the file pool and sets the block count to one: dsi: data set identifier. block size: #character in a block. block count: # blocks to allocate. The number of segments was calculated from the block size and the block count. A maximum of 63 segments could be allocated. If no segments were available, the task was placed in wait status until one or more became available.
SOPEN(dsi, block size)	Reopened a file with dsi previously allocated and block count set to one.
SEXPAND(dsi)	Increased the job's scratch file by one segment (hard record). If no segments were available, the task was placed in wait status until one or more became available.
SCLOSE(dsi)	Removed the job's scratch file definition from MASTER's executive tables. This prevented data transmission until the file was reopened.
SRELEASE(dsi)	Released the segments (hardware records) associated with the file named dsi. The records were returned to the job file pool

6.7.5 Managing User Files

Permanent files were user files on the mass storage system. The user had full control over access and manipulation of these files. The user program called functions in the package OCAREM to manage mass storage files. Table 6-7 presents the OCAREM functions.

Table 6-7. OCAREM File Management Routines

Routine	Description
ALLOCATE(<arguments>)	This function used information supplied in the call to build entries in the LABEL FILE, IDFILE, and the MSDFILE. The arguments were: owner: 1-8 chars as a name filename: 1-30 chars as a name edition: 1-2 alphanumeric chars acsc: Access security code (1-4 char) mdsc: Modification security code (1-4 chars) bksize: block size of 1-6 chars nbks: #of blocks in file, 1-8388607. expdate: expiration date, yymmdd. s: File to be allocated on devices in sector mode (S) or track mode (T). c: file was allocated in contiguous space (C) or segmented (S). dt: Model number of disk on which was to be allocated. dn: device numbers
MODIFY(<arguments>)	This function allowed the user to change the elements of the file definition that did not relate to the file's structure.. The arguments were similar to ALLOCATE with new values supplied for owner through expdate.
EXPAND(<arguments>)	This function allowed the user to expand the amount of mass storage space allocated to the file. The arguments were the same as ALLOCATE, except those that specified the number of contiguous blocks (C) or (S) the space to be segmented.
RELEASE(<arguments>)	This function allowed the user to remove a file definition from the MASTER mass storage tables. The arguments were owner through msdc plus: wait: If the file was open for use by another job, the request was completed after the file was released by that job. amount: the number of blocks to be released.

OPEN(<arguments>	This function allowed the user to prepare a file for data access. The arguments were the same as ALLOCATE for dsi through acsc with: wait: If the file was OPEN, data transfer depended on the usage specified by the other job. usage: If O, the file may be used for input and output, and if I, for input only.
CLOSE(wait,dsi)	This function closed a file by removing it from the MASTER mass storage tables. The arguments were: wait: If the file was in use by another job, closing was deferred until the file was released by the other job. dsi: the file identifier.

User files were not allocated across Class A and Class B devices. On Class A devices, MASTER minimized the number of segments per file by using the smallest contiguous area large enough to satisfy the request. Otherwise, it found the largest area as the first segment, the next largest area as the second segment, and so on.

On Class B devices, MASTER searched the device maps of each device starting with the device with the most available area so as to minimize the number of devices per file. An error terminated the allocation process.

6.8 Mass Storage I/O

Source: CDC 1966ca

A mass storage device was divided into segments which were hardware records on the device. The segment size varied with the device. Files were divided into logical records called blocks which were comprised of some number of characters. The number of characters in a block could vary with the file, but the maximum number was 128K. Thus, a block could have a size of one block or multiple blocks based on the size of the device segment.

When performing mass storage I/O, MASTER moved logical records to or from a buffer area, where a blocker/deblocker set of routines handled the I/O operations to a particular device. Tasks within a job called these routines to perform I/O on mass storage devices for both standard files (INP, OUT, and PUN) as well as user files.

6.8.1 Block Format

A block had the format depicted in Figure 6-5. A block was an alternating set of block headers and block data areas were terminated by a block header record set to 0.

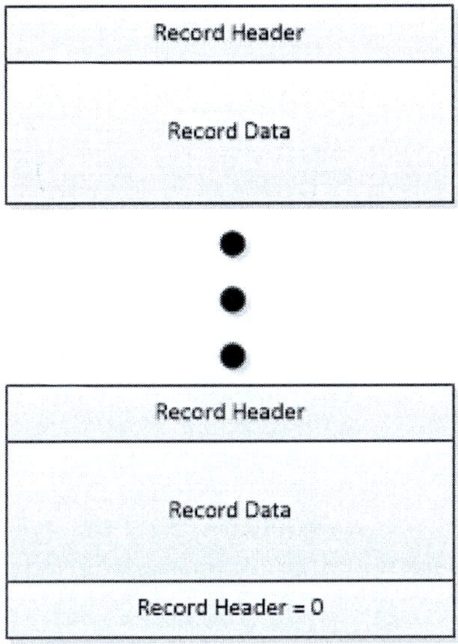

Figure 6-5. MASTER Block Format
Source: Adapted from CDC 1966ca

A record header was a 24-bit data word having the format depicted in Figure 6-6. The record length was the count of 24-bit words of record data in bits 0-14. X indicated the mode of record data with 0 = BCD and 1 = binary.

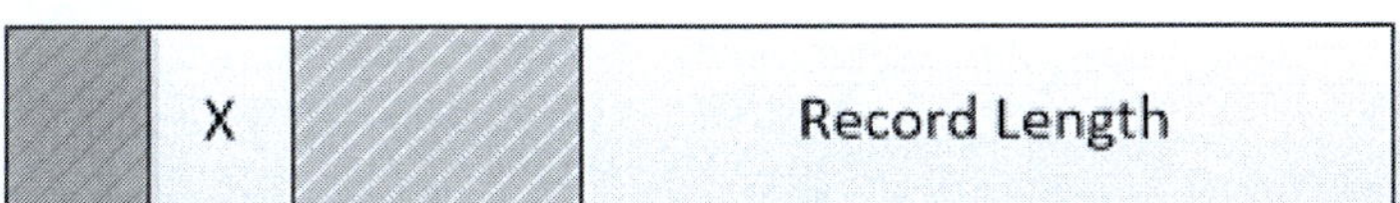

Figure 6-6. MSIO Record Header Format
Source: Adapted from CDC 1966ca

A block for a job file was always 1280 characters. The size of a user block varied with the size of the buffer area.

The blocker/deblocker functions used a buffer for each I/O operation. The standard files – INP, OUT, and PUN – each had a permanently assigned buffer within a job's core area. The user program was responsible for establishing buffers in a task's allocated area. A user file buffer had the same structure as Figure 6-5 except that it was preceded by a pointer. The pointer used one word of the buffer to point to available space in the buffer or a new logical record in the block.

6.8.2 Blocker Routines

The Mass Storage I/O system (MSIO) Blocker was a set of four routines that perform blocking on job files. These routines are described in Table 6-8.

Table 6-8. MSIO Blocker Routines

Routine	Description
PACKD(<arguments>)	This function defined a buffer area associated with a user file. The arguments were: dsi: the file identifier. reject address: if an error occurred, a return jump to this address was executed; otherwise, if blank, continue in normal sequence. bfwa: first word address of the buffer area. blength: block length in words.
PACK(<arguments>)	The task called this function to move a user record to the buffer area. While moving the record, it removed trailing zeros (binary record) or blanks (BCD record). The arguments were: dsi: the file identifier. mode: 0 = BCD; 1 = binary. reject address: if an error occurred, a return jump to this address was executed; otherwise, if blank, continue in normal sequence. fwa: first word address of record to be moved. rlength: record length (words).
PACKC(<arguments>)	This function wrote a block from the buffer to a user file before it was full (clearing the buffer). The arguments were the dsi and the reject address (as above).

PACKR(<arguments>)	This function removed a user file definition from the pack table. The arguments were the dsi and the reject address (as above).

Each user task could define a maximum of ten output file entries at a time. If an I/O operation was necessary for a task, the program could issue a PACKR request to remove an entry from the pack table in order to free up an entry for the required I/O operation.

6.8.3 Deblocker Routines

The deblocker routines are described in Table 6-9. Deblocking was the process of extracting logical records from blocks read from a mass storage device.

Table 6-9 MSIO Deblocker Routines

Routine	Description
PICKD(<arguments>)	This function defined a dsi for a file and its buffer area into which file blocks will be read for deblocking. The arguments were: dsi: the file identifier. reject address: if an error occurred, a return jump to this address was executed; otherwise, if blank, continue in normal sequence. bfwa: first word address of the buffer area. blength: block length in words.
PICK (<arguments>)	This function moved a logical record from the buffer area into the user program's record area. Alternately, it could pass a pointer to the first word of the corresponding record header. The arguments were the same as PICKD and included: key: a record passing specification with 0 = record moved and 1 = first word address of header returned.
PICKC (<arguments>)	This function allowed a user program to clear the buffer area to read a record from a new block before all logical records had been read from the current block. The arguments were dsi and reject address (as above).

PICKR (<arguments>)	This function removed a file definition from the pick table to make room for a new entry. The arguments were dsi and reject address (as above).

Each user task could define a maximum of ten input file entries at a time. If an I/O operation was necessary for a task, the program could issue a PICKR request to remove an entry from the pick table in order to free up an entry for the required I/O operation.

6.9 Unit Record Equipment I/O

Similar functions were provided for unit record equipment I/O that were specialized for the type of equipment and for magnetic tape. Some of these will be discussed in the chapter on peripheral devices.

6.10 MASTER Assessment

Considering CDC's limited development of operating systems for its supercomputers, the MASTER operating system was a sophisticated batch processing system comparable to that of other system vendors such as IBM, Honeywell, Univac, and Burroughs. The CDC 3000 series was intended to support both scientific and business data processing needs of its customers, so its operating system had to provide support for each mode of usage.

At the time that MASTER was designed, the notion of timesharing, supported for the CDC 3300/3500 systems, was actually multiprogramming, where programs had priority. In MASTER, the program that had the highest priority and was ready to execute was given control of the CPU. This was not interactive program execution, but sharing of the CPU by batch programs.

The reader will observe that MSIO tables had many options to preserve space in the operating system in order to accommodate user programs of varying sizes.

MASTER was the basis for the development of the Purdue MACE operating system, building upon the multiprogramming concepts, was able to introduce an interactive time-sharing capability, which was essential to the academic community.

CHAPTER SEVEN

CDC 3X00 SYSTEM SOFTWARE

The CDC 3x00 series supported several programming languages: Assembly, COBOL, and FORTRAN, of which Assembly and FORTRAN were enhancements of the compilers and languages developed for the CDC 1604.

7.1 SERIES 3000 COMPASS

Source: CDC 1967av

Series 3000 COMPASS was a comprehensive assembly language processing system. It compiled modules written in assembly language into binary modules which could be linked into an executable module. Table 7-1 describes some of its features (CDC 1964b). Figure 7-1 depicts a COMPASS coding form.

Table 7-1. Some COMPASS Features

Feature	Description
Address Arithmetic	Constants, symbolic addresses, and arithmetic expressions could be used for addresses.
Preloaded Data	Data areas could be specified by name and size; data could be preloaded at compile time.
Common Area Assignment	Common areas could be defined for sharing data among different subprograms.
Library Routines	Library routines for common functions, macro libraries, and I/O routines could be designated and invoked.
Diagnostics	Comprehensive diagnostics for source program errors detected during assembly could be included in the output listing.
Macro Library	Predefined and user-defined macro libraries could be accessed and code substituted for macro names.

```
          IDENT   AREA
          SPACE   1                                             NDB 01
          REM     THIS SUBPROGRAM COMPUTES THE AREA OF A CIRCLE NDB 02
          REM     GIVEN THE VALUE OF THE RADIUS, IN FLOATING POINT NDB 03
          REM     FORM, IN THE ACCUMULATOR, AND EXITS WITH THE AREA NDB 04
          REM     IN THE ACCUMULATOR.                           NDB 05
          SPACE   1                                             NDB 06
AREA      SLJ     **                                            NDB 07
          STQ     TEMP+1          SAVE Q REGISTER               NDB 08
          STA     TEMP                                          NDB 09
          FMU     TEMP            AREA = PI * R * R             NDB 10
          FMU     =D3.14159265                                  NDB 11
          LDQ     TEMP+1          RESTORE Q REGISTER            NDB 12
          SLJ     AREA            EXIT                          NDB 13
          SPACE   1                                             NDB 14
TEMP      BSS     2               WORKING STORAGE               NDB 15
          SPACE   1                                             NDB 16
          ENTRY   AREA                                          NDB 17
          SPACE   1                                             NDB 18
          END                                                   NDB 19
```

Figure 7-1. CDC 3x00 COMPASS Coding Form
Source: CDC 1964b

7.2 COSY

Source: CDC 1970aw

COSY/MSOS/RTS was a program that produced a Compressed Symbolic (COSY) deck from a source deck by replacing three or more consecutive blanks on a card by special BCD characters. The resulting deck was called a COSY deck. It was used to reduce the space occupied by source code decks on magnetic drums, disks, and tape.

7.9.2.1 COSY Library

A COSY library on tape or mass storage consisted of a group of COSY decks stored in blocks of 1280 characters (320 words). On magnetic tape, the COSY decks were separated by end-of-file marks and the library terminated with a double end-of-file mark. The MASTER transfer function (XFER) transformed unblocked tapes to the blocked format.

A directory was a 320-word block that contained a three-word entry for each COSY deck in a file. This entry contained a name and the number of the block in which the deck identifier appears,

7.3 ASCENT ASSEMBLER

The ASCENT assembler produced Chippewa Operating System (COS) binary decks from 3000 series assembly source code decks. The assembler was invoked by:

ASCENT(L,X,PA,PC,PB, FILE)

where the arguments were interpreted as depicted in Table 7-2.

Table 7-2. ASCENT Parameters

Parameter	Description
L	If non-zero, a listing of source and compiled code was written on the output file.
X	Specified a Load-and-Go file was written, if non-zero.
PA	If non-zero, specified a COS binary deck was written to P80C.
PB	If non-zero, a COSY deck was written to P80C.
PC	If non-zero, a relocatable binary deck was written to P80C.
FILE	Specified the file of COSY input. It could be either "INPUT" or "COSY".

ASCENT performed many of the same functions as COMPASS, but preceded it in development.

FORTRAN
COBOL
ALGOL

We mention ASCENT here because its input was CDC 3000 series source programs although the output was produced for the CDC 6000 series and later.

Note the overloading of the acronym COS.

CHAPTER EIGHT

CDC 3X00 PERIPHERALS

Source: CDC 1968l

The CDC 3x00 Family supported a wide range of peripherals – unit record equipment, such as printers, card readers, and paper tape devices – and mass storage devices, such as tapes and discs. This chapter will describe selected peripheral equipment used with the CDC 3000 series computer systems.

8.1 MAGNETIC TAPE CONTROLLER

Source: CDC1967ak

The CDC 3228/3229 Magnetic Tape Controllers (MTC) handled the transfer of data from CDC 6xx magnetic tape drives to and from the CDC 3x00 memory. The CDC 322x MTC could control up to four (CDC 3228) or eight (CDC 3229) tape drives. Each Magnetic Tape Unit (MTU) had an identifier from 0-3 or 0-7 depending the MTC model. The MTC was depicted in Figure 8-1. The CDC 322x was exemplary of the MTC's developed by CDC.

The CDC 322x MTC had one read/write control, which was physically attached to one CDC 3000 series data channel. Each MTU had a unique numerical designation determined by the Unit Select Switch on the MTU.

During write operations, data was received from the data channel as a sequence of 12-bit bytes. The MTU read or wrote data 6 bits at a time, so the MTC dissembled the 12-bit byte into two 6-bit characters. When an OUTC or OTAC instruction was executed, only the lower 6 bits were transmitted to the MTU.

During read operations, the MTU transmitted 6-bit characters to the MTC, which then assembled them into a 12-bit byte for transfer to the data channel. Similarly, this assembly was suspended for an INPC or INAC instruction and only the lower 6 bits were transmitted to the data channel.

Data could be written to or read from the MTUs in either Binary Coded Decimal (BCD) or binary format depending on the mode selected.

Figure 8-1. CDC 322x Magnetic Tape Controller
Source: CDC 1973a

The CDC 322x Panel held the Equipment Number switch and indicator lights. It was hidden behind a front door of the MTC. It is depicted in Figure 8-2 and Table 8-1.

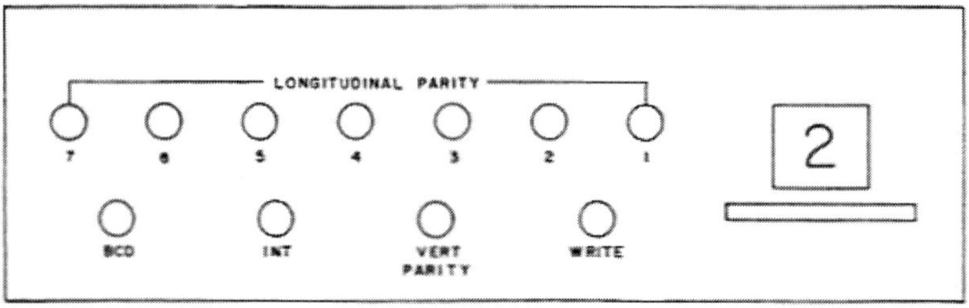

Figure 8-2. MTC Indicator Panel
Source: Adapted from CDC 1968ct

The *Longitudinal Parity* lights indicated if a parity error had occurred. At the end of an operation, none of the lights should be lit.

The Write Indicator was lit during write and Write File Mark operations.

The *Vert(ical) Parity* light was lit if a vertical parity error was detected during an I/O operation.

The *Int(erupt)* light was lit when interrupt occurred. It remained lit until the interrupt was dropped.

BCD light indicated that the MTC was operating in BC mode.

The square indicator on the right was an eight-position switch which allowed the operator to select the *Equipment Number* for the MTC.

8.1.1 Connecting an MTC to a Data Channel

An MTC had to be connected to its data channel before I/O operations could commence. This was accomplished using the Connect instruction (N00U) where N was the MTC identifier and U was the MTU identifier. The Connect code was the lower 12 bits of the instruction.

Each MTC examined the Connect code transmitted from its data channel. A reply, indicating a connection, was returned to the data channel from MTC if:

1. The N portion of the Connect code matched the setting of the Equipment Number switch on the MTC console;
2. The U portion matched the setting of the Unit Select Switch on an unreserved MTU; and

3. A transmission parity error was not detected.

An MTC accepted only one code at a time. First, it checked for parity errors. If none was found, the MTC returned a Reply if the code could be executed.

Parity was checked at several stages of an I/O Operation:

- Transmission parity checking, when connect codes, function codes, and data were transmitted between the data channel and the MTC;
- Parity error in the connect code prevented the MTC from connecting to the data channel;
- Parity error in the function code caused the requested function to not be performed;
- Parity error in output data caused the red indicator in the Equipment Number switch to be lit and a Parity Error signal sent to the data channel; or
- Parity error on input data caused the Parity Error signal to be sent to the data channel, an indicator set om either channel or console lights, and the faulty data to be entered into memory or the A register.

If a reply was not returned to the data channel because it did not match the MTC number, an Internal Reject was generated after 100 microseconds.

If the U portion did not match any of the MTU Unit Select Switches, a Reject signal was returned to the data channel.

If a parity error occurred, the Parity Error indicator was lit of each equipment detecting the error. Additionally, on the console the Equipment Number display was backlit in red.

Parity error conditions had to be cleared by a Channel Clear or Master Clear instruction.

8.1.2 MTC Function Codes

Function codes transmitted from the MTC to the MTU specified the operations to be performed. Function codes were user to prepare an MTC and/or an MTU for I/O operation. The function code was coded in the lower 12 bits of a Select/Function instruction. Table 8-1 describes the function codes.

Table 8-1. CDC 322x Function Codes

$Functions_8$	Description
	Non-operating Codes
0000	Release: Cleared the existing unit connection to the MTC.
0001	Binary: Set binary mode for reding/writing data.
0002	Coded: Set BCD mode for reading/writing data.
0003	556 BPI: Wrote/read all data at 556 bpi.
0004	200 BPI: Wrote/read all data at 200 bpi.
0005	Clear: Clear the existing unit connection to the MTC.
0006	800 BPI: Wrote/read all data at 800 bpi.
	Operating codes
0010	Rewind: Rewound the tape to the load point.
0011	Rewind Unload: Rewound tape to load point, then rewound until all tape was on the supply reel. All further operations on the MTU are locked until it was manually reloaded.
0012	Backspace: Moved tape backwards one record or until load point.
0013	Search Forward to File Mark: Advanced the tape until a file mark was detected.
0014	Search Backward to File Mark: Moved the tape backward until a file mark was detected.
0015	Write File Mark: Advanced tape 6 inches and wrote a 17_8 file mark followed by a 17_8 check character.
0016	Skip Bad Spot: Erased at least 4 inches of tape with vertical and longitudinal parity checks made to ensure complete erasure.
0040	Clear Reverse Read: Cleared Reverse Read condition.
0041	Set Reverse Read: Set Reverse Read condition, which must precede a reverse read operation.
	Interrupt Codes
0020	Select Interrupt on Ready and Not Busy: MTC sent interrupt to the CP when the MTU was Ready and Not Busy.
0021	Release Interrupt on Ready and Not Busy: Cleared an interrupt on the Ready and Not Busy condition.
0022	Select Interrupt on End of Operation: MTC sends interrupt to the CP when the data channel terminated a read or write operation.
0023	Release Interrupt on End of Operation: Cleared an Interrupt on of Operation condition.
0024	Select Interrupt on Abnormal End of Operation: MTC sends interrupt to the CP when an abnormal condition occurred.
0025	Release Interrupt on Abnormal End of Operation: MTC cleared interrupt when an abnormal condition occurred.

An MTC would accept a new operating code when the MTU was completely quiesced. Non-operating codes could be accepted prior to, after, or during an operating code execution.

8.1.3 BCD/Binary Modes

Data could read from or written to tape in either BCD or binary mode. Data was processing binary mode following a reset operation, which cleared the MTC registers), by selecting binary mode. Conversely, selecting BCD mode placed allowed the MTU to read/write data in BCD format.

8.1.4 1604 Mode

During a write operation in BCD mode, MTC automatically changed any character of all '0's to the value 12_8 as it wrote it to tape. Conversely, when reading from tape in BCD mode, it converted al characters with a value of 12_8 to '0's.if bit 4** was , bit 5 was complemented dur these operations, which converted the internal BCD codes to external BCD codes.

In 1604 mode, this conversion was not performed during a read or write operation.

8.1.5 Record/File Formats

The data written to tape by a single output instruction was a *record*. A *file* consisted of one or more records. The length of the records and the number of records was determined by the user program. Adjacent files were separated by a *file mark*, which an MTU wrote in response to function code Write File Mark (0015).

When the MTU detected a record gap or a file mark, it sent an End-of-Record signal to the data channel. This signal was used to terminate a read operation. A read operation could also be terminated when a specified number of words or characters had been read.

Data was written at different densities:

- At 200, 556, or 800 characters per inch for the CDC 604/607 MTUs, or
- At 200, or 556 characters per inch for the CDC 603/606 MTUs.

8.1.6 Interrupts

The MTC could be programmed to send an interrupt signal to the processor when any one of the conditions specified occurred. If a specific interrupt was selected and at least one of the conditions specified by it occurred in the connected MTU, the MTC send an Interrupt signal to the processor.

The processor had to be programmed to recognize the interrupt. If so, the main program was interrupted and control transferred to a specific program address for the specific interrupt handler. If desired, control can be transferred back to the main program after the interrupt was processed.

An interrupt signal remained raised until it was cleared by selecting the interrupt, selecting release, or master clearing the system

The Equipment Number of the MTU selected the interrupt line on which the interrupt signal was sent.

8.1.7. MTC Status

Twelve status lines connected the MTC to the data channel. A status code be sent over these lines after a connect attempt or rejection of it. Sense Status and Copy Status instructions transferred a status from the data channel to the processor.

8.2 Magnetic Tape Unit

Source: CDC 1973ak

The CDC 3000 series supported four Magnetic Tape Units (MTU): the CDC 603, 604, 606, and 607 models for the CDC 3000 series. Magnetic tape provided a non-volatile high speed storage medium for recording data. The tape was plastic with one side coated with a magnetic oxide. The oxide side was passed over electronic read/write heads to record and read data.

A Nonreturn-to-Zero (NRZI) recording scheme was used in which the magnetic particles were aligned in either a positive (1) or negative (0) direction. Each frame – a line across the width of the tape – consisted of six bits of data and one parity bit. Data was recorded using a Binary Coded Decimal (BCD) format for character data or in binary format for direct representation words as they appeared in core storage. Odd parity was used for binary format and even parity for BCD format.

A magnetic tape had reflective spots to mark the beginning and end points of the tape. These spots were located on the uncoated size of the tape and were sensed by photosensing circuits. A magnetic tape also had a ring that could be inserted into a circular slot on the back of the tape reel that indicated the tape was protected against writing as seen in Figure 8-3.

Figure 8-3. Magnetic Tape Reels Showing File Protection Ring
Source: CDC 1973ak

A magnetic tape unit drive unit is depicted in Figure 8-4 with its labeled components. Tapes were loaded onto a Supply Reel. The tape was threaded through rollers and across the magnetic heads in the Read/Write Assembly and then wound onto the Takeup Reel. The Unit Select Switch designated a unit number between 0 and 7 to indicate the unit when attached to an MTC.

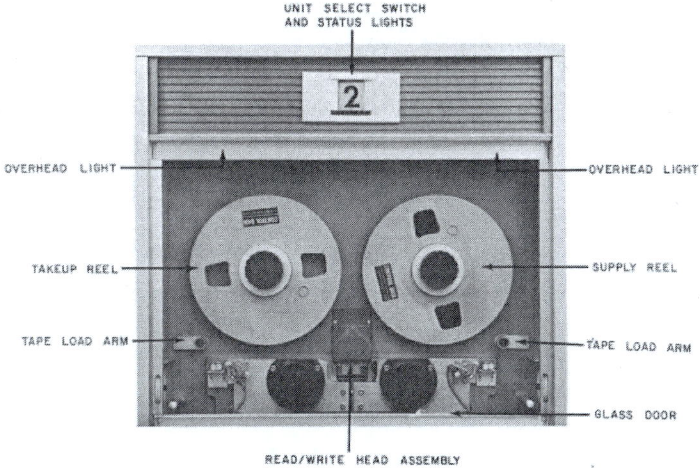

Figure 8-4. Model 600 Magnetic Tape Drive Unit
Source: CDC 1968ct

Figure 8-5 depicts a CDC 607 Magnetic Tape Unit in a cabinet configuration. The lower chassis provided a vacuum column that allowed the tape to be kept taught as unreeled from the Supply Reel, traversed the rollers and read/write assembly, and was reeled onto the TakeUp Reel.

A ten-position switch having the values 0-7 or STANDBY. 0-7 designated the MTU identifier to the MTC. STANDBY placed in a condition in which it could not be connected to an MTC.

Figure 8-5. CDC 607 Magnetic Tape Unit
Source: CDC 1968ct

The operator control panel is depicted in Figure 8-6. The controls are described in Table 8-2.

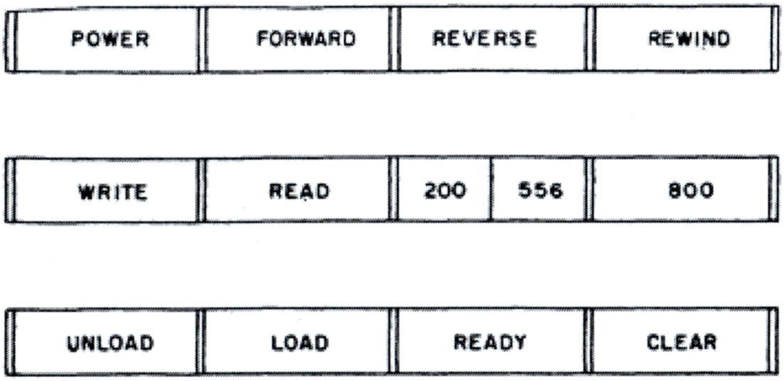

Figure 8-6. Model 607 Operator Panel
Source: Adapted from CDC 1968ct

Table 8-2. Model 600 Operator Panel Controls

Feature	Description
Power Switch	The operator pressed this switch to power up the MTU. Power was indicated by backlighting the switch.
Forward Switch	This switch initiated forward motion of the tape. Motion stopped when the CLEAR switch was pressed or the end of tape was reached.
Reverse Switch	This switch initiated rewinding of the tape. Motion stopped when the load point was reached or the CLEAR switch was pressed.
Rewind Switch	This switch initiated rewinding of the tape. Motion stopped when the load point was reached.
Write Indicator	This light was lit whenever writing was being performed on the tape.
Read Indicator	This light was lit whenever reading was being performed on the tape.
Numbered Switches	Pressing one of these selected the density for writing and reading the tape.

Unload Switch	Pressing this switch transferred all tape to the supply reel. It was lit to indicate unloading was in progress.
Load Switch	Once a tape had been threaded on the Takeup Reel, pressing this switch moved the tape forward to the load point. The switch was lit to indicate this operation was in progress.
Ready Switch	This switch placed the MTU under processor control. It was lit while this status was in effect.
Clear Switch	This switch cleared the status of the MTU, turned off the Ready light, and placed the tape under manual control.

8.3 Mass Storage Controller

Source: CDC 1976al

The CDC 3553 Mass Storage Controller (MSC) with attached CDC 841 Multiple Disk Drive (MDD) and/or CDC 821 Disk File provided a non-volatile mass storage subsystem. We will describe the CDC 3553-2 which had buffer memory.

8.3.1 Mass Storage Configuration

A CDC 3553 interfaced with one or two data channels. It synchronized data transfers between the disk drives and the CDC 3x00 memory. An MDD used a disk pack consisting of 11 disks mounted on a vertical spindle. Its data transfer rate was 2,148,000 bits per second. The CDC 821 Disk File consisted multiple disks mounted on two spindles. Its transfer rate was 2,232,000 bits per second. 18 disks were mounted on one spindle and provided 32 recording surfaces. The top and bottom surfaces of the disk stack were not used for recording. Two models were provided – the 821-1 with 36 disks or the 821-2 with 72 disks. A model 821-2 consisted of two Model 821-1 units coupled together.

An MSC could attach up to eight disk units and interfaced with a CDC 3x00 series data channel. For the MDD, an optional Dual Access Option allowed it to be interfaced to a second MSC. This provided a means of sharing data between two CDC 3x00 computer systems through data transfers across the intervening disk drives.

Data was recorded in discrete sectors on each disk. A data byte consisted of 12 bits. Each disk was divided into 14 sectors. An MDD had 4509 bits per sector, while the CDC 821 had 4380 bits per sector.

8.3.2 Controller Function Codes

The MSC was sent *function codes* by the operating system's I/O Subsystem to control the mass storage. Control and address codes which reserved the controller and the position of the read/write heads. Interrupt codes set and handled the interrupt processing. Error recovery codes handled the determination and correction of error conditions. I/O codes managed the transfer of data to and from the mass storage system. These functions are described in the following tables.

Table 8-3. Control and Address Functions

Function	Code	Description
Channel Release	0000	This function logically released a disk subsystem from the channel. It cleared all interrupts, removed all I/O code selections, and dropped the status response lines.
Restore	0001	This function initiated a seek of the disk arm to position zero.
Cylinder Seek	0002 0003	This function moved the disk forward one cylinder. Code 0003 moved the disk arm in the reverse direction.
Clear	0005	Clears the registers of all component in the subsystem, but left it attached to the channel and the unit selected.
Drive Release	0007	Logically released the drive unit and cleared the On Sector status.
Load Address At 1:1 Interlace	0010 0012 0014 0016	The next output data was loaded into the 24-bit controller address register continuously until the output operation was completed. Same as 0010, but at a 2:1 interlace. Same as 0010, but at a 4:1 interlace. Same as 0010, but at a 8:1 interlace.
Return Address	0011	For an input operation, continuously returned the contents of the 24-bit controller address register to the data channel until the input operation terminated.
Read Disk Address	0013	Returned the current address from the disk unit.

When the system setup an I/O operation for a disk unit, it also enabled an interrupt and set the status bit for the operation. If the system detected a follow-on operation, it could disable the interrupt and set up the follow on operation directly without incurring an interrupt.

Table 8-4. Interrupt Codes

Function	Code	Description
Select Interrupt on Ready and Not Busy	0020	Enables the interrupt line and sets the associated status bit when the subsystem was Ready and Not Busy.
Release Interrupt on Ready and Not Busy	0021	Removes the interrupt set up by the 0020 function.
Select Interrupt on End of Operation	0022	Enables the interrupt line and sets the associated status bit on the completion of the next operation.
Release Interrupt on End of Operation	0023	Disables the interrupt set by 0022 on completion of the operation.
Select Interrupt on Abnormal End of Operation	0024	Enables the interrupt and sets the status bit on the stopping of an operation due to an abnormal operation.
Release Interrupt on Abnormal End of Operation	0025	Disables the interrupt set by 0025 on the stopping of an operation due to an abnormal operation.
Select Interrupt on Opposite Channel Release	0026	Enables an interrupt whenever a channel ends its reservation of the controller.
Release Interrupt on Opposite Channel Release	0027	Disables the interrupt set by 0026.
Select Interrupt on End of Seek	0030	Enables interrupt and sets the status bit on completion of a seek operation
Release Interrupt on End of Seek	0031	Releases the interrupt set by the 0030 code.

Several functions were used to detect error conditions and, possibly, effect recovery operations. The margin selection function allows movement of the arm positioner in small increments to circumvent track defects, if necessary. It also provides for varying the read strobe to adjust for fluctuations in read timing.

The file status was displayed on the maintenance panel by setting the REGISTER SELECT switch to FILE STATUS. Some of the errors that could be detected included clock errors, voltage errors, pack errors, and logic and channel errors. Table 8-5 presents the Error Recovery Functions.

Table 8-5 Error Recovery Functions

Function	Code	Description
Disk File Status	0032	This function enabled the controller receive the was file status on the channel status lines.
Clear Disk File Status	0033	This function cleared the operation specified by 0032.
Disable Sector Verify	0034	This function suppressed the need to verify an address before a read, write, or search operation. If selected, the correct address for a pack or disk had to be specified in the last seek operation.
Write Address Normal	0035	This function wrote a new header in the sector specified by the address register, and had to be followed by a Load Address operation., which initiated the write operation. It should be preceded by a Read Disk Address operation to ensure that the read/write head was properly positioned.
Write Address Defective	0036	Same as 0035 except the defective sector bit was set in the header.
Write Address Lockout	0037	Same as 0035 except the write lockout bit was set in the header. Thus, a good sector could be made read-only once written with data.
Margin Selection	04xx	This function sent eight bits to the disk to facilitate fine tuning of arm positioning and read timing.

I/O Functions set the conditions for data handling operations on the disk units, including data transfer between the data channel and the selected device.

Table 8-6. I/O Functions

Function	Code	Description
Read	0040	Read words from the disk drive.
Write	0041	Write words to the disk drive.
Search Compare	0042	Search for a word through the specified sector(s) on the disk drive.
Masked Search Compare	0043	

Checkword Verify	0044	This function read the data within the current cylinder and checked it for an illegal checkword from the current address to the end of the cylinder.
Read Checkword	0045	Initiated a read operation from the selected disk unit at the address specified by the controller address register. All checkwords and data were transmitted to the data channel. Each sector had a 12-bit checkword.

Mode Select Functions specified the conditions under which function 0042 or 0043 was conducted.

Table 8-7. Mode Select Functions

Function	Code	Description
Magnitude Search	0050	If the Record <= Buffer, the comparison was successful.
Magnitude Search	0051	If the Record >= Buffer, the comparison was successful.
Equality Search	0052	If the Record = Buffer, the comparison was successful.
Buffer Mode	0053	Prepared the controller for a subsequent I/O operation for which successful completion was the word count specified for the I/O operation.
End of Record Mode	0054	Prepared the controller for a subsequent I/O operation for which successful completion was: 1. Write: a record mark was recorded at the end of a sector, or 2. Read: an End of Record mark was detected and signal sent.

8.3.3 Controller Status Codes

The MSC provided a 12-bit status code to the data channel to allow the computer system to determine the MSC status after function codes were sent to it. The computer system executed a Copy Status instruction which returned the status code held by the data channel. The status code may have multiple status bits set. Table 8-8 presents the status bits that can be set by the controller (Source: CDC 1976al).

Table 8-8. MSC Status Bits

Status code	Bit#	Description
Ready	0	This bit indicated that the last selected unit was connected to the data channel and in an operable condition for use.
Busy	1	This bit indicated the controller and/or device was performing an I/O operation and not available the requested operation.
Address Error	2,3	This bit indicated an address error had been detected due to" 1. An illegal address; 2. c(AR) /= address read from the device; 3. The address was beyond the capacity of the unit; 4. The seek operation initiated by Load Address was incomplete; 5. A defective track bit was detected; 6. A Checkword error occurred during address verification; or 7. A seek error occurred as reported by the file or disk unit.
No Compare	4,~2	A miscomparison occurred during the Search Compare operation.
Operation Error	4,2	An operation error occurred due to: 1. a failure to get a resume signal from memory on an I/O operation, or 2. a sector mark was received before the end of operation. (Mode 3532-2 only).
Lost Data	4,2	The unit did not respond soon enough to record all data correctly during a write operation. (Model 3553-1 only).
End of Record	5,~2	This bit indicated an End of Record bit was detected at the end of the last sector, when operating in End of Record mode.
Checkword Error	5,2	This bit indicated a checkword error occurred during a read, search compare, or checkword verify operation.
Write Lockout on Read	6,~2	This bit indicated it was permissible to read in a write protected area.
Write Lockout on Write	6,2	This bit indicated an attempt to write in a write protected area.
Positioner Ready	7	This bit indicated that the positioner had settled on the requested cylinder.

End of Operation Interrupt	8	This indicated an End of Operation interrupt was signaled.
Abnormal End of Operation Interrupt	9	This indicated an Abnormal End of Operation interrupt was signaled.
Seek Interrupt	10	This bit indicated the end of a seek operation on a unit. The unit was ready for a read or write operation.
Reserved	11,~2	This bit indicated that a Connect attempt of the unit to the data channel was rejected because the unit was already connected another data channel.
Defect Track	11,2	This bit indicated that a defective track bit had been detected at the unit address specified and prevented the I/O operation from being performed by generating an Abnormal End of Operation interrupt.

Note ~ indicates the bit must be not set.

A disk storage unit could become non-operable under the following conditions:

- Disk pack not loaded (disk drive unit only);
- R/W heads not landed;
- Disk motor not up to speed;
- File or disk drive in an unsafe condition;
- Unit does not exist in configuration;
- Unit reserved by another controller; Unit was in OFF linemode.

The last three codes caused an immediate reject of the I/O operation. If a unit became Not Ready during an operation, the I/O operation ceased and an Abnormal End of Operation interrupt was generated.

The logic and details of these operations is beyond the scope of the volume. The reader should consult the detail logic manuals for the specified MSC model and disk unit to fully understand the I/O operations.

8.3.4 MSC Control Panel

The MSC Control Panel is depicted in Figure 8-7.

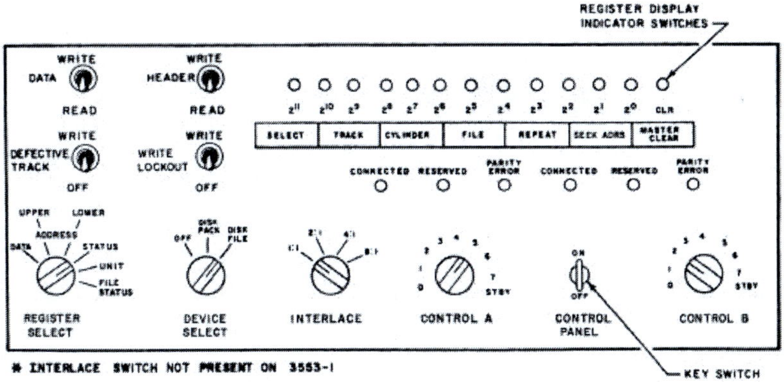

Figure 8-7. MSC Control Panel
Source: CDC 1976al

Table 8-9 indicates the functions of the switches and indicators.

Table 8-9. MSC Control Panel Switches and Indicators

Switches	Description
Control Panel (bottom Row, 2nd from right)	For normal programmed operation, this switch should be in the OFF position. When ON, other switches could be activated
Device Select	This rotary switch selected the device type (disk drive, disk file).
Register Select	This rotary switch selected the register/indicators to display and, possibly, to enter data.
Defective Track	For normal programmed operation, this switch should be in the OFF position. When ON, a defective track bit was written in each sector of the specified address headers.
Data	For normal programmed operation, this switch should be in the READ position. When in the WRITE position, data could be inserted from the panel by the register into the entire storage area selected by (Track, Cyl, and File) of the selected mode.

Header	For normal programmed operation, this switch should be in the READ position. When in the WRITE position, address headers could be read or written in the storge area.
Write Lockout	When in WRITE position, data was protected during write operations if the WLO bit was set in the address headers. When in the OFF position, data was not protected. Each sector has a lockout bit. When set to one, no write operations were allowed against that sector.
Interlace (3553-2 only)	Selected one of four interlace patterns for which headers would be written
Control A & Control B	These switches provided individual control for each data channel connected to the MSC. Positions 0-7 reflected unit STANDBY, and CONNECTED, RESERVED, and PARITY ERROR specified status.
Select, Track, Cylinder, File	These switches allowed operator to set data, which was indicated in the lights, to be entered into the register. (upper right panel row)
Repeat	The selected mode of operation was repeated with the specified device and address.
Seek Address	Initiated a seek operation on the selected device with the specified address data. When the seek was completed successfully, the On Sector status was returned from the MSC. This status was maintained until an I/O operation was executed against a unit.
Master Clear	Caused a Master Clear within the MSC; all write operations ceased. The Address Register was set to zero.
Register	Thirteen push-button switches (CLEAR and bits 0-11) provided for entering or displaying data into the register selected.
Indicators	**Description**
Register	In the upper right corner are indicators that display the contents of the selected register. Or, data to be entered into the machine.

8.4 Card Reader Controllers

CDC provided three Card Reader Controllers – Models 3248-A, 3447-A, and 3649-A, to handle a card reader. Each of these had different features to meet user's needs. Table 8-10 presents the basic characteristics and Table 8-11 presents their unique features.

Table 8-10. Card Reader Controller – Basic Characteristics

Characteristic	Value
Read Rate	1200 80-column cards per minute 1600 51-column cards per minute
Input Tray	4000 Cards
Output Tray	4000 Cards - primary tray 240 Cards – secondary tray
Data Transfer Rate	With Buffer Memory, 390 microseconds per 80-colum card

Table 8-11. Card Reader Controller – Special Features

Model	Feature
3649-A	May be connected to up to two data channels.
3649-A	Provided an input to A path directly to the A register.
3447-A/3248-A	Connected to a single data channel only.
3649-A/3447-A	Provided a Buffer Memory

Figure 8-8 depicts a Card Reader Controller in a CDC 405 Card Reader cabinet with the card reader mechanism at the top left.

Figure 8-8. A CDC 405 Cabinet with Card Reader Controller
Source: CDC 1968ct

The CRCs accepted both 80-column and 51-column cards. They read data in either Hollerith or binary format. The controller converted each 12-bit code read from a card into a 6-bit BCD code. It assembled two 6-bit characters into a 12-bit word and transmitted it to the data channel. An odd-numbered column's code was placed in the upper 6 bits of the word, while the even-numbered column's code was placed in the lower 6 bits.

For 51-column cards, the lower 6 bits of the last input byte were all zeroes to indicate the source.

8.4.1 Reading Operation

The CRC was controlled by the data channel, Card motion began when the data channel requested data in response to a Read instruction from the CPU. The punched card was then read column-by-column beginning with column 1. Reading stopped as soon as the last card has been placed in the output hopper After each card was read, the controller sent an End of Record signal to the data channel. This signal could cause the data channel to terminate the Read operation.

8.4.2 BUFFER MEMORY

CRC Models 3649 and 3447 contained a buffer memory that held one 80-column card image of 12-bit words. The reader entered data into the buffer memory at the rate of 50 msecs/card. Once a card was read, the data channel could read the card image from buffer memory at a rate of 390 microseconds/card into CP memory. While the buffer was being refilled, the data channel could service another device.

8.4.3 INPUT TO A REGISTER

CRC Model 3649 could transmit one 12-bit byte to the A register via a direct path without intervention of a data channel. Each time the CPU executed an Input To A instruction, the CRCR sent one 12-bit byte to the lower 12 bits of the A register as a binary number. No conversion was performed.

Only CDC models 3600 and 3800 had the direct path features.

8.4.4 INTERRUPTS

The CRC could notify the processor when it could start an operation, when it had completed an operation, or when an abnormal condition occurred. With normal operation, the processor could initiate an I/O operation via the data channel and then continue executing user programs. The card reader notified the processor via the CRC when it required service.

Interrupts were selected by function codes. When an interrupt condition occurred, the CRC sent an interrupt via the data channel to the processor. The processor then handled the interrupt according to established procedures in the operating system.

8.4.5 FUNCTION CODES

All operations were controlled by function codes. The CRC had to be connected to the data channel before functions could be executed. When a function was executed, a Reply signal was sent to the processor. If an error occurred, a Reject signal was sent, which directed the processor to execute the next instruction from the reject jump address.

Function codes were contained in the lower 12 bits of a function instruction. Table 8-12 presents the CRC function codes.

Table 8-12. CRC Function Codes

Function Code	Description
N000	Connect Reader: B specified the controller equipment number.
0000	Release and Disconnect: This function disconnected the CRC, cleared the channel reservation, and cleared all status conditions.
0001	Negate Hollerith to Internal BCD Conversion: Normally, a Hollerith to BCD conversion was performed on all cards read, but this function eliminated that conversion.
0002	Release Negate Hollerith to Internal BCD Conversion: Resumed normal conversion operation.
0004	Set Gate Card: Allowed the reader to do a limited sorting operation by directing cards to the secondary output hopper.
0005	Clear: Cleared any interrupt condition and signal.
0020	Select Interrupt on Ready and Not Busy: Sent an interrupt when data was available in the buffer memory for input and the data channel had ini231wtiated a read operation.
0021	Release Interrupt on Ready and Not Busy: Inhibit interrupts on Ready and Not Busy.
0022	Select Interrupt on End of Operation: Sent an interrupt when the data channel terminated a read operation and the reader was not busy.
0023	Release Interrupt on End of Operation: Inhibited an End of Operation interrupt.
0024	Select Interrupt on Abnormal End of Operation: Sent in interrupt on an abnormal condition.
0025	Release Interrupt on Abnormal End of Operation: Inhibited sending an interrupt on an abnormal condition.

Several abnormal operating conditions could be detected by the CRC upon a signal from the card reader, including:

- Stacker full or jammed for output hopper(s);
- Input tray empty on read operation;
- Feed failure (possibly card jam in read station);
- Illegal 6-bit operation;
- Compare or preread error (reader malfunction);
- The AUTO/MAN switch was in manual position on read operation;
- A file card (punches in rows 7 and 8 of column 1) was read.

More detail regarding these conditions can be found in CDC 1968ct.

8.4.6 Control Panel

Figure 8-9 depicts the CDC 405 Card Reader Control Panel with switches and indicators.

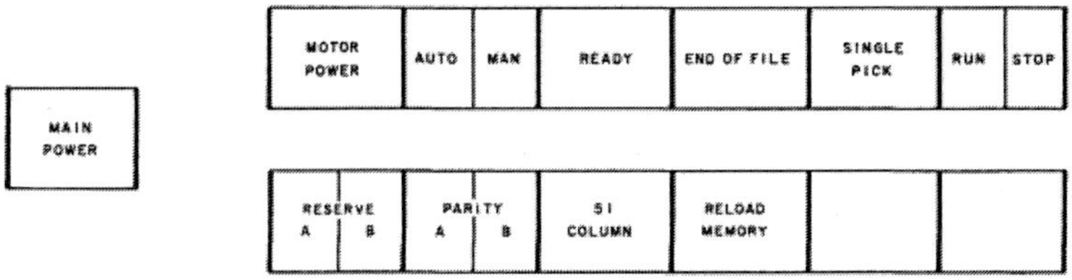

Figure 8-9. CDC 405 Card Reader Control Panel
Source: CDC 1968ct

Table 8-13 describes the switches and indicators on the 405 Card Read control Panel.

Table 8-13. 405 Card Reader Control Panel

Switch/Indicator	Usage
Main Power	Enabled power to the CDC 405 Cabinet, when lit.
Motor Power	Enabled power to the drive motors, vacuum-pressure system, and hopper-stacker vibrators, when lit.
Auto/Man Switches	A two-position switch selected manual or processor-controlled operation. The appropriate button was lit for that mode of operation.
Ready	This switch made the reader ready, if the Input tray was empty, No error conditions existed, and primary and secondary hoppers were not full.
End of File	Pressing this switch caused the reader to generate an end of file condition when the last cards was read; active when lit.
Single Pick	When MAN switch was lit, cycled one card through the card reader.
Run/ Stop	When MAN switch was lit, allowed manual control of the card reader.
Reserve (A/B) (3649)	Indicated if either of the associated data channels had reserved the reader.

Parity (A/B) (3649)	Indicated if an error had occurred one ither of the associated data channels.
51 Column	Allowed reading of a short (51-column) card by CDC 3649 or CDC 3447.
Reload Memory	When pressed in AUTO mode, fed data from a new card into the Buffer Memory (3447/3649 only).
Par/Conn	If PAR was lit, indicated a transmission parity had occurred; if CONN was lit, indicated the controller was connected to a data channel.

8.4.7 Control Panel Switch and Indicators

The CRC models had small control panel on the controller device itself. Figure 8-10 depicts the switches for the CDC 3447/3640 CRC. Table 8-14 describes the switches and indicators.

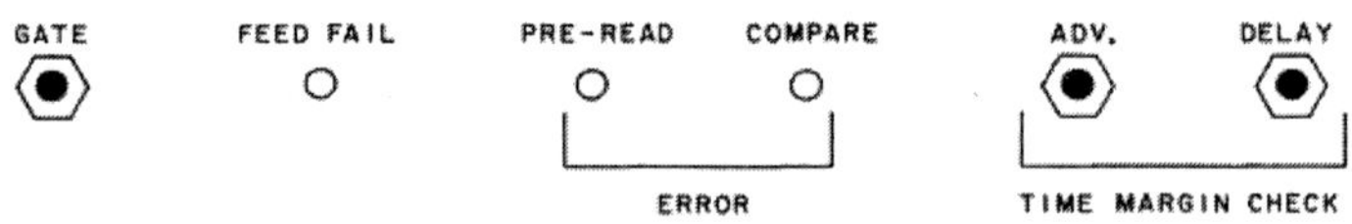

Figure 8-10. CDC 3447/3649 Control Panel Switches and Indicators
Source: CDC 1968ct

Table 8-14. CRC Control Panel

Switch/Indicator	Usage
Gate	Used by maintenance personnel only.
Feed Failure	This indicator was lit if a feed failure occurred, e.g., a card was likely jammed in moving through the read mechanism.
Pre-Read Error	This indicator was lit if an error had occurred in the photocell logic.
Compare Error	This indicator, when lit, indicated a hole count difference between the read and checkout stations. The card should be reread.
Time Margin Check	These were used by maintenance personnel in tuning the machine.

8.5 Line Printer Controller

The CDC 3458 Line Printer Controller (LPC) operated with either the IBM 1403 Model 2 Chain Printer or the IBM 1403 Model 3 Train Printer. These printers were acknowledged for years as the most rugged, reliable printers available. However, at full operating speed, they sounded like a buzz saw. The 1403 Printer characteristics are presented in Table 8-15.

Table 8-15. 1403 Line Printer Characteristics

Characteristic	Value
Line Length	132 characters.
Line Density	Six or eight lines per inch.
Printing Rate with Single Spacing	Model 2: 600 lines per minute Model 3: 1100 lines per minute with 48-character set Model 3: 950 lines per minute using 59 preferred characters of the 64-character set
Paper Motion	High Speed during spacing of eight lines or more.
Operating Mode	Internal or External BCD.
Data Word	6-bit (no assembly) or 12-bit.
Error Checking	Program, print, sync, and memory parity.

Figure 8-11 depicts the CDC 3458 Line Printer Controller. The panels swung outward to access the internal systems. Behind one panel was the console for the LPC.

Figure 8-11. CDC 3458 Line Printer Controller
Source CDC 1068ct

8.5.1 1403 Line Printer

The IBM 1403 Line Printer printed data on continuous-form paper that moved vertically between horizontal rows of hammers and type faces. It was a workhorse printer of the 1960s and 1970s as represented a long product lifetime. Printing and paper movement were controlled by the LPPC and the user program.

8.5.1.1 Chain Assembly

The chain assembly was a steel-coated plastic tape to which were attached a series of type slugs to form an endless loop. Each type slug contained type for two characters; the slugs were arranged in groups called arrays. Each array contained 48 characters. This 48-characcter set chain had a total of five arrays.

8.5.1.2 Train Assembly

The *train assembly* was constructed from a series of *type slugs* containing gear teeth which moved along a track channel on a guided track. The type slugs were not connected. The type slugs were moved by a drive gear at one end of the assembly. Each type slug contained 3 characters. The 48-character set contained five arrays with 48 characters in each set. Each array contained 26 alphabetic, 10 numeric, and 12 symbol characters.

The 64-character set contained four arrays with 60 characters in each set with arrays differing slightly. The four arrays had a different character as the 60th character, so this assembly was often referred to as the 59 preferred, four-array assembly. Each array contained 26 alphabetic, 10 numeric, and 24 symbol characters.

8.5.2 Printing Operations

Printing was accomplished by the timed firing of *print hammers* striking the paper and printing ribbon against the slugs as characters on the chain or train assembly passed beneath them. The chain or train assembly moved continuously at a constant speed. When the paper and ribbon made contact with the slug, the character was imprinted on the paper.

Each line could contain up to 132 print positions, which could be filled by a character or a blank (created by the hammer not striking the paper and print ribbon). Each print position had a separate hammer and an associated position in the controller buffer.

There was less space between the hammers than between the characters on the chain assembly. Thus, consecutive characters did not align with consecutive characters. A printing sequence of every second character and every third hammer was used to achieve the printed images aligned evenly on the paper. At any instant, one character and one hammer were perfectly aligned to cleanly print a character on the paper.

To print a line of characters from the 48-character set, the assembly had to be scanned 48 times. Each scan was called a *print scan*, which was the time required to allow each hammer the opportunity to print one character. Each print scan was divided into three subscans such that each subscan enabled one-third of the hammers to print one character.

8.5.2.1 Paper Advance

The continuous-form paper moved upwards from a bulk supply in a tray under the printer at the front of the printer. The paper passed between the print hammers and the type faces on the assembly and over the curved guides at the top of the printer. It then moved down through the stacker at the rear of the printer. As the paper was arranged in sheets that were punched with holes along the width of the paper, it fell into a bin in a fan-fold arrangement.

8.5.2.2 Carriage Control

A *carriage control tape* was as trip of plastic which was formed into a loop and rules with parallel lines along its length and width. The lines along the length corresponded to the 12 channels or hole positions. The line intersections were used to locate the punch positions for the rectangular control holes. The circumference of the tape was usually a multiple of the vertical length of the paper, e.g. the number of lines that could be printed on the paper. A row of round drive holes runs lengthwise through the center of the tape to into which the sprockets fit to drive the paper. A control hole pattern could be designed to allow different printing arrangements.

8.5.2.3 Running Time

Printer operating time was recorded on a running-time meter located on the printer. The first write signal after the printer was connected initiated the conditions for recording running time. A Channel Busy or Computer Running signal directed the accumulation of running time. After a user program completed, sending a CARRIAGE SPACE or CARRIAGE RESTORE prevented running time record until the next program began operation.

8.5.3 CDC 3458 Operation

The CDC 3458 Line Printer Controller (LPC) handled the transfer of data from the computer to the line printer. It received commands from the user program via the data channel and executed them to transfer data to the line printer.

8.5.3.1 Line Loading

Line loading was the process of transferring data to be printed to the LPC memory. Data was transferred as 12-bit bytes, with each byte representing two BCD characters. The two characters were printed upper 6-bits, then lower 6-bits. Character codes were converted to external BCD by the LPC if they entered as internal BCD codes.

A character translator matrix converted an incoming character to a code that represented a position within the array on the chain or train assembly. This position code was stored in the PC memory to be used for printing out the character. Different translator matrices were required because the two assemblies had different arrangements of print characters within a print array. A parity it was generated for each position code and stored with it in the LPC memory.

The LPC did not load a new line of data until the Write signal was dropped, meaning the line had been sent to the printer, and then brought again for the next line of data.

8.5.3.2 Printing

In printing one line of data, a comparison was made between the character aligned with the hammer and the character in memory. If the two were identical, the character was printed. The characters on the assembly are continually scanned until the 132 print hammers have had the option of printing each of the stored characters.

If a memory parity error was detected for a character position code, the error was registered with the LPC based on its column in the line to be printed

.

8.5.3.3 Paper Advanced

After each line was printed , the paper automatically advanced one line if n other spacing operations were programmed. Paper advanced was controlled by the user program through functions sent to the LPC. Spacing options can be applied both pre-print and post-print.

8.6 Peripherals Assessment

Initially, CDC acquired peripheral devices from third-party OEM sources. Eventually, it realized that it could increase its profit margin by manufacturing its own storage devices and unit record equipment. Additionally, with adaptations of the device controllers, peripherals could be used across system families, which eased the transition to new systems because users did not have to acquire all new hardware to move up to a more capable computer system.

CHAPTER NINE

THE CYBER 1700 SERIES MINICOMPUTERS

Somewhere along its journey, CDC, became enamored of minicomputers, perhaps as front-ends to some of their larger machines. CDC developed a series of minicomputers the CDC 1700/Cyber 17/Cyber 18 series. Unfortunately, CDC was a latecomer to the minicomputer marketplace and never really established a position that would allow it to be successful.

9.1 CDC 1700

Source: CDC UNKas, CDC 1965q

The CDC 1700 computer system was a compact computer system that was largely intended for data-handling applications, such as associated with industrial control processes, and re-routing of messages in a data collection/communications system. It used one's complement arithmetic and the ASCII-based character set. It was developed in the early 1960s with first deliveries made in 1966.

The CDC 1700 was a 16-bit minicomputer developed during the 1960s. It had a 1.1 microsecond cycle time. It used technology developed for the CDC 6000 series to provide the required performance and miniaturization. Several models of the CPU were sold with increased capabilities. The 1704 CPU was the most basic, while the 1705 CPU was an enhanced version. A CDC 1700 system is depicted in Figure 9-1.Table 9-1 presents the basic features of the CDC 1700 series.

Figure 9-1. CDC 1700 Computer System
Source: CDC1965q

Table 9-1. CDC 1700 – Basic Characteristics

Characteristic	Value/Explanation
Internal Representation	Fixed Point Binary Base 16 (Hexadecimal)
# Bits/Word	18 (16 data/instruction, Program Protect Bit, Parity Bit)
# Instructions/Word	1
# Instructions	
# Bits/Instruction	16
Instruction Type	One-Address
CPU Technology	Solid State Logic
CPU Registers	(2) Index registers
Main Memory	Magnetic Core: 4K – 32K words; Cycle Time: 1.1 microseconds
Add Time	Fixed Point: 2.2 microseconds
Multiply Time	Fixed Point: 7.0 microseconds
Divide Time	Fixed Point: 9.0 microseconds

The minimum configuration was a CDC 1704 computer 4K words, a CDC 1720 Card/Paper Tape Data Channel, and associated peripherals.

There were several models of the CDC 1700 – the 1704, 1714, 1774 – and its successors the Cyber 17, Cyber 18-17 (1784), 18-20, and 18-30.

Documentation is lacking in the public space on some of these models. This chapter will discuss the CDC 1704. A later chapter will discuss the Cyber 17/18 series.

9.1.1 CDC 1700 System Architecture

The system architecture of the CDC 1700 is depicted in Figure 9-2.

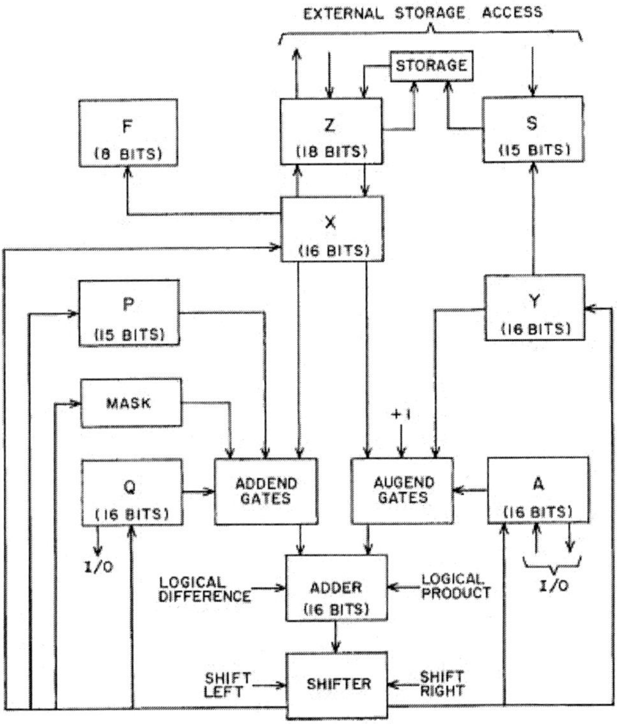

Figure 9-2. CDC 1700 System Architecture
Source: Adapted from CDC 1965q

The 15-bit P register acted as the program address counter, which held the address of the instruction being executed. After instruction execution, the value in P was appropriately incremented depending on the instruction executed or had a new address inserted if it was a branch condition. If the value in P was $7FFF_{16}$ and was incremented by 1, it rolled over to 000016.

The F register held the opcode of the current instruction and was used to generate the signals to execute the instruction. Other registers are described in Table 9-2.

9.1.2 Central Processor

The CDC 1704 Central Processor Unit (CPU) was designed for high-speed computation and I/O speed (based on CDC 6000 series technology). The CPU performed all instructions specified by programs stored in memory. It initiated I/O operations through specific commands, and handled all interrupts.

The Control Section directed the selection of the next instruction to be executed and established the internal signals to execute it. It also handled program protection, interrupt processing, and I/O and storage operations.

9.1.3 Registers

Multiple registers were accessible by the programmer as described in Table 9-2.

Table 9-2. CDC 1700 Registers

Register	#Bits	Description
A	16	Accumulator: Primary register for arithmetic and logical operations.
Q	16	Auxiliary Arithmetic Register: A multipurpose register used in multiply and divide operations, as the primary index register. It also supplied the addressing for peripheral devices for unbuffered I/O operations.
I	16	Index Register: A second index register
M		Mask Register: Any bit set to 1 inhibited the corresponding interrupt.
P	15	Program Address Register: P held the address of the current instruction. Incremented or set after the execution of an instruction.
X	16	Exchange Register: Held data being transferred to or from memory. Also held one argument in most arithmetic operations.
Y	16	Address Register: Used to compute the effective address for memory reference.
F	8	Function Register: Held the operation code for an instruction during decoding.

Z	18	Storage Buffer Register: Held the 18 bits of data being transferred from the memory to the computer or external storage or vice versa.
S	15	Memory Address Register: Contained the actual address used to access memory.

9.1.2 Memory

Memory consisted of one to eight 4K word CDC 1708 Storage Modules with a 1.1 microsecond cycle time. Special hardware could increase the maximum capacity to 64K words. Physical memory consisted of 18-bits words: a 16-bit data/instruction portion, a 1-bit parity bit, and a 1-bit protection bit.

If the protection bit (bit 17) was set, the memory word could only be modified by privileged instructions. Bit 17 could be set by the operating system for any program to indicate it was an element of a protected program.

9.1.3.1 Memory Protection

The Memory Protection system allowed the memory to be divided into foreground (protected) and background (unprotected) areas. The foreground job ran at a higher priority. Four program protect violations were detected:

- A non-protected instruction attempted to write into a protected area. Reads from protected areas were allowed.
- An attempt was made to write into a protected area from an external source where the write was initiated by a non-protected instruction.
- An attempt was made to execute a protected instruction after a non-protected instruction.
- An attempt was made to execute interregister instructions with bit 0 set.

The Program Protect Bit (bit 17) was used to protect a program from any other program in the system. All instructions and operands of the protected program had to have bit 17 set. The Program Protect Bit in each storage location was set or cleared by the SPB and C PB instructions.

Program protection was manually enabled by a two-position switch on the operator console. If the switch was not set to protect mode, none of the possible violations above were recognized.

9.1.3.2 MEMORY ADDRESSING

Memory was accessed using 15-bit addresses. A 15-bit address was composed as shown in Figure 9-3.

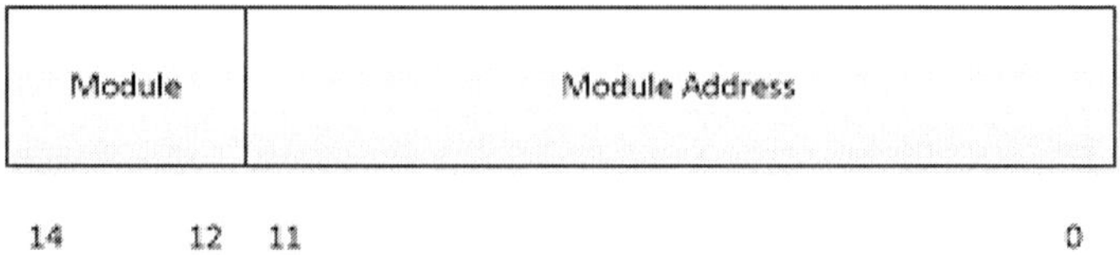

Figure 9-3. CDC 1700 Storage Address
Source: Adapted from CDC 1965q

The Module number selected one of eight modules of 4096 words. The Module address selected a location within a memory module.

The Z Register was the 18-bit storage register. It was used to transfer data between the computer, external storage, and the magnetic core storage. When a word was read from storage, it was placed in the Z register and the parity was checked. A parity bit was generated in the Z register when a word was transferred from storage to an external device.

The S register was the 15-bit storage address register which held the location to be read from or written to in storage.

9.1.3.3 ADDRESSING MODES

The CDC 1700 had seven different addressing modes as described in Table 9-3. The Address Mode bits are included in the Storage Reference instructions described in Section 9.2.1.

Table 9-3. CDC 1700 Addressing Modes

Mode	Mode Bits	Description
Absolute	0, 1, 2, or 3	Specified an absolute address in storage. The content of an index register, when specified, was added to the base address.
Indirect	4, 5, 6, or 7	Indirect: The value of the base address was an indirect address, e.g., it was the address of the address of the operand. Indirect flag was set to one.

Relative	8, 9, A, or B	Relative flag set to one. The base address was c(P) + c(address). The content of an index register, when specified, was added to the base address.
Relative Indirect	C, D, E, or F	Relative Indirect: Relative and Indirect flags were set to one. The base address was c(P) + c(address). The content of an index register, when specified, was added to the base address. If bit 15 of the indirect address was set to one, indirection continues until bit 15 was zero.
Constant	8, 9, A, or B	Relative flag set to one. If no index registers are specified, then the effective address was c(P) + 1. Otherwise, the content of the index register was added to c(P+1).
Storage	C, D, E, or F	Relative and indirect flags were set to one. Bit 15 of c(P+1) was set to 0. The base address was c(P+1). If indexing was specified, the content of the index register was added to the base address.
Storage Indirect	C, D, E, or F	Relative and indirect flags were set to one. 15 of c(P+1) set to 1. c(P+1) was an indirect address whose content was the base address. If bit 15 of the indirect address was set to one, indirection continues until bit 15 was zero.

9.1.4 Interrupt System

After each instruction was executed, the CPU tested for an internal or external condition that required handling. If the condition existed, c(P) was stored at a fixed location and an interrupt handler was initiated. The interrupt handler processed the interrupt and then returned to the next unexecuted instruction in the program.

For each condition that could cause an interrupt, two alternatives existed. The CPU could select an interruptible condition (possibly, from several available) and initiate the interrupt, or it could choose to ignore that condition. The program could also enable or disable the interrupt system based on the needs of the program using the IIN and the EIN instructions.

The 1704 CPU provided two interrupt lines. Line 0 provided entry for interrupts generated as a result of a storage parity error, a program protect fault, or power failure. Instructions could check for parity error or protect fault. Power failure was assumed if one of the other two conditions did not exist. In the case of power failure, approximately 8 milliseconds of programming time were available; then the computer generated a master clear before the power actually shut down.

Line 1 provided for interrupts from the low-speed peripherals controlled by Equipment #1, the *slow channel synchronizer*. Any of the four stations (TTY, Card Reader, Paper Tape Reader, Paper Tape Punch) on the slow channel synchronizer could send its interrupt to line 1.

The CDC 1705 Central Processor Unit incorporated an Interrupt/Data Channel option which increased the CDC 1704 computer by adding 14 interrupt lines. It also implemented the nonbuffered AQ I/O channel and the direct -access channel into storage from external sources.

Interrupt trap locations were established for each interrupt line at fixed storage addresses. For the basic system, these addresses were 0100_{16} and 0104_{16}. If the 1705 option was configured, they extended – in blocks of four words to $013C_{16}$.

9.1.4.1 Mask Register

The 16-bit Mask Register (MR) contained one bit for each interrupt line that was configured in the system. Bit 00 corresponded to line o, bit 01 to line 1, and so on up to line 15. To enable an interrupt on an interrupt line. The corresponding MR bit had to be set to 1. The MR was set by the interregister instruction.

The MR allowed the program to enable or disable selected subsets of the interrupts that could occur in the system. For the basic system, the program could enable or disable internal and external interrupts. With the 1705 option, greater flexibility in managing interrupts was available.

9.1.4.2 Interrupt Handling

When an interrupt occurred, c(P) was stored in the low-order 15 bits of the storage location reserved for that interrupt line. Bit 16 was set to record the current value of the OVERFLOW flag, which was then cleared.

The interrupt system was inactivated and control was transferred to the Interrupt Handler (IH). The interrupt handler was responsible for saving the contents of the registers, including the MR, storage locations reserved for that interrupt. The IH then loads the MR with the mask to be used while it was active. One's in the mask denoted interrupts that had a higher priority than the one being handled; the current interrupt had to have a zero in the MR. The IH then activated the interrupt system and processed the interrupt. This allowed a higher priority interrupt to interrupt the current IH.

9.1.5 I/O SYSTEM

The normal I/O channel for the CDC 1704 was the AQ channel. The 16-bit A and Q registers operated together to transfer data, status, and commands to the AQ channel. The Q register contained the address and commands for the peripheral device, while the A register received or transmitted the data and status. A maximum of eight devices could be attached to the AQ channel.

9.1.5.1 AQ CHANNEL PROCESSING

The A and Q registers were used to send data to peripheral controllers, and were referred to as the AQ Channel. The Q register contained the address and command for the peripheral device. Data and status were received or transmitted from the A register. The format of the Q register is depicted in Figure 9-4.

C	W	E	command
15	14 – 11	10 – 7	6 – 0

Figure 9-4. Q Register Format
Source: CDC 1965q

where	C	Continue Bit
	W	Converter Code
	E	Equipment Code
	Command	Consisting of Station Code (S) and Director Code (D)

The equipment contained logic shared by the stations. It compared the value of E with the setting of the equipment number switch to select the device to respond.

The Station contained logic unique for each unit. The station translated the command as required for each device. Sometimes, the station was the unit.

A unit was a physical piece of hardware, such as a magnetic tape drive. Units were controlled by high-level controllers.

The contents of the Q register were interpreted as presented in Table 9-4.

Table 9-4. Q Register Interpretation

Field	Description
E	Each equipment was assigned an equipment number $(0\text{-}F)_{16}$ via switch on its console. The equipment responded if its equipment number matched the contents of E.
S	This field selected a station within the equipment class. It varied from 1 bit to 6 bits and specified a particular station.
W	Bits 11-14 plus C bit 15 were reserved to address special devices called converters.
D	The Director Code (bit 0) specified the type of operation to be performed by the combination of the A and Q registers.
Command	Specified the operation to be performed by the station.

The commands used by the AQ channel are described in Table 9-5.

Table 9-5. AQ Channel Commands

Command	Description
Data Transfer	If Q_6-Q_0 were zero except for the station designator, a 16-bit input or output operation was performed by the A register using the Input to A or Output From A instruction.
Director Function	If $Q_{00} = 1$, and the computer executed an Output From A instruction, and all station bits were zero, c(A) controlled the function of the station within the equipment. Assigned bits of A were: A0 Clear Controller A1 Clear Interrupts A2 Data Interrupt Request A3 End of Operation Interrupt Request A4 Alarm Interrupt Request A5 Start Motion A6 Stop Motion The action of the specific codes was dependent on the type of the equipment the command was sent to.
Director Status	If $Q_{00} = 1$ and the computer executed an Input To A instruction and all station bits were zero, the status of the specified equipment was loaded into A. If the station bits were present, then the status of the specified station was loaded into A. The primary status codes were: A0 Ready A1 Busy A2 Interrupt A3 Data

	A4 End of Operation A5 Alarm A6 Lost Data A7 Protected A8 Parity Error A9-A15 Unassigned. The interpretation of the specific codes was dependent on the type of the equipment the command was sent to.

9.1.5.2 Output on the AQ Channel

A single word was output to the AQ channel from the A register by the Output From A instruction. The peripheral equipment whose address was the content of Q had to respond with a Ready or Reject signal within four microseconds.

If no response occurred within 6 microseconds, the computer generated an internal reject signal and reinitiated execution of the instruction. If a Reply was then received, the instruction P+1 was executed. If an external Reject was received, the instruction at P+1+lowest eight bits of the output instruction. If an internal Reject was received, the instruction at P+ lowest eight bits of the output instruction.

9.1.5.3 Input on the AQ Channel

A single word was input to the A register whenever the Input To A instruction was executed. The computer signaled the request by raising a "1" signal on the read line. The peripheral equipment, whose address was contained in the Q register, responded with a Reply when the data was available in the A register.

If no data was available, the peripheral device responded with a Reject. In either case, it had to respond within 4 microseconds. If no response occurred, the computer generated an Internal Reject. A Reply caused the next instruction to be executed from P+1. If an external Reject was received, the instruction at P+1+lowest eight bits of the input instruction. If an internal Reject was received, the instruction at P+ lowest eight bits of the input instruction.

9.1.6 CDC 1705 Option

Source: CDC 1969j

If the CDC 1705 Interrupt Data Channel option was configured, it provided three additional channel types for communicating with peripheral equipment.

9.1.6.1 Interrupt Data Channel

The CDC 1705 Interrupt Data Channel (IDC) was the basic I/O path between the CPU and the peripheral equipment. It provided a multi-level interrupt system that allowed the system to assign priorities for handling different types of interrupts.

The IDC provided direct access to both the A and Q registers and to a Peripheral Equipment Channel, which transferred data via the combined AQ registers. Words were transferred through the A register at a rate of 90,000 word per second.

9.1.6.2 Buffered Data Channel

The CDC 1706 Buffered Data Channel (BDC) provided a 16-bit buffered I/O path from the CPU via the IDC to up to eight peripheral controllers. The CDC 1706 received commands from the IDC and transferred blocks of data via DMA. Up to three BDCs could be connected to a CDC 1705 via the AQ Channel. A maximum of eight devices could be connected to a BDC.

The BDC was addressed by Q11-15, denoted as CW in Figure 9-x. The contents of CW were as two digits – the C digit as binary, the W digit as hexadecimal. C was always zero since it was specifying special devices connected to the AQ Channel.

A buffered output was initiated on an output command. c(Q) was stored in the BDC, then placed on the BDC channel. c(A) was transferred to the BDC. c(A) specified the first word address minus one (FWA-1) of the data blocks to be transferred. The contents of FWA-1 specified the last word address plus one (LWA+1) of the data blocks.

The BDC transferred one word at a time to the peripheral device. It cycles repeatedly until the data block was transferred. If a Reject was received form the peripheral device, the BDC indefinitely repeats the transfer of the word until the word was accepted.

An interrupt to the computer was generated when the CDC 1706 terminated a buffered transfer of data. The interrupt was enabled by an Output To A instruction. The W field of the Q registers, bits 11-15, selected a function in the 1706. B A_{15} and A_{00} were set. When the function was performed, A15 was cleared.

A similar procedure occurred when data was to be input to the BDC from a peripheral device. In this case, c(A) specified the location in memory where the data block was to be stored, FWA-1. c(FWA-1) specified the LWA+1 of the data block. Similarly, if on input, a Reject was received from the peripheral device, the BDC repeatedly tried to transfer the word until it was accepted.

9.1.6.3 Coupling Data Channel

The CDC 1716 Coupling Data Channel provided a direct, bidirectional 16-bit data path between two CDC 1704 CPUs. It was coupled to a CDC 1705 IDC on each computer system. It also provided a buffered data channel to which up to eight peripheral controllers could be attached. A CDC 1716 could replace any or all CDC 1706s attached to the computer system. Maximum data transfer rate across the CDC 1716 was 900K characters per second. Figure 9-5 depicts the placement of the CDC 1716 between the two CDC 1704 systems

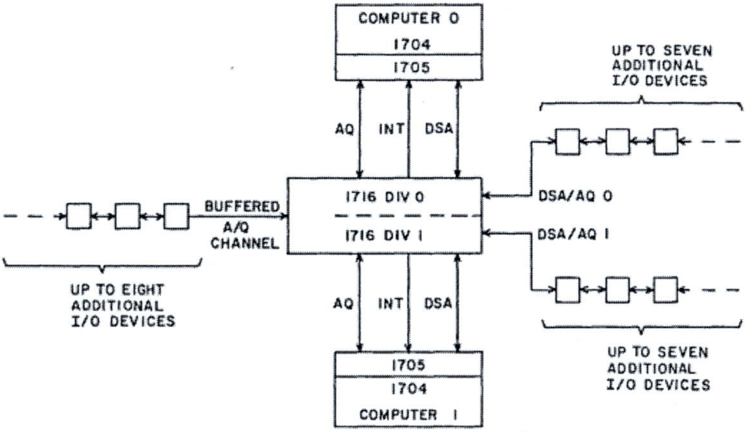

Figure 9-5 CDC 1716 Coupling Data Channel
Source: Adapted from CDC 1969j

A CDC 1716 was divided into two sections: Division 0 and Division 1. Each division was connected to a CDC 1705 IDC and a CDC 1704 CPU.

The CDC 1716 was controlled by the Input to A and Output from A instructions issued by either of the CDC 1704 computers. The operations were the same as for the CDC 1706 with the addition of the Buffered Transfer operation which effected a transfer of data between the storage of the two computers. Data transfer was mediated by the Program Protection switches on the CDC 1716 – one for each computer. When a switch was ON, only those instructions having a "1" on the protect line were recognized; all others were rejected.

A particular CDC 1716 was selected by bits 15-11 of the Q register. Bits 10-0 of the Q register selected a particular peripheral device. The contents of the A register were used to modify the operation, principally to clear and set bits or to specify flags and masks. Bit A_{00} was used to signal the End of Operation.

The CDC 1716 had one interrupt line into each of the CDC 1704 CPUs. Interrupts were generated by an End of Operation interrupt which was sent by the computer that initiated the transfer.

9.1.6.4 Satellite Coupler

The CDC 1718 Satellite Coupler provided coupling between a CDC 1700 and a CDC 3000 or 6000 series computer system. The CDC 1718 was connected to the 1705, 1706, or 1716 Data Channel. Data was transferred between the two systems in 12-bit bytes. Software was provided to allow the user to write specialized programs for transferring information between the two systems. Figure 9-6 depicts a CDC 1718 Satellite Coupler.

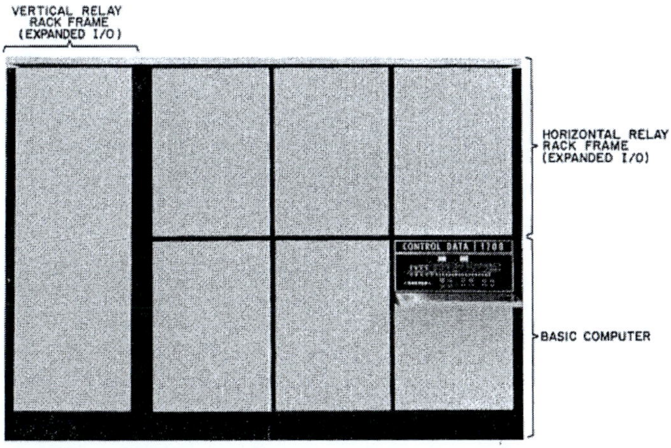

Figure 9-6. CDC 1718 Satellite Coupler
Source: CDC 1965q

Note: We use CDC 3000 as a generic reference for any model of the CDC 3000 family.

The coupler consisted of two divisions – A connected to the CDC 3000 computer and B connected to the CDC 1700 computer. To transfer data, the CDC 3000 wrote data into the Data register via Division A and the CDC 1700 read data form the Data register via Division B. Transfers from the CDC 1704 to the CDC 3000 reversed the roles of writing and reading. Each division contained an 8-bit Mask register. They shared an 8-bit Flag register. Each computer set bits in its own Mask register and either computer could set bits in the Flag register. The Flag register was used to communicate status and control between the two computer systems.

Character Mode was used to facilitate 6-bit characters from the CDC 3000 to the 8-bit CDC 1700 and vice versa. Parity was checked in transfers from Division A to Division B. A Program Protect switch controlled transfers from Division B as explained above for the CDC 1716.

Figure 9-7 depicts the CDC 1718 Control Panel.

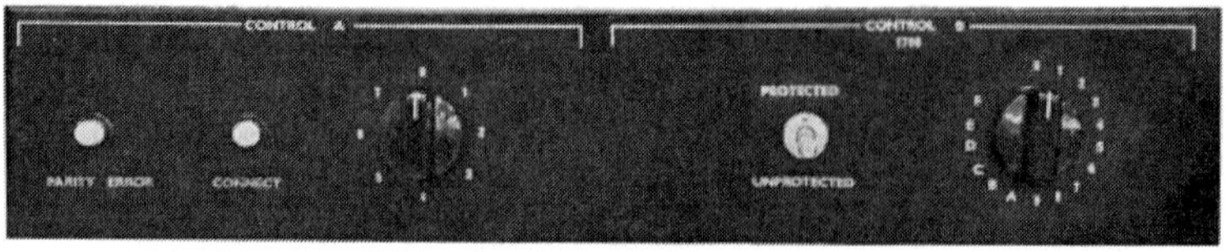

Figure 9-7. CDC 1718 Control Panel
Source: CDC 1969j

The elements of the CDC 1718 console are described in Table 9-6. It was divided into Division A on the left and Division B on the right.

Table 9-6. CDC 1718 Control Console

Switch/Indicator	Description
PARITY ERROR	A: This indicator was lit if Division A detected a parity error during transmission.
CONNECT	A: This indicator was lit when the CDC 3000 connected with Division A.
PROGRAM PROTECT	B: This switch had two positions: PROTECTED and UNPROTECTED. PROTECTED enable the program protect feature on the CDC 1704 computer system.
Equipment Number Switch	B: This 16-position switch selected the address number of Division B. Its positions were identified hexadecimally.

9.1.7 CDC 1700 CONSOLE

The CDC 1700 console is depicted in Figure 9-8. Table 9-7 describes the switches and indicators on the console.

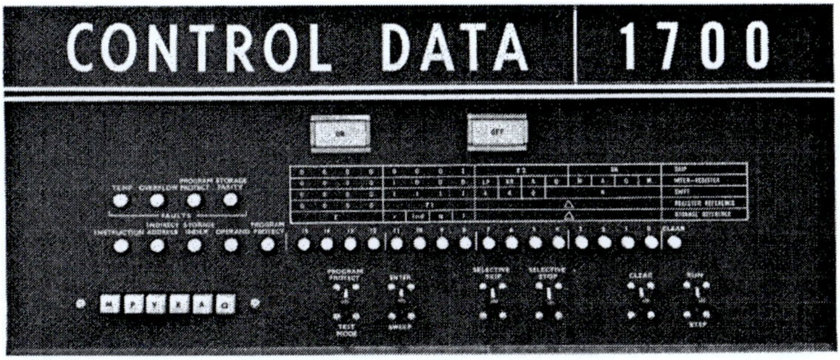

Figure 9-8. CDC 1700 Console
Source: CDC 1965q

Table 9-7. CDC 1700 Console Switches and Indicators

Switches	Description
Master Clear	A 3-position key/lever switch, which cleared CPU and peripheral equipment to initial conditions, when pressed and released. (Bottom Row Right, Left Switch).
Run/Step	A 3-position key/lever switch. When placed in the up position, the CPU began executing the program who address was in the P register. Pressing the switch down momentarily halted the computer. By repeatedly pressing the switch down, then releasing it, the operator could step through a program stopping after each storage reference.(Bottom Row Right, Right Switch).
Enter/Sweep	A 3-position switch key/lever switch. In center, no action. In up position, enter mode allowed the contents of the X register to be stored in location P+1, after which P+1 was incremented, when the RUN/STEP switch was repeatedly pressed and released. In the down position, sweep mode read the contents of location P+1 into X, then incremented P+1 every time the Run/Step switch was pressed. (Bottom Row Left, Right Switch).
Selective Stop	A 3-position key/lever switch, which either up (maintained) or down (momentary), halted the computer when a Selective Step instruction was executed. (Bottom Row Middle, Right Switch).

Selective Skip	A 3-position key/lever switch, which either up (maintained) or down (momentary) skipped a cycle, when a Selective Skip instruction was executed. (Bottom Row Middle, Left Switch).
Program Protect/ Test Mode	A 3-position key/lever switch. Up position selected program protect mode; down position caused a (1) Master Clear, (2) then executed a 100 microsecond program at location P, and then repeated 1 and 2. (Bottom Row Left, Left Switch).
Emergency Off	Pressing this button terminated all power to the computer system. (Top Row, Right Button)..
Indicators	**Description**
Registers	The X, A, Q, P, Y and M registers were available for display and data entry by pressing the appropriate button, which was lit for the selected register. (Bottom Row, Leftmost Buttons).
Program Protect	This indicator displayed the value of the program protect bit for the last storage location referenced by the computer. (Left Bottom Row, Right Indicator).
Faults	**Description** (Left Top Row Lamps)
HI TEMP	Lit when operating temperature exceeded safe limits.
OVERFLOW	Lit for arithmetic register overflow.
PROGRAM PROTECT	Lit for program protect violation.
STORAGE PARITY	Lit for parity error on storage read for operand or instruction.
Instruction Sequence Indicators	**Description** (Left Bottom Row, Leftmost Four Lamps)
Instruction	c(X) was an instruction.
Indirect Address	c(X) resulted from indirect addressing.
Storage Index	c(X) contains value of Storage Index Register.
Operand	c(X) contains the value of an operand read from or written to storage.
Reference Lamps	**Description**
15-0	These lamps indicated the contents of system registers (Middle Rows, bits 5-0 for selected system registers.

9.1.8 Peripheral Equipment

The CDC 1700 supported a full complement of peripheral equipment. All peripheral equipment had a Program Protect switch on their respective consoles which should be set if a protected program was running and the equipment was essential to that program.

9.1.8.1 CDC 1711 Teletypewriter

The CDC 1711 Teletypewriter served as the operator's console for the system and supported manual insertion of day and instructions directly in the CDC 1700's memory. The operator communicates with the operating system by typing commands and the console and receiving messages and results from the operating system. The integrated printer provides a hard copy of all communications between the operator and the operating system.

9.1.8.2 CDC 1746 Single Station Entry Display

The CDC 1746-1 Single Station Entry Display was a CRT device that displayed a 6-inch page on an 18-inch tube. The page consisted of 20 lines of 50 alphanumeric and special ASCII characters each. The CDC 1746 was attached to the CDC 1706 BDC via a controller which contained a 1000-character buffer and a character generator.

9.1.8.3 CDC 1732 Magnetic Tape Controller

The CDC 1732 Magnetic Tape Controller (MTC) handled I/O operations for up to eight CDC 608/609 Magnetic Tape Drives. The MTC was attached to the CDC 1700 via any of the data channels described in Section 9.1.4. The CDC 608 was a 7-track magnetic tape drive, while the CDC 609 was a 9-track drive.

9.1.8.4 CDC 1738-B Disk Drive Controller

Mass storage consisted of one or more CDC 853/854 Disk Storage Drive (DSD) units each with a capacity of 7.2 Mbytes. These were attached to a CDC 1738-B Disk Drive Controller (DDC). Figure 9-9 depicts the connection to the CDC 1704.

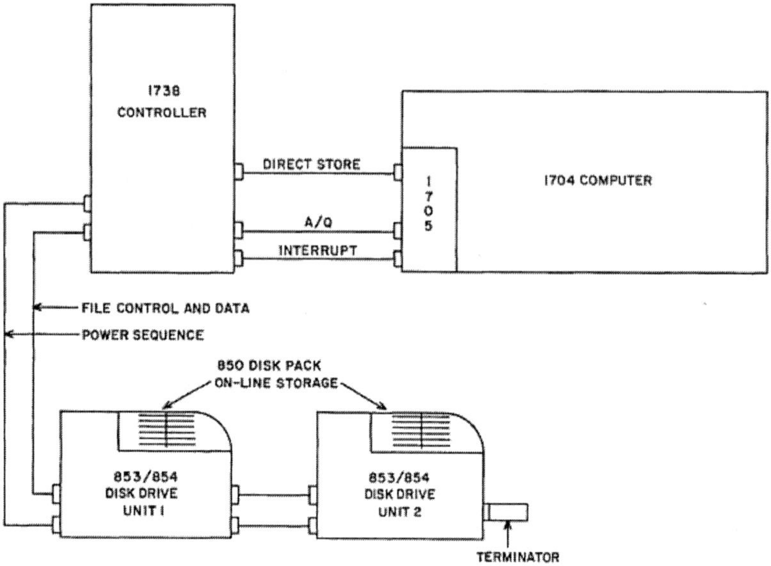

Figure 9-9. CDC 1738-B Disk Controller Configuration
Source: CDC 1969j

The CDC 1738-B controlled one or more free-standing Disk Storage Drives. The disk drives used multi-platter disk packs for storage. The six platters provided ten surfaces for recording data. The CDC 1704 computer issued instructions to the CDC 1738-B to handle I/O operations.

Three interfaces were used to communicate with the CDC 1738-B DDC:

1. A/Q Interface, which was used to transmit function codes and address data to the DDC and receive back status and address data.
2. Direct Storage Interface, which was used for all data transfer the DDC and the computer. It also transferred the Last Word Address+1 (LWA+1), which specified the end of the memory area where data was to be read from or stored to.
3. Controller/File Interface, which was used to select the file, track, and cylinder where data was stored and transfer the difference count. It also transferred serial data between the DDC and the computer.

Record Addressing

Records in a file were addressed by a 16-bit address, called the Sector Record Address (SRA), sent to the DDC. The SRA contained the sector number, the head/surface number, and the cylinder number. The format of this address is depicted in Figure 9-10.

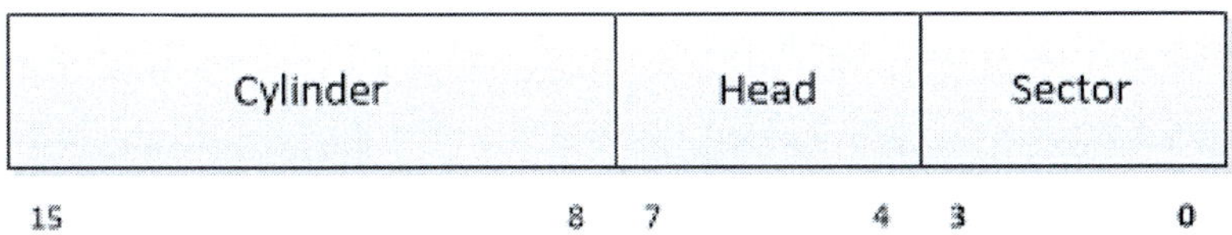

Figure 9-10. SRA Format
Source: Adapted from CDC 1969j

The Cylinder number was 0-99 for the CDC 853 and 0-202 for the CDC 854. The Head number was 0-10 and the Sector number was 0-15.

Each Sector Record was assigned a unique address in the file. The record address tags were written into the sector using the format for a sector shown in Figure 9-11.

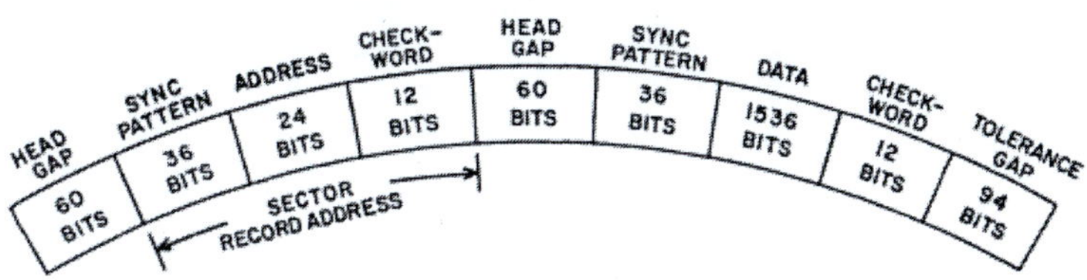

Figure 9-11. DSD Sector Format
Source: CDC 1969j

As seen in Figure 9-x, the sector address was included the lead part of the sector. Head gaps followed by synchronization patterns were used to ensure that the head arrived over the proper location at the right time. The size of the head gap was due to the physical characteristics of the disk drives. Each sector stored 128 12-bit words of data with check words for parity.

Direct Storage Access

The DDC had direct access to core storage. The LWA+1 was loaded into the DD. It was also held in the Storage Address Register (SAR) to be compare with the current address. The initial current address was FWA-1, which was loaded form the A/Q interface. The current address incremented by one very time a word was placed into storage. When the current address equaled LWA+1, the End of Operation status bit was set, which signaled the CPU that the specified operation had completed.

Function Codes

The function codes for the Output from A and Input to A instructions are presented in Table 9-8.

Table 9-8. Function Codes

Code	Description
	Output From A
001	Director Function: c(A) bits are used to select interrupts and the drive unit.
010	Load Address: c(A) specified the Sector Record Address (SRA). The SRA was loaded into the DDC File Address register. The difference between the current and requested cylinder was determined and transferred the difference and the new cylinder address to the DSD unit. The DDC then initiated the repositioning of the drive head to the new cylinder.
011	Write: c(A) contained FWA-1. Data was transferred from core storage to the DSD. When the current address equaled LWA+1, the operation was completed. If the transfer stopped within a sector, the controlled padded the rest of the sector with zeroes and the check word. If the transfer moved beyond the last sector of the cylinder, then the DDC moved the heads to the new cylinder and continued the transfer. An Address Error resulted if the transfer moved beyond the last cylinder.
100	Read: c(A) contained FWA-1. Data was read in from file storage. On each read, the current address was compared with LWA+1. The operation stopped when the buffer limits were reached. The controller will read to the last word in the sector. If the data does not compare, the No compare bit was set.
101	Compare: c(A) contained FWA-1. Data read from file storage was compared with data read from core storage. The comparison stopped when the buffer limits were reached. Otherwise, a status bit was set.

110	Checkword Check: c(A) specifies the Sector Record Address (SRA). All sectors in the track were read by the controller specified by c(A). The End of Operation status was set if no errors occurred.
111	Write Address: c(A) specifies the Sector Record Address (SRA). If the ADDRESS WRITE switch was set, then the DDC wrote tags in all tracks specified by c(A).
	Input to A
001	Director Status: A received the status condition of the DDC and DSD unit.
010	Address Register Status: A received the File Register A (FRA) status.

Table 9-9 presents the status bit assignments when loaded into register A by Function Code 001 under Input to A.

Table 9-9. DDC Status Bit Assignments

Bit	Status
15	Not Used
14	Protect Fault
13	Storage Parity Error
12	Defective Track
11	Address Error
10	Seek Error
9	Lost Data
8	Checkword Error
7	Protected
6	No Compare
5	Alarm
4	End of Operation
3	On Cylinder
2	Interrupt
1	Busy
0	Ready

The program selected the controller and the DSD via the Director function. The code 001 and the DSD number are loaded into the D and E fields of the Q register. All I/O operations were initiated by an Output From A instruction. Additional information for the DDC was contained in the A register. The computer checked the status via an Input To A instruction. The DSD number was stored in Q_{7-10} with all other bits zero.

9.1.8.5 CDC 10128 Dual Mode Option

The CDC 10128 Dual Mode Option (DMO) allowed a CDC 1700 computer system to communicate with a CDC 3000 series machine via a CDC 1748 or CDC 3316 Multiplex Controllers. This enabled the two machines in a network to receive the same data simultaneously and store it to prevent the loss of data due to machine failure or network problems.

9.2 CDC 1700 Instruction Set

Source: CDC 1974a

The CDC 1700 had different instruction formats for different classes of operations. The source form presented to either of the CDC 1700 assemblers had the following form:

Location Opcode Address Comment

which will be seen in the examples in the following sections.

9.2.1 Storage Reference Instructions

Storage Reference Instructions used core for its operands. Because of the 16-bit word size, some two-word instructions were used to fully address all of memory. The format of the Storage Reference Instructions is depicted in Figure 9-12. Table 9-10 describes the fields of these instructions.

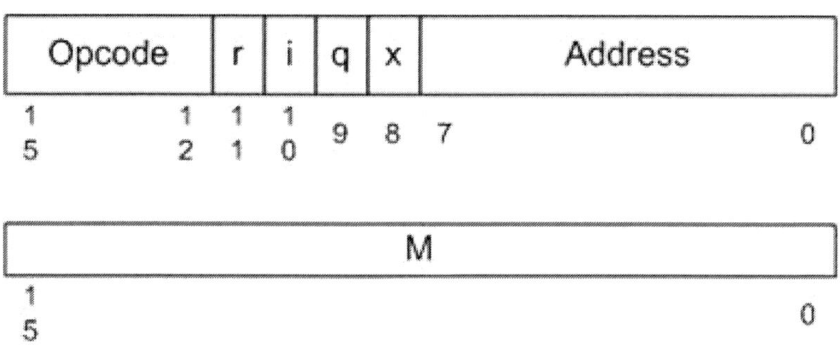

Figure 9-12. Storage Reference Instruction Format
Source: Adapted from CDC 1974a

Table 9-10 SR Instruction Fields

Field	Description
r	relative address flag
i	indirect address flag
q	index register q flag
x	index register 2 at $00FF_{16}$
address	non-zero if local addressing; 0 if two-word instruction format was used.
M	In two-word instructions, the memory address to be accessed.

The effective address was computed from the r, i and address bits in the instruction.

The storage reference instructions are presented in Table 9-11.

The CDC 1700 had two indexing registers: index register 1 was the Q register and index register 2 was memory location FF_{16}. A base address could be modified by one or both of the index registers to form the effective address. Using index register 2 required an extra memory cycle to fetch the value from FF_{16}. Index register values were treated as signed 15-bit quantities.

In the following, EA refers to the effective address.

In the arithmetic instructions, the OVERFLOW indicator was set if the magnitude of the result exceeded the capacity of the target register.

Table 9-11. CDC 1700 Storage Reference Instructions

Opcode	Mnemonic	Description
1	JMP	Jump: PC <- EA.
2	MUI	Multiply: A,Q <- c(A) * c(EA).
3	DVI	Divide Integer: A,Q <- c(A)/c(EA).
4	STQ	Store Q: EA <- c(Q).
5	RTJ	Return Jump: PC <- c(EA).
6	STA	Store A: EA <- c(A).
7	SPA	Store A, Parity to A: EA <- c(A); A <- Parity.
8	ADD	Add to A: A <- c(A) + c(EA).
9	SUB	Subtract from A: A <- c(A) - c(EA).
A	AND	And with A: A <- c(A) AND c(EA).
B	EOR	Exclusive OR with A: A <- c(A) XOR c(EA).
C	LDA	Load A: A <- c(EA).
D	RAO	Replace and Add 1 in Storage: EA <- c(EA) + 1.
E	LDQ	Load Q: Q <- c(EA).
F	ADQ	Add to Q: Q <- c(Q) + c(EA).

Suppose we wanted to add together a set of numbers at memory addresses 1000 through 1002. This simple routine does that:

```
TEMP        0        0
START       LDA+     $1000
            ADD      $1001
            ADD      $1002
            STA*     TEMP
```

But, if the set of numbers was larger, in memory addresses 1000 to 2000, we could use the following routine:

```
TEMP        0        0
START       LDQ      =X$2000-$1000     Difference in Q
            LDA+     $1000
LOOP        ADD+     $1000,Q           Index by Q
            ADQ      =N-1              Decrement Q
            SQZ      DONE-*-1          Finished?
            JMP*     LOOP              No
DONE        STA*     LOOP              OK
```

9.2.2 Skip Instructions

Skip Instructions made conditional tests and skipped forward in the program depending on whether the instruction's operand(s) met the actual condition being tested. The format for these instructions appears below:

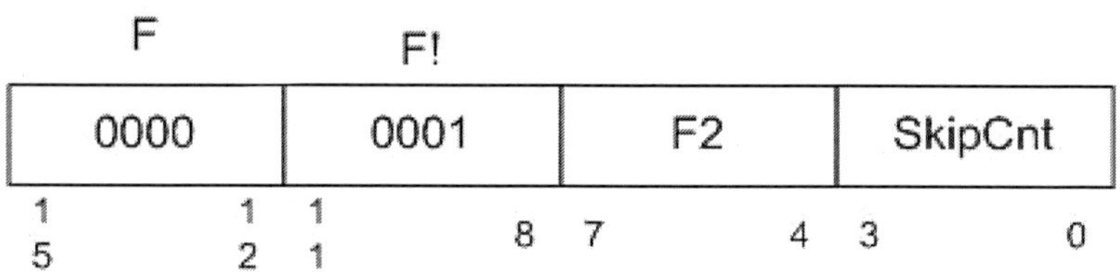

Figure 9-13. Skip Instruction Format
Source: Adapted from CDC 1974a

Fields F and F! have constant values. Field F2 indicates the subinstruction in the Skip class. SkipCnt specifies the number of words to skip from the present address. It was treated as a positive value from 0 … 15, so skips only occur in a forward direction.

Table 9-12. CDC 1700 Skip Instructions

F2	Mnemonic	Description
0	SAZ	Skip On Zero: Skip if c(A) = 0.
1	SAN	Skip not Zero: Skip if c(A) /= 0.
2	SAP	Skip if Positive: Skip if c(A) >= 0.
3	SAM	Skip if Negative: Skip if c(A) < 0
4	SQZ	Skip On Zero: Skip if c(Q) = 0.
5	SQN	Skip not Zero: Skip if c(Q) /= 0.
6	SQP	Skip if Positive: Skip if c(Q) >= 0.
7	SQM	Skip if Negative: Skip if c(Q) < 0
8	SWS	Skip Switch On
9	SWN	Skip Switch Off
A	SOV	Skip Overflow
B	SNO	Skip No Overflow
C	SPE	Skip On Parity Error
D	SNP	Skip No Parity Error
E	SPF	Skip on Protect Fault
F	SNF	Skip No Protect Fault

The Skip Switch was on the programmer's console and allowed the programmer to select alternate paths in a program at runtime.

9.2.3 Shift Instructions

Shift Instructions shifted the data bit by bit either in the A register or the Q register singly or together. The data can be shifted either left or right bit by bit. For these instructions the format appears below:

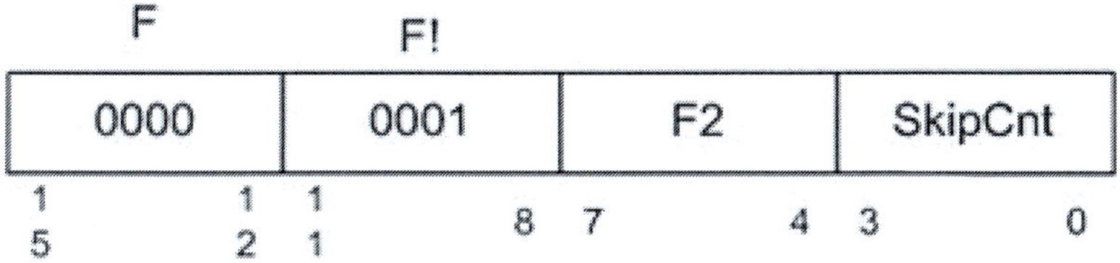

Figure 9-14. CDC 1700 Shift Instruction Format
Source: Adapted from CDC 1974a

Bit 5 selects the Q register.
Bit 6 selects the A register
Bit 7 determines whether the shift was left or right.

If both were set, the A and Q Registers were shifted as a pair. The shift count was 5 bits which allowed a shift in 31 positions when applied to the AQ register pair. Left shifts were end-around while right shifts were end-off with sign extension.

Notice there was just one shift instruction which was parameterized by bits 5 through 8. Table 9-13 presents the mnemonics and bit settings.

Table 9-13. CDC 1700 Shift Instructions

Bits 5-7	Mnemonic	Description
010	ARS	A Right Shift by SkipCnt.
001	QRS	Q Right Shift by SkipCnt.
011	LRS	Long Right Shift of QA by SkipCnt.
110	ALS	A Left Shift by SkipCnt.
101	QLS	Q Left Shift by SkipCnt.
111	LLS	Long Left Shift of QA by SkipCnt.

9.2.4 Interregister Instructions

The Interregister Instructions performed arithmetic or logical manipulation with the contents of the A, Q or M registers or any combination of the three. The format for this class of instruction is:

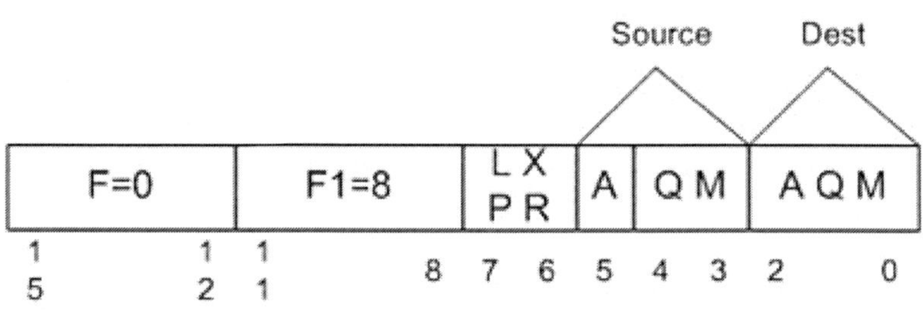

Figure 9-15. CDC 1700 Interregister Instruction Format
Source: Adapted from CDC 1974a

Bits 6-7 were used as follows:

- LP was the logical product indicator.

- XR was the exclusive OR indicator.

Most instructions had two operands. Operand 1 was the A register. If bit 5 was 0, the operand was FFFF, else it was the content of the A register. Operand 2 was selected by the combination of bits 3 and 4 as indicated in Table 9-14.

Table 9-14. Source Operand Selection

Bit 3	Bit 4	Operand
0	0	FFFF
0	1	M
1	0	Q
1	1	Q v M

The destination register was selected by bits 0–2. The operator selection was controlled by bits 6 and 7 as indicated by the following table.

Table 9-15. Operator Selection

LP:Bit 6	XR:Bit 7	Operation
0	0	Arithmetic Sum
0	1	Exclusive OR
1	0	Logical Product
1	1	Complement of Logical Product

Using these entries, the total number of possible instructions was 22 as given by Table 9-16. Let R be the destination register selected as above.

Table 9-16. Interregister Instructions

Opcode	Mnemonic	Description
40	CLR	Clear Register:
A0	TTRA	Transfer A: R <- c(A)
90	TRQ	Transfer Q: R <- c(Q)
88	TRM	Transfer M: R <- c(M)
98	TRB	Transfer Q v M: R <- c(Q) v c(M)
80	SET	Set to Ones: R <- '1's
60	TCA	Transfer Complement A: R <- NOT c(A)
50	TCQ	Transfer Complement Q: R <- NOT c(Q)
48	TCM	Transfer Complement M: R <- NOT c(M)

58	TCB	Transfer Complement Q v M: R <- NOT c(Q v M)
39	AAQ	Add A and Q: R <-c(A) + c(Q)
28	AAM	Add A and M: R <-c(A) + c(M)
38	AAB	Add A and (Q v M): R <-c(A) + c(Q v M)
70	EAQ	Exclusive OR of A and Q: R <- c(A) XOR c(Q)
68	EAM	Exclusive OR of A and M: R <- c(A) XOR c(M)
78	EAB	Exclusive OR of A and Q v M: R <- c(A) XOR c(Q v M)
B0	LAQ	AND A and Q: R <-c(A) AND c(Q)
A8	LAM	AND A and M: R <-c(A) AND c(M)
B8	LAB	AND A and (Q v M): R <-c(A) AND c(Q v M)
F0	CAQ	Complement AND A and Q: R <-c(A) AND c(Q)
E8	CAM	Complement AND A and M: R <-c(A) AND c(M)
F8	CAB	Complement AND A and (Q v M): R <-c(A) AND c(Q v M)

Register transfers could be accomplished by setting both LP and XR to zero and either operand 1 or operand 2 to $FFFF_{16}$.

Magnitude comparisons could be accomplished by setting both LP and XR to zero, selecting no destination register, and testing the OVERFLOW indicator.

Complementing registers could be accomplished by setting LP to zero, XR to one and either operand 1 or operand 2 to $FFFF_{16}$.

9.2.5 Register Reference Instructions

The Register Reference Instructions required one-word. The F field was always a zero and the Fl field will signify the instruction within this class. The format for the Register Reference Class of instructions is:

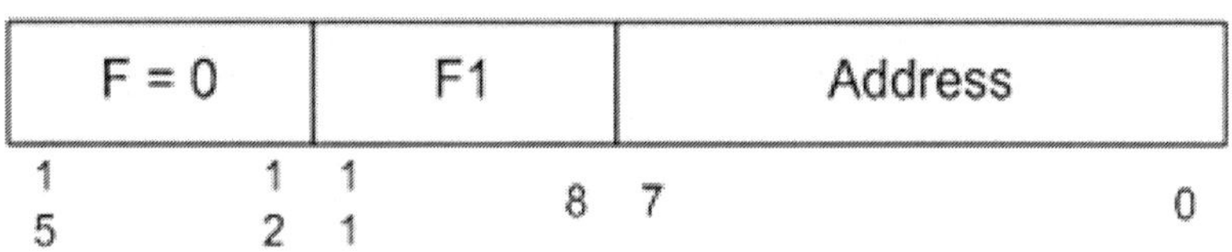

Figure 9-16. Register Reference Instruction Format
Source: Adapted from CDC 1974a

Table 9-17 describes the instructions in this class. For some instructions, bits 0-7 were treated as a number or arithmetic operations and referred to as 'delta'.

Table 9-17. Register Reference Instructions

F1	Mnemonic	Description
0	SLS	Selective Stop: stops the computer if the STOP switch was on.
1		I/O Instructions
2	INP	Input to A: Read one word from an external device into the A register.
3	OUT	Output from A: Write one word from a to an external device.
4	EIN	Enable Interrupts: Activates the interrupt system.
5	IIN	Inhibit Interrupts: disables the interrupt system.
6	SPB	Set Program Protect: Sets program bit specified by Q to one.
7	CPB	Clear Program Protect: Sets program bit specified by Q to zero.
8		Interregister Instructions.
9	INA	Increase A: Increase A <- c(A) + delta.
A	ENA	Enter A: a <- delta.
B	NOP	No Operation: Uses a machine cycle to fetch next instruction.
C	ENQ	Enter Q: Q <- delta.
D	INQ	Increase Q: Q <- c(Q) + delta.
E	EXI	Exit Interrupt State: Returns from an interrupt handler to a previously executing program – user or OS.

For INP and OUT instructions, c(Q) selected the specific peripheral device. If the device sent a reply, the next instruction was taken from c(P)+1.

9.2.6 Jump Instructions

Jump Instructions changed the current program execution sequence of instructions to a new sequence at a different location in storage. Table 9-18 describes the instructions in this class.

Table 9-18. Jump Instructions

F	Mnemonic	Description
1	JMP	Jump to the effective address to fetch the next instruction, e.g., P <- EA.
5	RTJ	Return Jump: Return from a subprogram. EA <- P+1 or P+2; P <- EA + 1.

9.3 Mass Storage Operating System

The Mass Storage Operating System (MSOS) was the primary CDC 1700 operating system for use with disc-based systems. This operating system evolved as it was adapted to the System 17/18 family of computer systems. Primary programming languages were assembly, and FORTRAN. Pascal was available via a cross-compiler from a CDC 6000 series computer system. It will be described in Section 10.3.

9.4 CDC 1700 and Ticketron

Source: Dubner and Abate 1970; https://en.wikipedia.org/wiki/Ticketron

TICKETRON was a real-time system for making reservation and distributing printed tickets at remote terminals for the entertainment industry. In effect, it was an extension to the box office concept in that it could be accessed from remote locations. It consisted of three central facilities located in New York, Chicago, and Los Angeles. Each facility could support around 900 terminals and could handle sales of almost 50,000 tickets per hour. The main office was located at the Beverly Hilton Hotel on Wilshire Boulevard in Los Angeles, California.

CDC acquired most of the parent corporation Ticket Reservations Systems (TRS) in 1969. When Computicket, owned by Computer Science Corporation (CSC) folded in 1970, Ticketron was the sole computerized ticketing provider in the US. CDC acquired the remaining asset from Cemp Investments to become the sole owner.

A remote terminal consisted of a keyboard, a ticket printer, and a receive-only teletype. A customer could visit a remote station to make inquiries about the availability of a performance. The terminal operator accessed the system locate the desired information. A teletype message indicated what seats were available. The user could select the seats he or she wanted. The operator used the system to sell the seats. Once the customer paid for them, the ticket printer printed out the tickets purchased by the user.

With direct access to the seat inventory for a performance, the customer was guaranteed the best availability seats at the time. The system also printed out certain management reports for the operators of the terminals.

9.4.1 System Architecture

The TICKETRON central system architecture consisted of four major elements (Dubner and Abate):

1. Remoter terminals with their communications networks;
2. Line controllers and buffers;
3. Processing unit and core storage; and
4. Auxiliary storage with connecting data channels.

The Central System was based on a duplexed CDC 1700 computer system used to provide a distribute the processing load. One system handled communications while the other processed messages. The front-end system performed the communication functions and managed the line buffers. The back-end system examined the messages and processed them. The processing system configuration was duplicated to provide reliability.

Each processor had 32K words of memory. Each processor had a CDC 1713 Typewriter console by which the operator communicated with the system. A CDC 1751 magnetic drum with a capacity of 512K words hosted the system software. Application data was maintained on four CDC 854magnetic disks with 3.1M words capacity each. Two CDC 601 magnetic tape units held near-line data and were also used to load up new versions of the system software to the magnetic drum. A CDC 1729 card reader was used to make intermediate updates to the system software and provide addition data.

Communications was handled by a separate CDC 1770 processor with 20K words attached to each processor and switched between the full duplex I/ lines.

System peripherals were connected to the two systems by a dual-pole, single position switch which allowed either one of the computers to access them at a time A CDC at a time. Two CDC 1716 Coupling Data Channel provided redundant communications between the two processors. A CDC 1742 300 lpm Line Printer and a CDC 1722/1724 Paper Tape Reader and Punch were shared between the two systems via a dual-pole, single position switch.

9.4.2 System Software

The TICKETRON system software consisted of three program modules: the communications program, the message processing program, and the on-line utility program.

The communications program, resident in the front-end processor, accepts input from the terminals and placed it in the input buffers and sent data from the output buffers to the remote terminals. Each communication line had its own input and output buffers.

The message processing module was organized as a single thread processing system. It received messages from the input buffers, processed them, and placed response messages in the output buffers. It only accepted another message after it had finished processing the current one. This placed a high value on short processing times for messages in order to have high thruput. To select a message, the program scanned the input queue. If it found a full buffer, it checked to see if the output buffer was not empty, and, if it was, it moved to another communications line. If it found no messages awaiting processing, it exited to the main scheduling module to execute a loop that continually checked for new input.

All program modules were written in FORTRAN because it offered the following advantages (Dubner and Abate):

- Minimized programming cost and time;
- Enabled machine independence;
- Was partially self-documenting;
- Was easy to modify; and
- Allowed easy communication between subroutines.

9.4.3.1 Overview

TICKETRON was an example of a stochastic, real-time service system. Inputs occurred at random, and generated service requests to be processed which varied in type based on the inputs. Throughput was the principal consideration in system design coupled with a reasonable response time given the communications lines. The designers focused on avoiding congestion which could lead to near system shutdown.

9.4.3.2 Communications Program

The TICKETRON system was expected to support over 500 terminals, which led the designers to design the communications subsystem as the critical element of the overall system. Communications was handled via the following functions:

- Iterating though a polling list which was dynamically maintained;
- Efficient transfer of messages between the terminals and the main processing program;
- Maintaining the physical status of terminals connected to the system; and
- Distinguishing between physical message errors as opposed to message content errors.

Associated with each I/O line were two input buffers and two output buffers. The system issued a poll on a line only if one of the input buffers was available to accept a message. Further, the system would only start processing a message if an output buffer was available to accept data to be sent to a terminal. This approach avoided congestion on individual I/O lines.

Each I/O line was full duplex transmitting asynchronously. The system output 9 bits per character (1 start bit, 6 data bits, 1 parity bit, and one 1 stop) at 1200 baud and input 7 bits per character (1 start bit, 4 data bits, 1 parity bit, and 1 stop bit).

Only four bits was required on input because the terminal was configured with function keys and special codes for ordering tickets. Every input message was a fixed size of 19 characters.

If the transmit button was pressed when a poll was issued, a character was transmitted to the front-end processor.

9.4.3 Operation

The TICKETRON system evolved over time. Initially, it was aimed at the New York theater and sports events advanced sales. The first system had 50 to 100 terminals selling some 50,000 tickets per day. Each CDC 1700 had 16K words of memory, two hard disk drives with 3.1 million words each, two magnetic tapes, a console teletype, and communications hardware support 16 voice grade, 1200-baud lines. This system became operational in March 1968.

Soon, it became apparent that sporting events used more of the system capacity. The number of communications lines was increased to 32 and core storage was increased to 32K words. This system handled 500 terminals and ticket sales of over 100,000 per day. A magnetic drum was added to store and serve up high-frequency file usage for the inventory for same day sporting events. This system became operational in January 1969.

A later enhancement, circa 1970, increased communications line to 56 and the communication processor was replaced with a newer model to handle 900 terminals. The magnetic drum size was increased to 512K words and two additional disks were added.

The TICKETRON system continued to evolved with newer and different computer systems. It operated until 1990, when its industry position was overtaken by Ticketmaster. Its assets were sold to Ticketmaster after its market share decreased below 40% (https://en.wikipedia.org/wiki/Ticketron).

9.4.4 TICKETRON Assessment

The early ticket processing systems, such as TICKETRON led the way to interactive communication with remote systems and pioneered some of the key techniques in real-time processing of data. They pioneered a new application of computing as the hardware and software evolved, which made it easier for people to accomplish simple tasks. Such point-of-sale systems swiftly expanded to many other areas of commerce and were early exemplars of eCommerce.

9.5 CDC 1700 Assessment

The CDC 1700 was the first "minicomputer" created by CDC in that it started out as a data processing system, but evolved to a multi-user system. Its competition was the IBM 14xx series, early Honeywell machines, and others of the late 1960s and early 1970s. Smaller than the CDC 1604 and, perhaps, somewhat less powerful, its use of CDC 6600 technology made it a strong competitor except that it was priced considerably more than competing machines.

The CDC 1700 was also used as a front-end processor for the CDC 6x00/7600/Cyber machines to handle the unit record peripherals and allow the PPs to focus on mass storage operations.

A CDC 1700 emulator was added to the SIMH package (https://virtuallyfun.com/2016/07/26/cdc-1700-emulator-added-to-simh/), which can boot and run a version of MSOS 5.

CHAPTER TEN

CYBER 17/18 SERIES

The Cyber 17 was an enhanced version of the CDC 1700 that increased the memory size to 64K words. It had a cycle time of 0.9 microseconds, which was reduced to 0.6 microseconds in later models. It was a microprogrammed machine.

10.1 CYBER 17 SERIES

Source: CDC 1973cu

The System 17 was the enhanced successor to the CDC 1700 system. It was targeted for many types of applications, but particularly for industrial control. As a general-purpose computer system, it could be used to do accounting, data processing, and laboratory analysis, and engineering and scientific calculations as the primary system for a small business or departmental-level system as an element of a larger organization's computing suite.

The Cyber 17 was a minicomputer intended as a system for growing organizations. A Cyber 17 could also be used as a remote subsystem to act as a front end to a CDC 6600/7600 system. In this role, it supported on-site batch submission with output delivered to the Cyber 17 for printing or punching. The Cyber 17 could support and control the submission of jobs to be executed on the CDC 6600/7600 systems.

Figure 10-1 depicts a Cyber 17 Console. Figure 10-2 depicts typical Cyber 17 system. This incorporates supports the processor, memory, magnetic tape drive, and power supply in the tall cabinet and the removablel disk drive in the small cabinet. The table supports a video display terminal as the operator's console along with a small impact printer. Note the relative size of this system to the CDC 160A and the CDC 1604.

Figure 10-1. CDC Cyber 17 Console
Source" CDC 1973cu

Figure 10-2. Cyber 17 System
Source: CDC 1973cu

Since the Cyber 17 was succeeded by the Cyber with a year or so, further discussion will be focused on the Cyber 18.

10.2 Cyber 18 Series

The Cyber 18 was an enhanced version of the Cyber 17 that increased memory size to 128K words in the largest model and operated at a faster speed. It had a cycle time of 0.75 microseconds. It also had eight GPRs and several instructions to support timesharing operation. It ran an enhanced version of MSOS 5. (CDC 1976s)

The Cyber 18 family consisted of four models as depicted in Table 10-1.

Table 10-1. Cyber 18 Models

Feature	18-05	18-10M	18-20	18-30
# Processors	1	1	1	2
Memory (Kbytes)	16	32-128	32-256	64-512
Memory Type	Core	MOS	MOS	MOS
# Operator Stations	1	5	16	
Peripherals	Limited	Full	Full	Full
Line Printer (lpm)		300	600	600
Disk System	One diskette and controller	17.6M byte disk cartridge system.	200M byte SMD	200M byte SMD
Operating System	Batch	MSOS/ RTOS	Enhanced MSOS 5	Enhanced MSOS 5

The Cyber 18-05 was a processor used primarily to process data to and from peripherals and computers on a terminal communications network. It could service multiple lines and served as a telecommunications line data concentrator. The Cyber 18-10 was a small processor used primarily to emulate the CDC 1700 with improve performance as a transitional system to the larger Cyber 18 systems.

The Cyber 18 microprograms were stored in a 512-word micromemory. The microprocessor emulated a CDC 1700 computer system. Each microprogram instruction was treated as a jump to a micromemory location that contained the routine to emulate the instruction.

An operator console, typically, a Teletype-like console or a CDC video console through

The Cyber 18-30 was a later version of the basic Cyber 18. The CPU and memory had been assigned to their own cabinet on the left end while the system console had its own cabinet with a card reader on top.

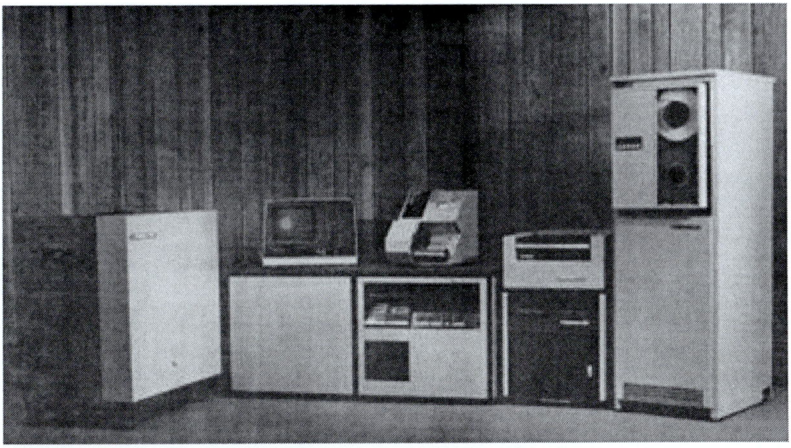

Figure 10-3. Cyber 18-30 Computer System
Source: CDC 1976s

One difference between the CDC 1700 and the Cyber 17/18, which may confuse readers, was that the CDC 1700 documentation referred to the MSB as bit 15 and the LSB as bit 0. However, the Cyber 17/18 referred to bit 0 as the MSB and but 15 as the LSB.

10.2.1 CYBER 18 IO SYSTEMS

Interrupt handling in the Cyber 18 was a slightly enhanced version of the interrupt system for the Cyber 17. Before an interrupt could be recognized, the mask bit for that interrupt type had to be examined to determine if the interrupt should be handled. A detailed examination of the interrupt system was provided in CDC 1983y.

10.2.1.1 MASK AND STATUS MODE REGISTERS

The Cyber 18 had two Mask Registers, labeled M1 and M2, which received bits from the ALU. M1 was used to enable microinterrupts and M2 was used to enable macrointerrupts. The purpose of a mask registers was to enable and disable interrupt handling. When an interrupt occurred, the corresponding bit in the mask register was checked to determine if the interrupt should be recognized (e.g., enabled).

The Status Mode Registers, SM1 and SM2, allowed the microcode to control the mode of operation and provide the status of internal and external conditions. Each register had 16 bits which were set by outputs from the ALU.

10.2.1.2 Interrupt register

The Interrupt Register had a bit for each interrupt line configured in the Cyber 18 system. It held the active interrupts with the highest priority interrupt identified at bit 15. If the appropriate bit in the mask register was set corresponding to the interrupt requesting service, the interrupt would eventually be handled based on its priority.

10.2.1.3 Interrupt Instructions

Three instructions controlled the interrupt system: EIN, IIN, and EXI. Enable Interrupt (EIN) caused the interrupt system to be enabled, which allowed interrupts to be possibly recognized and handled. Once enabled, interrupts that occurred would be handled in priority order. EIN could only be executed when the PROTECT bit was set. Attempting to execute EIN when the PROTECT switch on the console was set caused an illegal instruction error to occur.

The Cyber series was designed so that one instruction would be executed after an EIN instruction. This simplified interrupt routines.

The Inhibit Interrupts (IIN) instruction caused the interrupt system to b disabled. The IIN instruction had to be executed with the PROTECT switch set.

The Exit Interrupt (EXI) instruction was always the last instruction to be executed in an interrupt handler. The reason for this was that new interrupts could have occurred, e.g., setting their bits in the Interrupt Register, and thus might have priority than other bits that had been set previously. Alternatively, if no other interrupts were waiting to be recognized, control returned to the previously executing program. The EXI instruction had to be executed with the PROTECT switch set.

10.2.1.4 Interrupt Trap Region

The Interrupt Trap Region was a block of memory of 64 words reserved for the sixteen interrupts handled in the system beginning at 01008 and ending at 013F8. Each interrupt had four words assigned to it. The format of the interrupt blocks was described in Table 10-2.

Table 10-2. Interrupt Block Description

Word	Description
1	P Register Storage
2	Return Jump of the Interrupt handler
3	New Mask Register contents
4	Address of the interrupt handler

10.2.1.5 INTERRUPT PROCESSOR

An Interrupt Processor (IP) processed interrupts of a particular type (also known as an *interrupt handler*). Each interrupt type had its own interrupt handler. The last instruction of an interrupt handler had to be the EXI instruction, which cause a jump back to word 1 of the interrupt where the contents of the P register were stored. This value was used to restore the P register which caused the computer to continue with the execution of the interrupted program.

Figure 10-4 depicts the state after an interrupt occurs.

```
PROGRAM EXAMPLE:  M = 0008

Main Program

3000        0400 (EIN)
3001        XXXX
3002        XXXX
3003        XXXX        "Interrupt on line 3"
                  <--------------------------
3004        XXXX

Interrupt Trap Region (For state 3)

010C        0000
010D        RTJ
010E        Priority Level
010F        Address of interrupt processor
```

Figure 10-4. After an interrupt occurred.
Source: CDC 1983y

Since bit 12 of M was set, the interrupt on line 3 was recognized and the main program halted. The next instruction that would have been executed was at location 3004, so it would be stored in word 1 at location 010C. The next instruction was located at 010D; it was usually a jump to a common interrupt handler, which was depicted in Figure 10-5.

5000	Address of next instruction in trap region 010F stored here.
5001	STA
5002	STQ
5003	XXXX
5004	XXXX
5005	XXXX
5006	JMP

Figure 10-5. Common Interrupt Handler
Source: CDC 1983y

The A, Q and X registers were stored; the Mask Register was replaced by the contents of the ITR word 3, which was located at 010E. The last instruction was the jump to the interrupt handler whose address was located at 010F.

10.2.2 I/O Operations

In the Cyber 18, there were three modes of I/O operation: the CDC 1700 A/Q, the M05 set/sample mode, and the automatic data transfer (ADT) mode. The Cyber 18_20 was the developed by CDC and NCR (National Cash Register), so it includes I/O modes from both companies.

10.2.2.1 A/Q Mode

The A/Q mode uses the input (INP) and output (OUT) instructions direct from the A register. Prior to I/O, the Q register was loaded with the address of the peripheral sending or receiving data. The A register contained data, status, or functions depending on the value of the director bits in Q. Table 10-3 presents the use of the director bits in A.

Table 10-3. Use of Director Bits

Director Bit	INP	OUT
0	Read Data	Write Data
1	Read Status	Writ Function

The status and function bit assignments were similar to the CDC 1700 in Tables 9-4 and 9-5 except for the different numbering of MSB and LSB.

10.2.2.2 M05 Set/Sample Mode

The M05 Set/Sample Mode was used to transfer data to and from magnetic tape units. This mode was initiated by the SIO instruction. Like the A/Q mode, Q held the device address and A held or received data to be transferred. Table 10-4 presents the bit assignments of the Q register.

Table 10-4. Q Bit Assignments -M05 Mode

Bits	Description
0-4	M05 Mode Selected – Always 00000.
5	Always 1.
6-8	0xxx-Send Port ; 1xxx-Send Line.
9-11	Device Number
12-14	Select Mode: 1xx – Set; 0xx – Sample.
15	Always 0.

10.2.2.3 Automatic Data Transfer Mode

The Automatic Data Transfer (ADT) mode was used when blocks of data were to be transferred to or from the peripheral device. This type of transfer was faster than a/Q mode, but slower than a DMA transfer. Only certain devices were capable of handling ADT operations

To initiate an ADT operation, the DMI instruction was used. It specified the direction of transfer and the addresses in memory of the first and last word of the block of data to be transferred or stored. The Q register held the device address. Bit 9 of the A register was set to 1. Then, an I/O instruction was executed – INP, OUT, or SIO.

The block of data was transferred one word at a time. Whenever a word was to be transferred, a microinterrupt was generated, which was processed by a microroutine. When the ADT operation was completed, a macrointerrupt was generated, which allowed another ADT operation to be initiated or ADT interrupts to be disabled.

10.3 Operating Systems

Source: CDC 1977ae, 1977bc

Model 18-10M, -20, and -30 ran the Mass Storage Operating System 5 (MSOS 5). MSOS 5 was a modular multiprogramming system designed to support a variety of applications requiring dedicated system utilization, batch processing, and program checkout features in a real-time environment. It supported both batch operations and real-time support. Batch operations supported both foreground and background jobs.

A typical configuration that would be used with MSOS 5 is depicted in Figure 10-6.

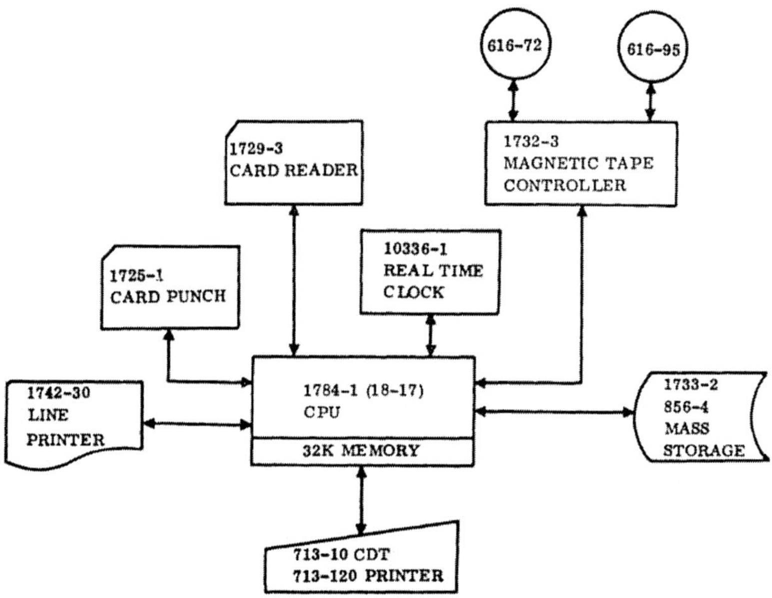

Figure 10-6. MSOS Typical configuration
Source: Adapted from CDC 1977ae

Note: Figure 10-6 references the Cyber 18 (CDC 1784) processor which had a minimum of 32K words of memory. MSOS 5 ran on smaller configurations on the CDC 1704, 1714, and 1774 processors.

10.3.1 MSOS System Architecture

The MSOS 5 system architecture is depicted in Figure 10-7

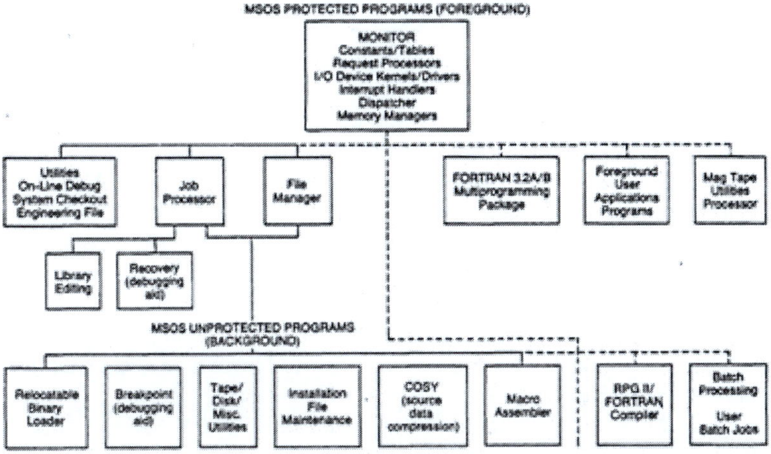

Figure 10-7. MSOS 5 Subsystem Structure
Source: CDC 1980d

10.3.2 MONITOR

Source: CDC 1977bc

The MONITOR was the real-time executive for MSOS 5. It allocated system resources and invokes other subsystems on a priority basis. Real-time programs were run at the highest priority level – 15. Other programs ran at various priority levels, but user programs typically ran at level 0.

MSOS 5 regulated all multiprogramming based on a priority level assigned to a particular operation, whether the operation was program execution or input/output. The system queues for input/output, data transmission and program execution were organized by priority level, with no restriction on the number of requests which may be queued at a given time. The program selected for execution was the one with the highest priority level. It remained in execution until completed unless a higher priority level program was scheduled. The lower priority level program was then suspended until the higher priority interrupt program was completed.

10.3.3 Memory

Memory was allocated in several ways: by priority level, by partitions, and by protected/unprotected status. The basic objective was that important programs had a relatively large area in which they could be loaded and executed. Two partitions were supported: foreground processing and background processing. If a foreground program needed more memory, the entire background area could be swapped to disk.

The on-line programs (the monitor, job processor, and recovery) all ran in a protected area. Batch programs ran in an unprotected area. Programs in the unprotected area gained access to monitor services through monitor calls, which generated a memory protect violation interrupt. This interrupt was handled to allow the service routine to execute on behalf of the unprotected program in protected space.

Timeshare 3 ran on the Model 18-30 and provided a timesharing interface to the large Cyber systems. It supported up to 64 users on dedicated or dial-up lines. It converted the Cyber 18 to a communications multiplexor.

10.3.4 Interrupt System

There were 16 priority levels to allow users to ensure that critical tasks were performed in a timely manner. All interrupt handlers were assigned to the highest priorities to ensure that interrupts were serviced in a relatively short time. Background programs were given it the lowest priority.

Each interrupt line was assigned a specific priority and an associated interrupt handler. The priority level of an interrupt determined whether it was processed immediately or deferred until higher priority interrupts were completed. Device drivers were executed in preference to foreground programs. Table 10-5 depicts the MSOS priorities.

Interrupted programs were entered into interrupt stack on a last-in first-out basis because a higher priority program could interrupt a running program.

The interrupt handlers, when they received control of the CPU, set an interrupt mask so that only higher priority interrupts can interrupt the interrupt processor. Once n interrupt handler completes its actions, the interrupt mask dropped to a lower level.

Table 10-5. MSOS 5 Priorities

Priority	Description
15	Internal errors: stall alarm, parity, and protect violations.
9-14	I/O drivers that were most time-critical.
4-8	Foreground programs
2-3	Foreground idle loop (job processor, protect processor)
1	Background programs
0	Background programs - Batch
-1	CPU Idle Loop

Level 15 was also available for process control programs that were very time-critical and whose failure to run in a timely basis might cause substantial harm to the user's process.

10.3.5 Request Processor and Dispatcher

The Request Processor was a scheduler that checked each monitor request for validity. If the request was valid, it was directed to the appropriate device or service. If a scheduler request was submitted, it was either scheduled immediately or queued for later processing.

The Dispatcher worked off the scheduler and interrupt queues., executing the highest priority task in either stack. If equal priority requests occurred in both stacks, the interrupt stack task was given control of the CPU.

The timer routine periodically checked the queued TIMER requests in the scheduler stack. If the requested delay had elapsed the request was queued with other requests on a FIFO-within-priority basis.

The Dispatcher allocated control of the CPU to the highest priority task from a queue of tasks, which may either be a program element or a monitor request. Interrupted programs had priority over scheduled programs of equal priority.

10.3.5 I/O System

Each peripheral and element of the computer system had its own driver (e.g., a software module that handled requests for service to the device. MSOS I/O drivers were interrupt-driven. DMA/DSA devices operated asynchronously to CPU operations.

I/O drivers set up the I/O equipment for data transfer using parameters specified in the service request. They established buffer sizes if block data transfers were requested. They started the data transfer. Subsequent requests to the same device were enqueued to the driver on a priority basis. The I/O driver fetched requests from the queue and service them. These queues were ordered in a FIFO-within-priority basis, such that requests of the same priority were executed in the order in which they were requested.

10.3.6 Job Processor

The Job Processor was a system program that monitored unprotected programs in the background partition running at low levels of priority. It was mass-storage resident and loaded as needed into any portion of protected memory.

Scheduled programs were queued in a scheduler stack. Deferred queuing of a program until a time period had elapsed was supported by TIMER requests.

10.3.7 Libraries

Three libraries were supported by MSOS, which stored their programs on mass storage. The system library contained copies of all foreground programs except those programs which resided in the system area of mass storage and were stored in absolute binary format. These programs were loaded into memory at autoload (initialization) time.

The program library contained all background programs. These were mostly represented in relocatable binary format.

The macro library stored standard macro definitions used by the macro assembler.

Several utilities were used to manage and maintain libraries:

- A skeleton editor and library builder allowed the user to change the order and the content of both libraries via the installation files as the system was rebuilt; and
- A library editor allowed internal change to programs in both libraries. The system library could have system programs added to the limit of library slots and deleted from them. The program library could have new programs added to it up to the mass storage space available.

10.3.8 Linking and Loading Binary Programs

The two types of binary programs were linked and loaded by the LOADER. At system initialization, memory-resident programs were linked and loaded and saved in the system region of mass memory. Similarly, mass-memory-resident programs, which were dynamically loaded into main memory as needed, were linked and loaded and stored in the system library in absolute binary format. After initialization, additional foreground programs could be inserted in the system library by LIBEDT.

At startup, the autoload procedure transferred the main memory image of resident programs from mass memory to main memory.

A memory map was created during the loading process which specified data and common storage locations, and the name and core location of each program. Data was loaded first, followed by common storage, and, then, the name and starting location of each program.

During loading, the Loader also created a table of external and entry point names consisting of four-word entries: the first three words contain the six-character name followed by the address of the first routine in the program to use that name. Subsequent uses form a link address in word four which points to the address of the previous four-word block. When the Loader matched an external name in the table. Each link address had the actual address of the entity replace the link address and the link was removed.

A control block for each program loaded was created in the Loader buffer area. Blocks were variable length and terminated by a carriage return. When the Loader completed its task, it transferred control to the Job Processor giving it the buffer area address.

After startup, LIBEDT was called to build the program library using either absolute binary or relocatable binary format. For absolute binary programs, all external references were linked when it was loaded into the program library.

As noted, absolute and relocatable binary programs could be loaded from the program library. Relocatable binary programs could be loaded from designated I/O devices.

10.4 System Software

The Cyber 18 system software included a set of utilities for MSOS 5 as well as language processors for a macroassembler, microassembler, and FORTRAN.

10.4.1 Utility Software

Three types of system utilities were provided as presented in Table 10-6.

Table 10-6. MSOS 5 System Utilities

Utility	Description
	Hardware Performance Checking
Small Computer Maintenance Monitor (SCMM)	This program was executed by the operator using a manual interrupt at the console. It was used to detect hardware errors and to test i/o equipment.
Engineering Log	This program was used to save hardware deice failure data. Data was entered by an I/O device driver when an unrecoverable device error was encountered by the driver. When the log was filled, the operator was notified. But, the contents of the log could be inspected at any time.
	Program Debugging
ODEBUG	An on-line debugging program used to debug foreground programs that treated them as files. It could load, dump, and alter programs.
Breakpoint	This program ran in the background and allowed the operator to inspect program performance at selected decision points and alter data and instructions at these points.
Recovery	This program checked the performance of batch programs after they had been executed.
Trace	An on-line program to trace the execution of a foreground program.
	Other Utilities
System Checkout (SYSCOP)	Dumped the image of a failed system to be written to mass storage. After autoload restarted the system, SYSCOP examined the image and printer error information.
LIBEDT	Library editing routines to allow the user to manage the system and program libraries,
COSY	A compression program.
Listing and Sorting	LULIST, LISTR, OPSORT.

10.4.2 Assembly System

The assembly system was oriented to the low-end model Cyber 18-10 with just 4K word of memory, paper tape reader and punch, and a teletypewriter.

For larger systems without disk drives, the Utility System assembled modules producing relocatable binary objects that could be integrated by a linking load with library routines into a relocatable binary program.

A cross-assembler that ran on the Cyber 170/6x00/7x00 computer systems allowed programs to be assembled there and transferred to the Cyber 17/18 systems.

The MacroAssembler, a variant of COMPASS, provided programmer-defined macro capabilities, symbolic naming, and assembler-directed pseudo-operation. The Assembler could generate absolute loading executables, relocatable program modules, and library modules for inclusion by the linking loader.

10.4.2 File Manager

The File Manager was a package consisting of a request supervisor and a collection of request processors that handled file management operations. The supervisor resided in core while the request processors were loaded from mass storage as needed. User programs made requests to the File Manager through a set of macros from assembly programs or FORTRAN subroutine calls.

10.4.2.1 File Types

The File Manager created and stored and retrieved data from three file types as described in Table 10-7.

Table 10-7. MSOS 5 File Types

File Type	Description
Sequential	Records were stored and retrieved one at a time in order with no gaps.
Indexed	Each record was stored and accessed by a key, whose value was translated into an index which yielded an address for the record.
Direct	Records were accessed by file pointers in a contiguous area of storage or linked by a pointer from one record to the next.

10.4.2.2 Record Format

Each variable length record was composed of three sections as shown in Table 10-8.

Table 10-8. Record Fields

Field	Description
Header Word	The first word contained the length of the record, which could not be changed after the record was stored. This field was set by the File Manager.
Record Pointers	In indexed files, the record pointer pointed to a two-word mass storage address, which contained: 1. the sector of a file record block 2. the offset in the file record block where the record was stored.
Data Words	Zero or more words which contained the record's data in binary or ASCII.

10.4.3 FORTRAN

MSOS FORTRAN was a multipass compiler that supported both reentrant and non-reentrant ENCODE/DECODE packages and a FORTRAN I/O library. ENCODE/DECODE ran in the foreground and provided a multiprogramming interface and an enhanced system call interface to MSOS 5. The FORTRAN compiler was an optimizing compiler that generated efficient code (CDC 1976s).

10.4.4 PASCAL

A PASCAL cross-compiler ran on the Cyber Series and the 6000/7000 systems and provided relocatable binary output. A BASIC compiler ran on the 18-30 and provided a timesharing capability. RPGII ran on either the 18-10M or the 18-20 and was largely compatible with IBM's System 3 RPG compiler.

10.5 CDC 2550

The Cyber 18 was used as the processor for the CDC 2550 Host Communications Processor (HCP) which was used in communications networks by Cyber 70 & 170 mainframes. It was produced by CDC's Communications Systems Division, Santa Ana, California

The CDC 2550 was a medium-sized data communication system that served as a communications system as a front-end for the CDC and Cyber mainframes. Model 2 also interfaced with selected terminal devices. And, with a CDC 2550-1 communications coupler could connect two computers together. The CDC 2550provided multiplexor capabilities to as many as 32 communications line adapters. It was housed in two cabinets collocated with the mainframe. The initial version used a CDC MP17 processor while later versions used the MP18 MOS processor.

10.6 System 17/18 Applications

Source: CDC 1973h

The Cyber 17/18 supported a diverse set of application programs too numerous to document all of them here. CDC developed data acquisition devices to support collection of data and control of application peripherals. A select set of applications is presented in Table 10-9.

Table 10-9. Selected Cyber 17/18 Applications

Application	Brief Description
Petro-Chemicals	Cyber systems were used to control and monitor a petro-chemical refinery to provide monitoring, logging, and alarm functions. Links to other Cyber 17 systems provided control over refining process, including optimization and supervisory control of processes, analysis of data, and production scheduling.
Steam-Electric Generation	One system was developed for a coal-fired, steam-electric generating unit that could produce up to 550,000 kW. The unit consisted of a B&W cyclone boiler that produced steam at 1000 degrees F at 3500 PSI, a Westinghouse turbine and generator, and a coal-handling facility - all controlled by an analog system for which a Cyber 17 supplied the analog set points.
Chromatography	This application provided on-line analysis of gas chromatograph data to identiy the components and concentration of a gas trace from several instruments. The system controlled sampling intervals, and controlled for baseline drift, peak height, and retention times, and computer molecular weight and volume fraction.

Seismic Data Processing	Cyber 17's have been used for multiple geophysical applications to process data in near real-time. Application programs computed trace collection, convolute filtering, and time depth analysis and were written in FORTRAN.
Electric Utility Control	Multiple Cyber 17s were configured with CC 40-100 Process Interface Controllers to assist in managing an electric utility generation and distribution system, including circuit breaker control, connect/disconnect of distribution switches, and trans former taps for high-voltage bulk power supply. It performed the calculations to monitor and control power distribution, load balancing, and load frequency.
Telemetry Acquisition and Analysis	The Telemetry Acquisition/Reduction application to handle a variety of telemetry data processing, including data formatting, bit synchronization, buffered I/O, and real-time analysis. Data could be passed to larger systems of the CDC 3000 family for more extensive data analysis.

CHAPTER ELEVEN

CDC PERIPHERALS

CDC systems supported the usual suite of peripherals of most mainframes, but where it made its mark was its high-performance disk drives. CDC recognized early on that high performance computer systems need to get data in and out of the computer memory at a fast rate in order to keep the central process speed. CDC also developed the CDC 38500 Mass Storage System to support was Data-Set approach.

11.1 CDC 6603 DISK FILE

Source: CDC 1968bq

The CDC 6603 Disk File was the primary mass storage system for the CDC 6000 series systems. It was manufactured by Bryant-Excello as an OEM peripheral. It provided a capacity of 74,111,040 characters. It had a transfer rate of 1,093,850 characters per second. The rotational speed was 66.6 msecs per revolution. It featured 96 magnetic heads – four per disk surface – which moved in unison by a single positioning arm. The CDC 6603 Disk file cabinet was depicted in Figure 11-1.

As can be seen in the figure, the disks were mounted horizontally on shafts, 7 platters on each of the drives. This yielded 12 'surfaces" which read or written in parallel – one bit per surface. Each surface was organized as four concentric zones with each zone containing 128 tracks swept by one head. The two inner zones had 100 sectors while the two outer zones had Each sector was 351 bits 128 sectors, but the programmer thought of it as 351 words spread over the 12 surfaces. Of these, 322 were used for data, 2 for control bytes, and the rest used by the hardware.

Figure 11-1. CDC 6603 Disk File
Source: CDC 1968bq

11.2 CDC 6638 Disk File System

The CDC 6638 Disk File System (DFS) consisted of a CDC 808 disk file coupled with a CDC 6639 Disk File Controller (DFC). The DFC interfaced between the computer system and disk file via the Data Channel. Data was buffered in 12-bit parallel format. The DFC accepted function codes which it translated into operations on the DFS, such as connect a DSU and read or write data.

The maximum capacity of the CDC 808 was 175,685,632 characters. It had a rotational speed of 1200 rpm with a 163 msec access time, including positioning, verification, and latency. It had 64 read/write head groups each of which contained 12 read/write heads. Half the heads were attached to each of two positioners which could move independently, which allowed concurrent reading and writing.

The CDC 808 was logically divided into two sections: unit 0 and unit 1, which were mechanically and electrically independent of each other. A PPU Data Channel could connect with either unit.

11.3 CDC 844 Disk Storage Unit

A disk pack was divided into cylinders, tracks, and sectors as depicted in Figure 11-x. A cylinder consisted of all the data accessible by all heads in one position. A track contained all the data accessible by one head in one position. A track was divided into sectors, which were the smallest addressable area on the disk.

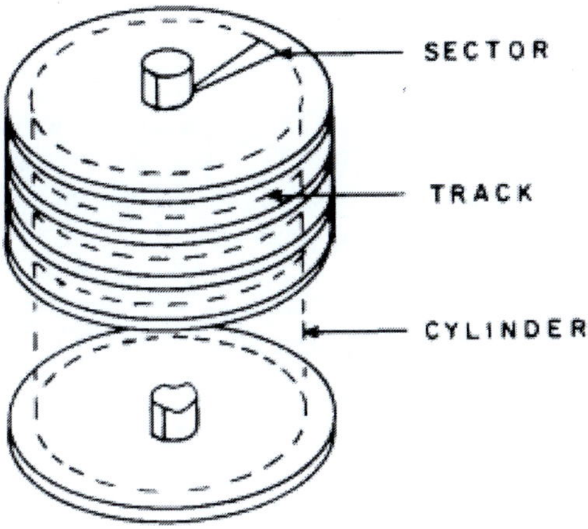

Figure 11-2. CDC 844 Disk Pack Structure
Source: CDC 1980ac

All CDC 844 disk packs were formatted at the factory A surface analysis was also performed to detect bad spots, which were then recorded in utility flaw map sectors. The capacity of a disk pack was 118,640,256 6-bit characters. The average access time was 30 msecs for a random seek and 6 msecs for a move from cylinder to another.

11.4 CDC DISK CONTROLLERS

Source: CDC 1980ac

The CDC 7X54 Disk Storage Controllers (DSC) were designed to handle CDC 844 Series Disk Storage Units (DSU). They supported the CDC 6000series, the CDC 7600, and the Cyber 70 and 170 computer systems. Up to two of the DSCs could be attached to these computer systems with up to four DSUs per DSC. Each DSC could interface with up to four PP /O channels. Each DSU could attach to one or two DSCs.

The Standard Option 10302-x Mass Storage Extenders (MSE) could increase the number of DSUs to a maximum of 22 (Model -1) or 36 (Model -2) per computer system.

A 7152 Disk/Tape Controller consisted of a disk controller and a tape controller mounted in the same cabinet. The 7152 included a PROM for autoloading controlware.

DSCs were initialized by a PPU autoloading controlware via a start memory command executed by the DSC. After the software was loaded, the DSC could then respond to other commands. Selected DSC commands are presented in Table 11-1. A command was 12 bits with its bits numbered from the left as 11 to 0.

Table 11-1. Selected DSC Commands

Command	DSC Codes$_8$	Description
Connect DSU#	0000	Allowed a PPU to reserve a DSU without initiating head movement. The DSU was reserved until one of commands complete, drop seeks, or drive release. Bits 2-0 DSU number If accessed through an MSE: Bits 2-0 MSU number Bits 5-3 DSU number
Seek, Interlace	0001 0002	A PPU issued this command with a four - word argument to prepare a DSU for a 1:1 interlaced data transfer.
Read	0004	Initiated a data transfer from a selected disk sector through the coupler buffer memory to the PP. The coupler memory had a capacity of one disk sector which was transferred to the PPU memory at channel speed. The PPU had to initiate a block input to receive the data.

Write	0005	Initiated a transfer from a PPU to the specified disk sector from the prior seek command. A PPU had to initiate a block output to send the data.
Drop Seek	0015	This command caused the DSC to release all DSUs reserved to the DSC.
Drive Release	0020	This command released the last DSU reserved for the specified DSC.
Start Memory Load	0414	A PPU used this command to initiate the autoloading a DSC from PPU memory.

The reader is referred to the source manual for a detailed exposition on DSC operations. Over 40 commands are accepted by the DSC. There are some differences in the commands issued by a 6000 series PPU versus a 7000 series PPU.

11.5 7021 Magnetic Tape Subsystem

Source: CDC 1982ab

A 7021 Magnetic Tape Subsystem (MTS) provided a CDC 6x00/7x00/Cyber series computer with a near-line storage capability. A 7021 MTS consisted of:

- 7021-1 Magnetic Tape Controller (MTC) or 7622 Magnetic Tape Controller, depending on the computer system family and model. Each MTC included the following components:
    - An MTS processor;
    - Couplers for the specified computer family and model; and
    - Tape Control Unit (TCU).
- 1 to 8 Magnetic Tape Transports (MTT).

The MTTs provided 7- or 9-track recording density using either NRZI recording or NRZI/PE recording. NRXI recording density was either 556 or 800 characters per inch, while Phase Encoding (PE) was 1600 characters per inch.

11.5.1 MTS Functions

An MTS had an integrated processor which executed functions based on commands sent by the PPUs. Each function was a 12-bit word to invoke functions residing in the MTS processor memory.

An MTS function was issued from a PPU to a selected MTS. The MTS processor accepted a function by sending an inactive signal to the PPU within 500 microseconds of arrival. Function parameters were sent by the PPU within 1 msec after the function request was accepted. The PPU sends a General Status function to check that the parameters were correctly received. An alert bit was in general status was set and the PPU had to query for the cause of the error. The MTS translated the function request into one or more TCU commands and sends them one at a time to the TCU.

When an error occurred, the TCU advanced the tape to the next interblock gap or the end of the tape so that the tape may be either at the beginning of a "good" record or at the end of the tape. Either condition was returned to the PPU.

There were many MTS functions of which a selected few are described in Table 11-2. Where subfunctions were issued for functions, the subfunction was indicated by "/x", where x was the code. The reader is referred to the document CDC 1982bu for a comprehensive discussion of the 7021 MTS functions.

Table 11-2. Selected MTS Functions

Function	Code	Description
Format Unit	30	This function specified the characteristics of the data being read or written on the selected MTT. It required two parameter words which included these fields: Code translation, which was used to translate to or from an external encoding to an internal encoding. Assembly/Disassembly Mode, which packed 6-bit characters into words or unpacked words to 6-bit characters. TCU number Parity Selection Density Selection.
Connect Unit	20-27	This function reserved an MTT for all subsequent functions until a release command was issued.
Rewind	10/0	This function issued a rewind command to the TCU back to the loadpoint of the tape.
Rewind/Unload	10/1	Similar to Rewind, but the operator was notified to unload the tape.
Search Tapemark Forward	15/0	The MTT moves the tape forward past the next tapemark into the interblock gap.

Backspace	13/1	The MTT moved the tape backwards one tapemark or on block
Write Tapemark	51	The MTT erased about 6 inches of tape and wrote one of three tapemarks, which depended on the encoding method.
Read Forward	40/0	The MTT read one block of data on the tape, assembled the data in 12-bit words, and transferred the data to the PPU. The last Format Unit function the features of parity, recording density, assembly/disassembly mode.
Write	50	This function wrote one block of data in the forward direction on the MTT. Data was transferred from the PPU in 12-bit words which were transmitted to the MTT as 6-bit frames (&TRK) or 8-bit frames (9TRK).

Numerous functions were provided for precision movement and error handling for the selected MTT.

11.6 CDC 38500 Mass Storage System

Source: CDC 1975ai

As large scientific applications were developed for the CDC computer systems, CDC realized that large data sets needed an efficient storage mechanism that was many multiple of their disk systems capacity. In general, magnetic tape systems could store more data than contemporary disk systems, but the tape systems had to be on-line to provide the performance improvements in the end-to-end processing of large data sets. Waiting for off-line tapes to be loaded had a significant impact on this performance.

CDC devised the data-set approach as the mechanism for handling large data files. Data was stored on a CDC 38500 Mass Storage System (MSS) for long-term storage. When data files were requested they were loaded from the MSS to disk systems for analysis. Processed data and results could then be written to the MSS. Here, "long-term storage" did not mean archival storage, but large data files that might be used frequently over a matter of weeks or months.

11.6.1 Magnetic Tape Cartridges

The MSS was based on the Magnetic Tape Cartridge which stored 8M bytes. A single MSS could store 2000 cartridges or about 16G bytes. In an era when large data files were typically a few megabytes, this provided the ability to store hundreds of these files from many different users. 8 tape cartridges were held in an Octopak as depicted in Figure 11-3.

The MSS used a storage magazine filled with tape cartridges which were arranged in an X-Y grid. A specific cartridge was selected by a mechanical arm which moved to the particular grid coordinates for the tape cartridge, fetched it from its slot, and then moved it to a read/write station. The cartridge was opened and the tape unwound and drawn into a two-vacuum column unit. The tape remained attached to the cartridge spool, so storing the tape just meant winding it back onto the cartridge spool. Once a tape had been rewound and the cartridge sealed, the cartridge was moved to an exit station from which the mechanical arm moved it back to its storage location. These operations could be overlapped to maintain a continuous flow to the computer system.

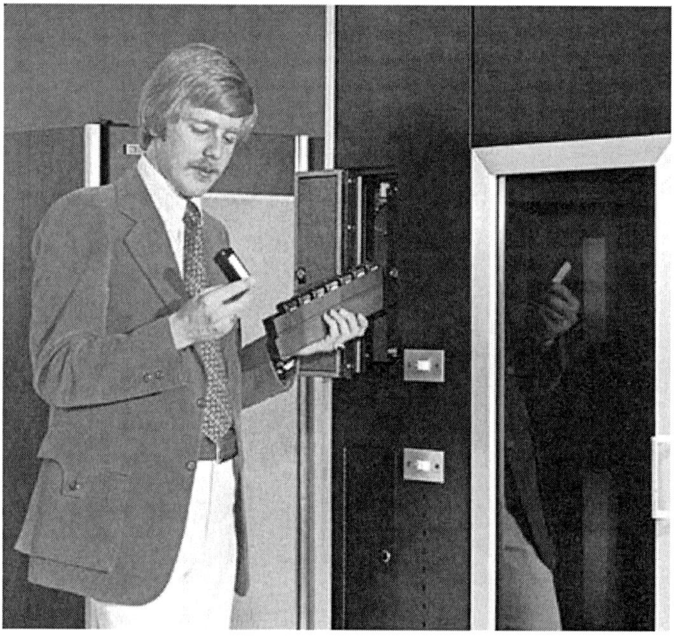

Figure 11-3. MSS Tape Cartridge and Octopak.
Source: CDC 1975ai

The base configuration for an MSS unit included two read/write stations, but this could be expanded to four stations. An access door allowed new Octopaks to be loaded into the tape magazine. This allowed for individual cartridges which were being replaced due to errors or archiving to be removed from or inserted into the Octopak as well as allowing Octopaks to be removed for servicing and reinserted into the magazine. Diagnostics could detect when a tape cartridge had failed and inform the system operator of the need to replace it.

The MSS could off-load a tape cartridge to any available contiguous space on a disk volume. Unlike other systems, it did not require dedicated disks to extract from or restore data to a tape cartridge. This reduced contention at disk controllers and data channels. Alternatively, the MSS could read data files directly into the CM for greater improvement in end-to-end data processing.

Figure 11-4 depicts the MSS cartridge storage with mechanical arm.

Figure 11-4. MSS Cartridge Storage and Mechanical Arm
Source: CDC 1975ai

As Coleman (UNK) notes:

"To access a file, the robot positioned itself in front of the desired cartridge, blew a jet of air over the top of the cartridge, which blew the cartridge into the robot's "picker". The robot then positioned itself at the receiving port of the tape drive and mechanically shoved the cartridge onto a small conveyor belt. The conveyor belt moved the cartridge to the back of the drive where it was "shuttled" sideways into the load position. The drive then popped open the door of the cartridge and sucked all 150" of tape into the vacuum columns. (Both ends of the tape were connected to the cartridge--one end to the door and the other end to the spindle.)

To read or write the cartridge, the drive "shoe-shined" the tape back and forth, in the vacuum columns, past the head. The tape was written in both directions, and the head was positioned to one of eight positions (nine data tracks were written for each head position). Thus, to read or write the entire cartridge, the tape was shoe-shined past the head sixteen times, one for each head position in each direction. When access to the cartridge was complete, the drive wound the tape back into the cartridge, pulling the door closed as the last of the tape was wound up. The drive then shuttled the cartridge onto an output conveyor belt, which moved the cartridge to the output port where the robot picked it up and returned it to its storage cell."

Figure 11-5 depicts an MSS with two tape cartridge magazines.

Figure 11-5. MSS Tape Cartridge Magazines
Source: CDC 1975ai

11.6.2 MSS AND LLNL

Source: Coleman UNK.

Lawrence Livermore National Laboratory (LLNL) has had a long history in exploring methods and mechanism for storing large amounts of data. Over the years, the magnetic disk systems and tape libraries overflowed with data. LLNL initially used IBM Data Cells, IBM Photostore, and the IBM 3850 system, but later settled on the CDC 38500 Mass Storage System.

LLNL eventually had eight CDC 38500 MSS each of which had two tape drives and held 2,000 cartridges. A cartridge held 8M bytes of data. The MSS wrote one cartridge at a time with files in the order in which they were received, which meant many user's files could be stored on one cartridge. Coleman and others developed the MASS system, which ran on a Texas Instruments TI-980 system, to manage the files on the various cartridges.

LLNL worked closely with CDC engineers to develop and test the MSS with initial loading in 1978 and full production in 1979. MSS was used until 1988 when it was retired after CDC declined to main the hardware. LLNL's MSS was the first to be installed and the last to be retired of the approximately 75 installations. It was replaced by StorageTek silos (which are discussed in the forthcoming volume on Supercomputers).

The CDC 38500 MSS served LLNL well for almost a decade and was instrumental in pioneering the use of large archival tape-based storage systems for near-line data storage.

CHAPTER TWELVE

ASSESSMENT OF CDC

CDC can be viewed as the rebel (much like James Dean of the same era) in the early days of computer systems. It was extremely successful in designing the fastest computers in the world due to one man, Seymour Cray. However, its success in delivering these machines rested on a supporting cast such as William Norris, Neil Lincoln, James Thornton, Les Davis, Dean Roush, and a host of other engineers and managers. Its heyday lasted for approximately 15 years – say to the mid-1970s.

When Cray left, CDC lost its visionary and did not have a major success in computer design thereafter. The STAR-100 and the Cyber Series were based on Cray designs, but just enhanced versions.

12.1 INNOVATIVE ARCHITECTURES

CDC's architectures were innovative and influenced the design of the next two generations of computer architecture.

The concept of functional units demonstrated parallelism at the instruction execution level as a means of greater speed, but also exposed the issues with dependencies in addressing memory locations and the use of registers.

The concept of PPUs demonstrated two key ideas. First, that multiple small computers operating in parallel could significantly increase the overall computational speed of the machine. Second, the idea of offloading I/O operations from the CPU to the PPUs led to reducing the size and complexity of the CPU operating system and freeing cycles for computation. Dividing the overall operating software of the machine into separate systems led to effective use of system resources.

The concept of loading a register (the A registers) which resulted in an automatic fetch from or store into the indicated memory locations eliminated at least one instruction in access data and instructions. On the whole, some 6x00/7x00 programs were much smaller than similar programs on contemporary systems.

A few of these ideas do not exist in current (circa 2022) system architectures nor have they been used since the late 1990s with the demise of CDC. The speed of current microprocessors was mostly due to improvements in semiconductor technology, and not due to architectural innovation.

12.2 Poor Operating Systems

One of the major problems that CDC had was its operating systems. Because of its orientation towards scientific computing, its operating systems often lacked the utilities and other accoutrements that were required for general purpose computing for academic or commercial environments, although a significant number of CDC machines were purchased by universities. And, CDC did not have a large application library. CDC's philosophy was that its customers wrote their own system and application software because they knew their environments best. Only reluctantly did CDC develop operating systems and utilities. As a result, there were competitors, notably the operating systems and compilers developed at Lawrence Livermore Laboratory, which provided some features that were comparable to major vendors like IBM, UNIVAC, and Honeywell.

12.3 Minicomputers

CDC was also a late entrant to the broader minicomputer and microcomputer market. Although it had the first minicomputer, the CDC 160, it didn't capitalize on this capability and rapidly lost ground to many other companies whose primary focus was the minicomputer. The Cyber 1700/1800 series were not powerful enough to compete with the established minicomputer vendors and did not have the range of software offerings. The CDC 110 microcomputer quickly faded from view because it, too, was underpowered.

12.4 Networking Services

CDC developed the CYBERNET Service, which was a large nationwide computer network that provided communications and time-sharing services to many companies.

CDC developed a system called CDCNET, which served as the intranet coupler with many different network protocols, but primarily Ethernet, HDLC, MCI's network among others. The CDCNET intranet layer connected specific user network protocols to the higher layer CDCNET protocol which supported long haul communications among various entities. The CDCNET software received traffic from a lower layer network protocol, wrapped it in a data package, and transmitted across CDCNET to a its destination where it was unwrapped and handed to the destination network.

12.5 Commercial Credit

After it successfully sued IBM, CDC received the Commercial Credit Corporation (CCC) as part of the settlement. This and its foray into the educational instruction market via PLATO diverted management's attention from its core competency. This eventually to financial problems which limited CDC's ability to continue research and development into newer models.

Through CCC, CDC pioneered the concept of developing and selling data processing services to a range of customers. CYBERLOAN was an on-line consumer loan system that automated the branch office operations of consumer loan companies

CDC offered it as a total package, e.g., a turnkey system, where CC provided all hardware, software, and communications equipment to the customer. CYBERLOAN terminals placed at customer premises communication with a centrally located Cyber 73 system running KRONOS to handle all of the operations. From this program, CDC tried to branch into providing and operating data centers based on its systems.

12.6 PLATO

Source: Van Meer 2003

Another activity that strayed from CDC's core competency was PLATO. CDC was very interested in breaking into the educational marketplace to challenge IBM's dominance there. However, poor software made CDC machines unattractive to educational customers.

Van Meer documents the evolution of PLATO from a computer-based education (CBE) system to a platform for corporate social responsibility. Ultimately it consumed funds that CDC did not have to spare and, thus could not be re-invested in significant enhancements to the Cyber architecture.

PLATO was one of the first educational support systems that "accommodated graphics, animation, simulation, and text-based instruction". Originally developed at the University of Illinois, it was initial supported by CDC's Norris with hardware donations. By the mid-1970s, CC had gained controlled of PLATO as it was prepared for the commercial market. While PLATO was effective in some learning environments, in other sites, it was not cost-effective for small groups of students.

Bill Norris retired in 1986. By this point, CDC was financially struggling and Lawrence Perlman sold off the PLATO division. It appears that PLATO never really turned a profit, and was a consistent drain on corporate finances and resources that might have been employed to modernize the architecture to make CDC more competitive.

12.7 University of Wyoming Experience

Jim Kirkpatrick has written an entertaining and informative review of the University of Wyoming's Central Computing experiences with CDC's Cyber mainframes. It describes both the good and bad of CDC mainframe computing and highlights some of the reasons why CDC eventually failed as an viable organization.

12.8 Lasting Influence

However, CDC's influence on the computer and software industry was large. CDC was an early backer of solar and wind power. Its distribution center in St. Paul, MN used solar power. It supported Jacob's Wind Energy which developed wind mill farms in Hawaii and California. Robert Price, former CEO of CDC noted:

> "Control Data was the Apple Computer of its time; innovation was at the core of Control Data's DNA. There were more than 100 spin off and other derivative companies ranging from Arbitron, which measures radio audiences, to Digital Biometrics, which builds digital fingerprinting equipment. Despite the extreme turbulence in the social, political and economic environments of the late 1960s and 1970s, Control Data achieved a greatness few companies ever realize."

In some sense, CDC created the supercomputer industry almost single-handedly. It showed how supercomputers improved computational capabilities for several industries. Success bred competition - some of it very effective. The market for supercomputers was not very large and competitors began to chip away at CDC's originally overwhelming presence.

The effect of the end of the Cold War was often cited as a reason for the demise of the supercomputer era. However, I am more convinced it was the technological improvements in microprocessor chips in size, speed, cost, and reliability that were the most significant factor. The corresponding developments in programming languages, operating systems, data base management systems, systems utilities, and networking systems meant that organizations could do a lot more with smaller, less expensive systems. Distributed systems and parallel processors could do much more than large mainframe systems.

EXERCISES FOR THE READER

1. Arguably, CDC had the first minicomputer in the CDC 160. It failed to capitalize on this in pursuit of "big iron" machines. Eventually, it came back to the minicomputer market with Cyber 17/18, but it was too little too late. DEC, DG and other manufacturers start with minicomputers, but also ventured into the mainframe market with various offerings. Pick a well-known minicomputer company. Compare and contrast its history with that of CDC, including drawing a timeline of major events and market moves. (Additional Research Required).

2. Examine the CDC 3300 instruction CPR. What programming language feature would this instruction implement? (Hint: Think FORTRAN IV).

3. The CDC 160 and the PDP-8 were both 12-bit minicomputers. Compare and contrast their instruction sets according to at least three features you select. Provide a rationale for your criteria selection.

4. The CDC 3300/3500 supported paging to extend memory allocation. These systems allowed a page to be divided into four subpages of 512 words. Discuss how this capability allowed MASTER to efficiently manage the available physical memory.

5. On the CDC 1706 Buffered Data Channel, once an output of a word was initiated, it was repeatedly retried until the word was accepted by the peripheral device. Could this approach generate a deadlock condition? How would it have to be cleared?

6. A similar case arises when buffered input was conducted on the BDC. If a word on input was not accepted by the BDC, it repeatedly requested a word transfer until the word was accept.

7. The CDC 3300/3500 included Business Data Processing instructions to improve the performance of the COBOL compiler. Compare these instructions with those provided in the IBM 7070/080 instruction set. What do you was the easier to use set of instructions. Provide at least four arguments pro or con.

8. The CDC 3000 series machines had a memory bit which indicated indirect addressing, e.g., if the bit was set, the value of the memory location contained the address of the actual operand. This evaluation was recursively applied to memory fetches if subsequent memory location indirect bits were set. Compare this approach with incorporating the indirect bit within the instruction. Assess both approaches in terms of memory utilization, access time to data, and complexity of programming (e.g., from the compiler viewpoint). What did the programmer need to know to use this bit effectively.

9. The CDC 3000 required the programmer to specify a new storage bank, when the bank address limit was reached rather than continuing across the bank address boundary to the next storage bank. Discuss the reason pro and con of this design.

10. The CDC 160A was generally operated as a single user machine in the sense. that it executed one batch job at a time. The operators were often the programmers who developed the code to be run and interacted with the machine through the console and the operator panel switches. Examining the CDC 160A operating system, suggest what CDC could have done to make it more useful to individual operators.

11. The execution model of programs supported by the operating system follows a common thread from the CDC 1604 models through the CDC 3000 series to the CDC 6000/CDC 7600 series/Cyber series. Assess whether that model contributed more than the speed of the hardware to the high performance of these machines.

12. Following question 11, did the distribution of I/O to small minicomputers modeled after the CDC 160A, significantly contribute to the overall speed. Of the systems. Present three arguments for and three arguments against this model.

13. CDC staked its future largely on high performance scientific and engineering computing rather than business data processing (BDP), although the CDC 3300/3500 had commercial instructions to targeted to BDP. Examining the architecture of the hardware and the operating systems and utilities, what else might CDC have done to gainer greater acceptance in the business marketplace?

14. Contrast the software offerings of the CDC 160A and the DEC PDP-8. The PDP-8 was a mature machine (having the lineage PDP-1 to PDP-4 to PDP-8). DEC early on realized that software was the key to enabling and retaining customers.

15. Early machines had 12, 24- 36, and 48 bits as their word length. Aside from IBM's decision to base the System/360 on 32 bits, explore why computer manufacturers settled on 32 bits. Discuss the benefits of each of the word sizes. (MS Thesis topic, extra research required).

16. Note that many machines of this era had fewer instructions than could be represented in their instructions format. after critically examining the CDC 1604 and CDC 3000 system, consider what instructions you would suggest to be added to their instruction set architecture and why.

17. Packing two instructions in one word provided some efficiency because it reduced memory references, which were much slower than CPU the CPU speed. However, it required some consideration of the programmer in writing assembly language code. Present three arguments fro and con why the use of packing two instructions per word might be useful other than the one just cited.

GLOSSARY

Acronym	Definition
BDC	Buffered Data channel
CDC	Control Data Corporation
CM	Computational Module (3600)
COSY	Complete Symbolic
CPU	Central Processor Unit
EOF	End-of-File
EOR	End-of-Record
GPR	General Purpose Register
IBM	International Business Machines corporation
lpm	lines per minute
MSIO	Mass Storage I/O Subsystem (Drum SCOPE)
MSOS	Mass Storage Operating System (1700/17/18)
MSS	Mass Storage System (CDC 38500)
MTU	Magnetic Tape Unit

REFERENCES

Many of the CDC manuals are available from www.bitsavers.org as PDF documents.

Bennett, R.P. and E.J. Rosenberg. 1963. 160-A Reference Manual, System Development Corporation, TM(L)-993

Coleman, S. UNK. "Early Archival Storage at LLNL", retrieved March 31, 2023 from: https://www.computer-history.info/Page4.dir/pages/Storage.dir/

Control Data Corporation (CDC), Minneapolis, MN:

(a) 1974. CDC 1700 Computer System: Codes, 60163500

(b) 1964. Control Data 3400 Computer System General Information Manual, No. 60058300

(c) 1964. Control Data 3400 Computer System Reference Manual, No. 60028200

(d) 1980. Cyber 18/1700 MSOS Analysis, Volumes 1, 2

(e) 1963. Control Data 160A Computer Programming Manual, 145e

(f) 1963. Input/Output Specifications for the Control Data 160/160A Computers, 025d

(g) 1967. 3400/3600/3800 COMPASS Training Manual, Vol. I, No. 60166700

(h) 1973. CDC System 17 Series: Computer Systems Application Guide. 200.

(i) 1970. 3300 Computer System Reference Manual, No. 60157000K

(j) 1969. Control Data 1700 Computer System Standard Peripheral Reference Manual, 60182700

(k) 2007. A Legacy of Innovation in Products and Services

(l) 1968. 3000 Series Peripheral Equipment Reference Manual, Volume I & II, 60108800. (m) 1960. 1604 Computer: Volume I: Description and Operation, 031a

(n) 1960. 1604 Computer: Volume II: Principles of Operation, 032a

(o) 1960. 1604 Computer: Volume III: Maintenance, 033a

(p) 1979. SCOPE System Programmer's Reference Manual, Model 72, 73, 74 Version 3.4, No. 60306500.

(q) 1965. 1700 Computer System Computer Reference Manual, No. 60153100.

(r) 1967. MSIO Reference Manual, 60174800A.
(s) 1976. Cyber-18 Computer Systems System Summary, No. 96767850A.
(t) 1966. 3300/3500 Computer Systems MASTER Reference Manual, 60176800.
(u) 1977. Cyber 18 Processor with MOS Memory, 96768300.
(v) 1961. Control Data 160A Computer, 55-0091 (brochure).
(w) UNK. Control Data 3000 Series: Total Technical Excellence Now! Hardware/Software/Personnel, 55-0111 (brochure).
(x) 1965. 3100/3200/3300/3500 Computer Systems Real-Time SCOPE: General Information Manual, 60134300.
(y) 1983. Cyber 18_20 Input/Output, 76361225.
(z) 1964. Control Data 160G Computer System.
(aa) 1969. 3100/3200/3300/3500 Computer Systems: Real-Time SCOPE Reference Manual, 60172500.
(ab) 1982. 7021 Magnetic Tape Subsystem, 60403900V.
(ac) 1980. CDC Disk Storage Controllers, 60363900, Revision P. (ad) 1965. Control Data 160A Computer: Reference Manual, 60014500.
(ae) 1977. Cyber 18 Models 17/20/30 Timeshare 1700: Mass Storage Operating System (MSOS) Version 5 Reference Manual, 96769400.
(af) 1964. Control Data 3600 Computer Systems Reference Manual, No. 60021300.
(ag) 1963. Control Data 1604A Computer: Reference Manual, 245a.
(ah) 1966. SCOPE Reference Manual, 60173800.
(ai) 1975. The Data-Set Approach to On-line Mass Storage, 201.196.
(aj) 1967. 3000 Series Computer System: Input/Out Specifications Manual, No. 60048800.
(ak) 1973. Control Data 3228-A/B, 3229-A/B Magnetic Tape Controllers, 60331700.
(al) 1976. Control Data 3553 Mass Storage Controller Computer System, 60278500C.
(am) 1967. 3400/3600/3800 COMPASS Training Manual, Vol. II, No. 60166700.
(an) 1967. 3400/3600/3800 COMPASS Training Manual, Vol. III, No. 60166700.
(ao) 1961. Characteristics of the Model 1604 Computer, 018c.
(ap) 1963. Control Data 1604A Computer: Programming Manual, 245c.
(aq) 1965. Control Data 1604-C Computer: Input/Output Specifications, 60003000.
(ar) 1961. 1607 Magnetic Tape Subsystem: Volume I: Description and Operation, 037B.
(as) UNK. Control Data 1700 Computer System (brochure).

(at) 1965. 3600 Computer System SCOPE Reference Manual, 60053300B.
(au) 1967. 3600/3800 Computer System: DRUM SCOPE Reference Manual, 60059200.
(av) 1967. 3100/3200/3300/3500 Computer System: COMPASS Programmer Training Manual, 60184200.
(aw) 1970. 3100/3200/3300/3500 COSY/MSOS Reference Manual, 60207300.
(ax) 1965. 3400 Computer System: SCOPE General Information Manual, 60055600.
(ay) 1977. CDC 2550-2 (MOS) Host Communications Processor, 74375500.
(az) 1965. Control Data 3300/3500 Computer Systems Equipment Bulletin: Timesharing, 60156000.
(ba) 1983. Introduction to Cyber 18 System, 76371235.
(bb) 1976. Real-Time Operating System, Version 3 Reference Manual, 96769500A.
(bc) 1977. Mass Storage Operating System (MSOS) Version 5 Reference Manual, 96769400.
(bd) 1964. OSAS-A/160A Assembly System, 6050700.
(be) 1966. Computer System Library Functions, 60056400B.

Donnelly, J.E. 1979. "Components of a Network Operating System", Fourth Conference on Local Networks, Minneapolis, MN. (also Computer Networks 3, 1979, pp. 389.398, North Holland Publishing Co.); updated version retrieved from web circa 2010 – no longer available).

Dubner, H. and J. Abate. 1970. TICKETRON – A successfully Operating System without an Operating System, Spring Joint Computer Conference, pp. 143-155.

Iverson, K. E. 1962. *A Programming Language*, John Wiley and Sons, New York, NY

Jones, D. 2005. The Control Data Corporation 160 Computer, http://www.cs.uiowa.edu/~jones/cdc160/

Kaisler, S. 2016. *Birthing the Computer: From Relays to Vacuum Tubes*, Cambridge Scholars Publishing, Newcastle-on-Tyne, England

Kirkpatrick, J. Unk. "The Cyber Era", https://www.uwyo.edu/infotech/aboutit/history/cyber-era.asp, retrieved Jan14, 2023.

Koudela, J. Jr. 1973. "The Past, Present, and Future of Minicomputers", *IEEE Proceedings*, 61(11):1526-1534

Leatherdale, D. 2009. "Pioneer Profile: Seymour Cray", *Resurrection*, Computer Conservation Society, 47.

Lincoln, N., Ed. 1975. "Reminiscences of computer architecture and computer design at Control Data Corporation", CBI OH 321, Charles Babbage Institute, Minneapolis, MN.

Lincoln, N. 1982. "Technology and Design Tradeoffs in the Design of a Modern Supercomputer", *IEEE Transactions on Computers*, C 31(5):349-362.

Masterson, Jr., K. 1960. "Compilation for Two Computers with NELIAC", *Communications of the ACM*, 3:p. 607.

Murray, C. J. 1997. *The Supermen*. John Wiley and Sons, New York An excellent book describing the supercomputer era from the founding of ERA up through the heyday of Control Data and Cray Research until the death of Seymour Cray in 1996.

Pope, D.A. and M.L. Stein. 1960. "Multiple Precision Arithmetic", *Communications of the ACM*, 3(12):652-654.

Rau, B., C.D. Glaeser, and R.L. Picard. 1982. "Efficient Code Generation for Horizontal Architectures: Compiler Techniques and Architectural Support", *ACM SIGARCH Computer Architecture News*, 10(3):131-139.

Stroud, A.H. and D. Secrest. 1962. "A Multiple-Precision Floating-Point Interpretive Program for the Control Data 1604", *The Computer Journal*.

Thelen, E. 1961. Characteristics of the Control Data Model 160A Computer, http://ed-thelen.org/comp-hist/CDC 160A-prel.html.

Turton, T. 2004. A Proposed High-Speed Computer Design, retrieved from: http://www.turton.co.za/pubs/virtualMultiprocessor.html.

Van Meer, E. 2003. "PLATO: From Computer-based Education to Corporate Social Responsibility" Iterations, November 2003 [published by The Charles Babbage Institute for the History of Information Technology}, Minneapolis, MN.

Worthy, J.C. 1987. *A Concise History of Control Data Corporation 1957 1986*, Control Data Corporation.

INDEX